Babylon and Beyond

'Here, there and everywhere, human beings are picking themselves up from the rubble of capital's eco-destruction and assembling the means for a worthwhile existence. Derek Wall does a beautiful job of weaving these threads into a strong fabric. The children of the future will look back on *Babylon and Beyond* with gratitude.'

Joel Kovel, Distinguished Professor of Social Studies, Bard College, New York and author of *The Enemy of Nature: The End of Capitalism or the End of the World?*

'Derek Wall has produced a thoughtful and inspiring guide to capitalism and anti-capitalism. This really is the first book that carefully explains the different varieties of anti-capitalist thought including green localism, ecosocialism and Hardt and Negri's autonomism. Drawing upon his experience as an economist he makes the most seemingly obscure ideas clear, while showing that there are practical alternatives to neo-liberalism and old fashioned socialism. I thoroughly recommend that you read *Babylon and Beyond*.'

Caroline Lucas, Green Member of the European Parliament and co-author of *Green Alternatives to Globalisation: A Manifesto*

'Funny, lateral and unique – an erudite Green primer on global justice. The idiot's Idiot's Guide.'
Matthew Tempest, Political Correspondent, *Guardian Unlimited*

'Usually the green perspective is simply tagged on to the red. Derek Wall is that rare breed: a real red-green hybrid. In this book, his eco-Marxism comes alive as he guides us through the major issues and leading theorists with a lightness of touch and personal warmth which makes even the most complicated of arguments accessible.'

Hilary Wainwright, Editor of *Red Pepper*

'There are far too many books on anti-capitalism out there already – but with *Babylon and Beyond*, Derek Wall has removed the need to read most of them. Just read this one: a succinct, intelligent and witty summary of what it's all about.'

Paul Kingsnorth, author of *One No, Many Yeses: A Journey to the Heart of the Global Resistance Movement*

'A synthesis of red and green is the future of progressive politics. Wall illuminates the interface of ecological and socialist ideas; divining common threads and offering the hope of a democratic, just and sustainable future for humankind.'

Peter Tatchell, human rights campaigner

'So you thought there was no alternative to global capitalism? Well there is – and you are holding the manifesto in your hands. Read this book from cover to cover – at least twice – to find out how to resist the worldwide tide of injustice and environmental destruction.'

Professor Andrew Dobson, Open University

Babylon and Beyond

The Economics of Anti-Capitalist, Anti-Globalist and Radical Green Movements

Derek Wall

Pluto Press

LONDON • ANN ARBOR, MI

First published 2005 by Pluto Press
345 Archway Road, London N6 5AA
and 839 Greene Street, Ann Arbor, MI 48106

www.plutobooks.com

British Library Cataloguing in Publication Data
A catalogue record for this book is available from the British Library

ISBN   0 7453 2391 X hardback
ISBN   0 7453 2390 1 paperback

Library of Congress Cataloging in Publication Data applied for

10   9   8   7   6   5   4   3   2   1

Designed and produced for Pluto Press by
Chase Publishing Services Ltd, Fortescue, Sidmouth, EX10 9QG, England
Typeset from disk by Stanford DTP Services, Northampton, England
Printed and bound in the European Union by
Antony Rowe Ltd, Chippenham and Eastbourne, England

To Jean-Pierre Faure and Brad Warner

Contents

Acknowledgements   x
Foreword by Nandor Tanczos   xii

1 Warm Conspiracies and Cold Concepts   1
2 Vaccinating against Anti-capitalism: Stiglitz, Soros and
   Friends   23
3 White Collar Global Crime Syndicate: Korten, Klein and
   other Anti-corporatists   44
4 Small is Beautiful: Green Localism   64
5 Planet Earth Money Martyred: Social Credit and
   Monetary Reform   84
6 Imperialism Unlimited: Marxisms   101
7 The Tribe of Moles: Autonomism, Anarchism and Empire   123
8 Marx on the Seashore: Ecosocialist Alternatives   153
9 Life after Capitalism: Alternatives, Structures, Strategies   171

Bibliography   193
Index   207

The Green Economics Institute
Directors: Volker Heinemann, Goettingen University, and Miriam Kennet, Mansfield College, Oxford University

The Green Economics Institute (GEI) seeks to promote an economy that puts people and planet before profit. Green economics opposes the commodification of life and democracy. It adds a spiritual and ethical element to decision making, while acknowledging the pivotal role of women and nature in real wealth creation. It also opposes the growth imperative, injustice and patriarchy inherent in capitalism. Prosperity, without cancerous expansion of GNP growth, can become compatible with ecological considerations through the principle of 'usufruct' where goods are shared rather than simply produced, consumed and thrown away by private owners. Green economists strive to reclaim economics from being the preserve of purely quantitative measurement, graphs and statistics.

Economics should focus on happiness rather than econometrics. The GEI series examines the pathologies of global capitalism as well as critically discussing green economic alternatives including commons regimes, fiscal measures and new monetary instruments. GEI titles build on insights from ecological and post-autistic economics, ecofeminism, stakeholder theory, Marxism, post-structuralism and post-Keynesian ideas, but moves beyond them to create a discipline that seeks to nurture radically new alternatives based on equity, intergenerational social justice as well as concern for non human species and the biosphere.

GEI titles argue for economic development based on cultural diversity, transparent community control and decision making.

www.greeneconomics.org.uk
www.inderscience.com/ijge Academic Journal International Journal of Green Economics

Email: greeneconomicsinstitute@yahoo.com

Mr. Lebeziatnikov who keeps up with modern ideas explained the other day that compassion is forbidden nowadays by science itself, and that that's what is done now in England, where there is political economy.

Dostoevsky 1993: 14

Acknowledgements

To Nandor, of course. Peter Lockley worked with heroic dedication, reading the whole thing and making lots of useful corrections and suggestions; also thanks for the *Rings of Saturn*, Open Source, Robin Hood, beer and conversation. Xanthe Bevis for her many virtues including being thorough, keeping me laughing in difficult situations and partnering me in several rash political projects. She is one of the people who keeps me doing 'real' things when the temptation is simply to hole out in trailer trash land, drinking, smoking *Bolivars*, reading the *Grundrisse* and Gary Snyder and writing in pleasurable isolation. Her academic contribution was also essential. X you shine. And thank Will for the Slough song. Also to Christina who was happy to roll a spliff or pass a can of red stripe in moments of stress … Christina Borgenstierna made me think deeply, introduced me to squatting, made me aware of that place known as Europe, read and commented, helped with lots of cool political interventions and was continually good for my sanity, thanks Chris, your merit is great. Matthew Tempest for some good advice on the chapter one, lots of encouragement and the hotel floor in Weston-super-Mare, immortal line 'lets share a room and the *Guardian* will pay'. Chris Cotton read the whole thing and was continuously enthusiastic while catching lots of typos. Andrew Copeman, another friend and a poet, was a source of great encouragement, we once walked 50 miles together which helped; Andrew, have fun with the trees. Adam Buick and Richard Kuper read my stuff on Marx with more care than I deserve. Victor Anderson, John Barry, Michael Babula, Molly Scott Cato, Steve Dawe, Richard Douthwaite, Brian Heatly, Gary Holden, Nadia Johanisova, Chris Keene, Miriam Kennet, Jim Killock, Brian Leslie, Brian Orr, Frank Rotering and Stephen Young also gave me detailed feedback.

David Castle for being a patient editor even when I was a desperately impatient writer. Kate Brennan for rescuing me from the gutter when I was homeless. Joel Kovel, may you live long and usufruct strongly, for carrying the ecosocialist cause into many difficult battles, your comments were as always erudite and relevant.

For those friends who I sit with in the South and West London Dojos, sesshins in Sheringham and Galway Bay, Zen days especially Alex and Jim.

Caroline Lucas for generally being right, always been inspiring and being as innocent as a lamb when it comes to deals, intrigue and manoeuvres, all the usual stuff politicians do but she doesn't, although it would be nice if she could sew some meetings up and do at least some Machiavellian deals just once in a while. Thanks for your continued support for Babylon.

For my band of travelling anarchists Larry Wall, Peter Wall and Vincent Wall for their enthusiasms for cookery, wildlife, Jackie Chan, Japanese popular culture (all right yu-gi-oh) hi to the women formerly known as Mrs Wall, if only by the secretary of St Francis primary school.

For my bosses, especially Clive Denning, for being to capitalism what Caroline is to backroom politics.

Walt Contreas Sheasby, whose death has robbed me of a good friend for whom all the important bases green, red and Zen were covered; a dear friend, the world diminished without you. Mike Woodin is also sadly missed. Both died from environmental causes, Mike, never a smoker, from lung cancer, something that is difficult to pin down to a precise cause but increasingly is a product of pollution; Walt from the West Nile Virus that global warming has brought to California ...

Peter Lockley and Beth Collar researched the illustrations, Xanthe Bevis completed the index, all with their usual flair and efficiency.

And thanks to anybody who I have forgotten in the rush to finish! The mistakes are all mine.

Derek Wall
July 2005

Foreword

by Nandor Tanczos

Human beings face the greatest challenge in the history of our species. We face the destruction of the life support systems on which our very existence depends, and we face it because of our own activity.

There are some who deny or diminish that threat. They mostly either retreat into fairy tale thinking – that technology, or the 'free' market, or UFOs will save us – or hope that by closing their eyes they can make it go away.

Yet the evidence is mounting almost daily that the threats are very real and are gathering momentum. A new report from the UK is saying that if we don't turn carbon emissions around in the next decade, we will not be able to stop runaway climate change whatever we do.

Authoritative voices are warning us that we are very close to the point where world demand for oil will outstrip the capacity of the oilfields to supply. Our total dependence on fossil fuels, the use of which has provided the energy for an enormous expansion of human activity and population, is like a chemical addiction. And as the US has recently confirmed in Iraq, strip a junkie of their supply and the temptation to turn to crime can be irresistable.

'The American way of life' said George Bush Sr, 'is not negotiable.'

A time of crisis, however, is also the time of greatest opportunity. More and more people are waking up to the need to change, to change at a fundamental level, and to change right now. People are waking up to the fact that the institutions of society that so many have put their trust in are failing us. Government won't do it. Big business can't do it.

Because the challenge we are facing is about more than changing a few policies or practises. It requires a fundamental rethink of what it means to be a human being. Government and business can become allies, but the power to make real change lies in the hearts and the lives of ordinary people.

It is already happening. The international people's movement against genetically engineered (GE) plants and animals has demonstrated how the reckless agenda of multinational corporations, aided and abetted by our own governments, can be stopped in its tracks and rolled back. One conglomerate has been outed bribing government regulatory officials in Indonesia, GE companies are pulling out of the EU and Australia, and GE agriculture firms are facing massive stock market losses. The promised gold rush is proving to be a fantasy, largely because of global consumer resistance.

While the campaign has significant support in the scientific community, for many ordinary people it began as a sense that something just didn't feel right. That feeling is often quickly backed up by investigation, but the sense of something being fundamentally arrogant and wrong about GE is the key – it is our humanness talking to us.

What is it to be human? Western society, at least, defines us as individuals whose value can be judged by what job we have, what colour credit card we have, what kind of car we drive and the label on our clothes.

Yet beneath these displays of status, real people are emotional, social and spiritual beings – intrinsic characteristics that cannot be considered in isolation from each other. We seem to have forgotten that our relationships – with one another and all the other beings with whom we share this beautiful planet – are fundamental to who we are.

There is a passage in the Bible that says 'where there is no vision, the people perish'. The inability to step back and clearly see and understand the 'big picture' is the central problem that we face in the world today. The main motivations for Western industrial society for the past few hundred years – belief in unlimited growth and technology as the solution to all problems – are the very things that are killing us.

We cannot grow forever on a finite planet. If we continue to assume that endless growth and consumption is possible, and disregard the biosphere's capacity to meet our greed, and if we continue to neglect social justice and fair and sustainable wealth distribution, we will reap a bitter harvest.

Neither will technology on its own fix the problem. Yes, we need better technology, more efficient technology that uses non-polluting cyclical processes and that does not depend on fossil fuels. But just more technology will not do, because the problem is in us and the way we see ourselves in the world.

We humans think that we can own the planet, as if fleas could own a dog. Our concepts of property ownership are vastly different from traditional practices of recognising use rights over various resources. A right to grow or gather food or other resources in a particular place is about meeting needs. Property ownership is about the ability to live on one side of the world and speculate on resources on the other, possibly without ever seeing it, without regard to need or consequence.

The ability to 'own' property is fundamental to capitalism. Since the first limited liability companies – the Dutch and British East India Companies – were formed, we have seen the kidnapping and enslavement of 20–60 million African people and the rape, murder and exploitation of indigenous people around the world. Colonisation was primarily about mercantile empires, not political ones. It was all about forcing indigenous, communitarian people to accept private individual ownership of resources, which could then be alienated, either by being bought or stolen. The subsequent political colonisation was just about how to enforce that ownership.

Today property rights are being extended through the General Agreement on Tariffs and Trade (GATT) and trade related aspects of intellectual prosperity rights agreements (TRIPS) and through institutions such as the World Trade Organization (WTO) and the World Bank. Private property rights are being imposed over public assets such as water, intellectual property and, through genetic engineering and biopiracy, on DNA sequences. Even traditional healing plants are under threat. In Aotearoa – New Zealand – we have had multinationals attempting to patent piko piko and other native plants. This is all part of the 'free' trade corporate globalisation agenda – to create tradable rights over our common wealth, accumulate ownership and then sell back to us what is already ours.

This is only possible because we have lost our place in the scheme of things. We think of the environment as something 'over there', as something separate from human activity, something to either be exploited or protected. The reality is that we are as much part of the environment and the planet as the trees, insects and birds.

It is time to relearn what it means to be human.

Nandor Tanczos was elected as the world's first Rastafarian Member of Parliament in 1999, when he won a seat for the New Zealand Green Party. A key element of the Rastafarian faith is the practice of italism. Ital means 'vital' and deals with all that lives and comes from the Earth. In Rastafarian italism means eating a vegetarian or vegan diet based wherever possible on locally grown organic products. Italism with its emphasis on local production is the opposite of a globalised, corporate economy based on monoculture and the shipping of commodities tens of thousands of miles. Italism shows that localism can be based on diversity rather than intolerance and reminds us of the diverse contributions of black culture and spirituality to a practical green politics. If you chop the word 'capitalism' and discard 'cap' the first three letters, 'italism' is the system that remains.

1

Warm Conspiracies and Cold Concepts

'It was you who told me,' I said gently, 'that capitalism, by its very nature, is a permanent state of war, a constant struggle which can never end.'

'That's true,' she agreed without hesitation, 'But it's not always the same people doing the fighting.' (Houellebecq 2003: 284)

Everything becomes saleable and purchasable. Nothing is immune from this alchemy, the bones of the saints cannot withstand it ... Ancient society therefore denounced it as tending to destroy the economic and moral order. Modern society, which already in its infancy had pulled Pluto by the hair of his head from the bowels of the earth, greets gold as its Holy Grail, as the glittering incarnation of its innermost principle of life. (Marx 1979: 229–30)

October 1998, Davos, Switzerland. Grey-suited civil servants are meeting to celebrate the 50th anniversary of the General Agreement on Tariffs and Trade (GATT) and the creation of its free trade successor the World Trade Organisation (WTO). A little ritualised cake cutting and mutual backslapping is all the local film crews are expecting. Instead of such self-aggrandisement, the cameras roll to the sight of:

a colourful crowd of demonstrators on the far side of rolls of barbed wire ... 'Free trade', they claim, 'despoils the environment and enslaves dispossessed peoples'. 'God is dead', reads one banner; 'The WTO has replaced Him.' The protest, organised by a new network Peoples Global Action, starts quietly but becomes noisier. Most of the demonstrators act peacefully but some start to throwing stones, and bottles, then overturn cars and set them ablaze. (*The Economist*, 1 October 1998)

Since 1998, international trade conferences, summits and other state-corporate jamborees have been disrupted on a continual basis (Anon. 2000). If Davos marked some kind of a start, Seattle is better known. In November 1999, huge protests involving hundreds of thousands of critics of free trade disrupted the WTO talks at Seattle. Since Seattle, a huge, militant and diverse anti-capitalist movement has emerged as a global force. The aim of this book is to explain the economics of this anti-capitalist movement and, in so doing, to examine how a fairer and more ecologically sustainable world can be created.

The movement challenges the misdeeds of powerful globalising elites who seek to redistribute resources from poor to rich, to open up areas of ecologically diverse wilderness to loggers and oil companies and to start profitable wars for weapons manufacturers. However, the removal of such elites is unlikely to be sufficient to achieve a just and ecological world. At its most subversive the anti-capitalist movement is about ideas, it attacks the key concepts of conventional economics. The movement has challenged not just genetically modified crops and social injustice but contested economic assumptions ranging from free trade and economic growth to property rights. This is a rebellion against cold economics concepts as well as assumed warm conspiracies by corporations and right-wing politicians. The most radical anti-capitalists tell us that almost everything we know about economics is wrong and, given economic logic is the logic that runs modern society, the implications of such a critique, if correct, are breathtaking.

The movement has been surprisingly successful, often slowing and sometimes reversing the supposedly irresistible march of global market forces. Not only did the Seattle trade talks collapse largely because of the protest but, in September 2003, some four years on, WTO agenda-setting discussions at Cancun, Mexico, fell apart after an alliance of developing countries put forward many demands of the anti-globalisers. In 2003, anti-capitalists who rose up to prevent water privatisation toppled the Bolivian government (*Guardian*, 21 October 2003). The once forgotten global financial architecture of the International Monetary Fund (IMF), the World Bank, the G8 and associated institutions is constantly in the news, visible and under almost continuous criticism. From opposition to genetically modified (GM) food to successful demands to reduce Third World debt, movement victories are multiple.

The movement's diversity is also important. American Midwest anarchists have come together with trade unionists, socialists and major non-governmental organisations (NGOs) like the World Development Movement and Oxfam, along with radical farmers like José Bové from France in the Confédération Paysanne, Greens and others. Revolutionaries in Mexico and Argentina have been part of a movement that stretches to local community groups in the more conservative parts of Birmingham or Kyoto. This has been the first radical movement to fully utilise the internet to coordinate days of action and other protests on a global scale. The movement in all its multiplicity argues that neo-liberal globalisation creates poverty, destroys diversity, wrecks the environment and erodes democracy. The globalisers on the contrary argue that there is no alternative to conventional market economics and neo-liberalism is the only secure path to prosperity. The stakes are very high.

For all these reasons and more, the anti-capitalist movement demands attention, but while its slogans seem self-apparent its ideas are often contradictory, sometimes complex and have deep historical roots. It is an amalgam of different schools of thought with different forms of analysis and varied demands. The aim of this volume is to unpick the intellectual knots in the protest network, to show how anti-capitalist ideas have developed. In this chapter, I briefly examine the origins of the anti-capitalist movement, outline the arguments of their opponents who support free market globalisation and describe the different variants of anti-capitalism discussed in later chapters.

THE ANTI-CAPITALIST MOVEMENT

The movement did not start on the streets of Seattle or Davos. Submerged and open networks of anti-capitalism flowered in 1999 but had been mobilising long before (Wall 1999). Anti-capitalist sentiments predate capitalism understood as an advanced industrial or post-industrial system based on profit and investment. Given that centuries before capitalism existed, Jesus threw the moneylenders out of the temple, one wonders how he would have reacted to contemporary church towers being used as mobile phone masts or the corporate enthusiasms of some American Protestants. Five centuries before Christ entered the temple, the Buddha, Gautama Siddhartha, set up a philosophical system in opposition to the notion of economic (wo)man and the desire for ever more consumer goods, before the term 'economics' had been coined by Aristotle. The fact that the Buddha's holiness was indicated, amongst other signs, by his long ear lobes, a symbol of nobility enjoyed by the then Nepalese ruling class whose lavish jewellery distended their ears, suggests that Zen is only half of the process. Rebellion against empire has a long history too. The Spartacus uprising where the slaves attempted to overthrow Roman power deserves a mention, immortalised as it was by Rosa Luxemburg's brave but failed Spartacist revolution of 1919 and put into celluloid by the Marxist scriptwriter Howard Fast (Bronner 1987; Fast 1990). From the peasant revolutionaries such as John Ball to the Anabaptists who took on and nearly defeated the Saxon Lutheran princes there is a tradition of struggle against established economic and political power that stretches back centuries (Strayer 1991).

The creation of the capitalist market in Britain, for example, during the eighteenth century was vigorously opposed with direct action by small producers, farmers and workers who insisted instead on the maintenance of a moral economy that placed need before greed (Tilly 1978). Land enclosure was fought with a series of peasant revolts and oppressive landlords were shamed in the seventeenth century by ritual processions known as charivari or skimmingtons (Wall 2004). In Ireland, oppressive landowners were humiliated by hunger strikers who starved themselves to death at their gates in the nineteenth century. The so-called utopian socialists continued the habit of resistance to the market, particularly in Britain and France. It is worth mentioning Robert Owen, the factory-owning radical, who attempted to build a socialist commonwealth in the early nineteenth century (Taylor 1982). Karl Marx, who spent his entire adult life attempting to understand capitalism, at the very time it was maturing, sought to create a system to help fight it (Harvey 1990; Wheen 2000). Marx's attitude to capitalism was akin to that of many of the utopian socialists and anarchists in its complexity; while he attacked capitalism as exploitative, he also saw it as a progressive force, which by developing the means of production would pave the way to a new society. For good and sometimes for ill, the twentieth century saw Marxist inspired revolutions over much of the globe.

In turn, Marx's anarchist detractors created militant movements opposed to capitalism during the nineteenth and twentieth centuries (Woodcock 1963).

The Frankfurt School of Western Marxists based around figures such as Adorno, Horkheimer and Marcuse saw capitalism as a totalitarian system that controlled the working class via parliamentary democracy and consumerism (Jay 1973). According to Marcuse, representative democracy seduces the public into thinking that they can participate politically, when in fact they are being manipulated by a capitalist elite who choose the real rulers of society. The radical New Left, who agreed with Marcuse's insight that consumerism is used to buy obedience, exploded out of the relatively conservative left parties of the 1950s and 1960s. Marcuse helped inspire the student uprisings of the late 1960s and early 1970s, particularly Paris in 1968 (Brown 1974).

Feminists have criticised the economic system as one that enslaves women and fails to value their contribution (Peterson and Lewis 1999). Women either work for free in the home or increasingly as low paid, part-time and poorly protected workers in the formal economy (Malos 1980). Drawing upon both the Frankfurt School and feminism, green movements have crystallised during the last quarter of the twentieth century to argue that a society focused on market economics diminishes human beings and manipulates spiritual and social needs into forms of consumerism (Snyder 1974). Greens have attacked capitalism, above all, because of its emphasis on economic growth, which they have seen as ecologically unsustainable (Douthwaite 1993; Porritt 1984).

Activists have increasingly targeted corporations as a source of ecological and human injustice. The UK based Corporate Watch was established in 1995 by campaigners who had worked to boycott the Shell oil company for its complicity in the execution of Nigerian activist Ken Saro-Wiwa. From the boycott of Nestlé over its high-pressure selling of powdered milk to mothers whose access to dirty water in developing countries raised infant mortality, to animal rights campaigns against vivisecting companies, anti-corporate protest has grown in the 1980s, 1990s and into the twenty-first century.

The Zapatista uprising of January 1994 is pivotal to any understanding of the recent wave of militant anti-capitalism. This previously obscure guerrilla army occupied five southern Mexican provinces to protest at the introduction of the North American Free Trade Agreement (NAFTA), which they believed would lead to the loss of their land by multinationals. Their spokesperson Marcos argued, 'NAFTA is a death sentence because it leads to competition based on your level of skill, and what skill level can illiterate people have? And look at this land. How can we compete with farms in California and Canada?' (Russell 1995: 6). The Zapatistas were reported as stating: 'There are those with white skins and a dark sorrow. Our struggle walks with these skins. There are those who have dark skins and a white arrogance; against them is our fire. Our armed path is not against skin colour but against the colour of money' (*Earth First! UpDate* 53, November 1994: 3).

In Mexico there is a tradition of hostility to prices, property and other market institutions, that predates Marxism and anarchism. The Zapatistas take their name from Emiliano Zapata who led the Mexican Revolution. He fought for 'tierra y libertad', the demand for communal land ownership and the defence of the peasant producers. A subplot of Malcolm Lowry's *Under the Volcano*, one of the most important novels of the twentieth century, is right-wing opposition to the Mexican state, which even in the 1930s retained some notion of its revolutionary roots (1967). The Zapatista leader Marcos was originally a Maoist and remains influenced by Marxist forms of anti-capitalism however, such Mexican and indigenous roots have shaped the movement. To join NAFTA the Mexican government abolished article 27 of Zapata's 1910 revolutionary constitution, which guaranteed the right to land for those who worked it. The Zapatistas fought to prevent these '*ejidos*', or communal landholdings, from being sold to private landowners. The Zapatista Army of National Liberation began as a local militia to defend the poorest people of Mexico's poorest provinces but mutated into a wider campaign against capitalism, motivated by fear that free trade would create even greater suffering in the Chiapas.

The Zapatistas exploited the power of the internet, a product of capitalism and driving force of globalisation, to help kickstart the anti-capitalist mobilisation of recent years (Anon. 1998; Holloway and Pelaez 1998). They have worked with a variety of groups including anarchists and radical environmentalists such as Reclaim the Streets (RTS) in the UK (Wall 1999). In 1996 they called an international *encuentro* or encounter to link opponents of neo-liberalism, which brought 6,000 participants to the Chiapas. A second *encuentro* in Spain in 1997 saw the creation of Peoples Global Action (PGA), who organised the 50th anniversary Davos demonstration against GATT in 1998. The PGA linked together ten grassroots networks including the

Brazilian Landless movement and the radical Indian Farmers Union. *Do or Die!* a journal produced by members of Earth First! and RTS reported back from the first *encuentro* that four hallmark principles were used to create a measure of unity:

> A very clear rejection of the institutions that multinationals and speculators have built to take power away from people, like the WTO and other trade liberalisation agreements.
>
> A confrontational attitude, since we do not think that lobbying can have a major impact in such biased and undemocratic organisations in which transnational capital is the only real policy maker.
>
> A call for non-violent civil disobedience and the construction of local alternatives by local people, as answers to the actions of governments and corporations.
>
> An organisational philosophy based on decentralisation and autonomy. (*Do or Die!* 8, 1999)

PGA used the internet to organise internationally and rejected the participation of formal NGOs and political parties including Greens and Marxists. In February 1998 the first meeting of PGA brought together 300 delegates from 71 countries, including the Uwa peoples of Colombia, Canadian Postal Workers, European Reclaim the Streets activists, anti-nuclear campaigners, French farmers, Maori and Ogoni activists, through to Korean trade unionists, the Indigenous Women's Network of North America, and Ukrainian radical ecologists. 'All were there to form a global instrument for communication and co-ordination for all those fighting against the destruction of humanity and the planet by the global market' (*Do or Die!* 8, 1999). A series of rolling protests at international events to promote the free trade hegemony was launched, as noted by *The Economist*, at the 50th anniversary of GATT, in Switzerland.

A global day of action against capitalism was organised for 18 June 1999 to coincide with that year's meeting of the G8. In Britain, the 'Carnival against Capitalism' was a carefully planned act of chaos. Fifty thousand gold flyers distributed at clubs and pubs, a global e-mail discussion list and vigorous fly posting, were used to draw 10,000 partygoers to the meeting point at Liverpool Street Station. Banners proclaimed 'Kill Capitalism', 'Global ecology not global economy'. Coloured masks were distributed and flags – green for ecology, red for communism and black for anarchy – were used to lead demonstrators in different directions. The entire financial centre of London was severely disrupted (Wall 2004).

Major protests followed at Seattle that, as noted, derailed the WTO agenda-setting talks. September 2000 saw the IMF meeting in the Czech Republic under siege. The World Social Forum met in a conscious parody of the World Economic Forum's traditional gathering, for the first time in February 2001. The event in Porto Alegre in southern Brazil was also accompanied by direct action:

> José Bové ... was the star turn at 'anti-Davos', especially after he joined leaders of Brazil's Landless Movement on an excursion to destroy a plantation of genetically modified soya owned by Monsanto, an American company. He was briefly arrested and threatened with deportation, but was later allowed to stay. Protesters trashed a nearby McDonald's in his honour. (*The Economist*, 3 February 2001)

In April 2001 a Quebec meeting to create a free trade area of the Americas had to be fortified to resist an assault by anti-globalists. The next WTO meeting was in Qatar, a remote police state, chosen to reduce the possibility of protest. Such actions at major international events have continued to occur since 2001, and a wave of protest is being planned as this book goes to press against the G8 meeting in Scotland in 2005. Many events have turned to violence with protesters being killed or severely injured. Local networks that undertake grassroots action of a less dramatic but no less important kind accompany such large-scale and vivid events (Plows 2004).

GLOBALISATION, CAPITALISM AND THE ARGUMENTS FOR NEO-LIBERALISM

It is important to define the key terms and to explore, albeit briefly, the arguments used to defend economic orthodoxy. Supporters of capitalist globalisation are most commonly termed 'neo-liberals' because of their renewed faith in the 'liberal' unconstrained free market. Globalisation is a much debated term but can be defined straightforwardly by the decline in the power of nation states and the growing flow of resources on a planetary scale. While technology, culture and other factors come into play, globalisation is first and foremost an economic process driven by market forces. The market is a system where we buy and sell items. In theory the market is made up of thousands of competing firms, whose desire for profit means they provide goods and services. Even some supposed 'anti-capitalists' such as David Korten, author of *When Corporations Rule the World* (2001), view the market as a positive and practical way of organising economic activity. However, the market tends to evolve into capitalism. Capitalism is, essentially, a system where profits are made within a market-based context and reinvested in new capital equipment, that is, machines and IT used to produce more goods and services. Some theorists have suggested that forms of 'state capitalism' can also be identified, where the state rather than private companies exploits workers and the environment.

Capitalism is based not on the intense competition of thousands of companies but on the creation of markets dominated by just a handful of enormous firms. Food retailing is a good example of the process. In Britain thousands of bakers, greengrocers and corner stores have disappeared and four or five large supermarkets control much of the market. To survive, a firm must, generally, make profit. Profit is reinvested to expand the size of the firm; if profit was frittered away rather than reinvested, the firm would risk being put out of business by more efficient rivals. Investment allows a firm to expand its market share, and as it sells more items it can exploit economies of scale. This concept is based on the idea that as a firm becomes bigger, production costs fall per item produced. Such economies occur because larger firms can bulk buy raw materials more cheaply than smaller firms; larger firms can make more efficient use of machinery, employ specialist staff and gain funds for expansion in the form of bank loans more easily. Smaller firms generally have higher costs and tend to be pushed out of business. There are numerous linked processes that help explain the evolution of markets into capitalist systems. The creation of public limited companies allows firms to borrow money in return for giving others a 'share'. Such share ownership allows swift expansion but aids the process of replacing small businesses owned by individual entrepreneurs with faceless corporations. Public companies gain an institutional existence, have the legal status of individuals and, like all good bureaucracies, tend to be self-perpetuating.

The capitalist system, as we shall see in subsequent chapters is a complex one; workers have to be made to work and consumers have to be persuaded to consume to sustain the growth of companies. Ever more complex financial instruments are used to allow capitalism to grow and change in order to survive. Banks, to cut a long story short, lend money from depositors to borrowers and create more money in the process. Banking has been one target of anti-capitalist concern because of the banks' ability to make money out of money and use this power to shape society. Share ownership and the basic banking functions are the first steps on a ladder of increasing financial abstraction, with ever more esoteric devices being used to make money out of money and, at the same time, to support capitalist growth. The drive for profit fuels globalisation as firms seek new markets to sell their products and new sources of cheap raw materials and labour. The creation of global markets is also strongly conditioned by the financial side of capitalist growth. 'Hot money', so-called because it moves from one country to another and is transformed from one currency to another and then back again, erodes the barrier between nations. If a country introduces policies hostile to capitalism, currency tends to flow out, creating economic crisis. To maintain a strong exchange rate, pro-capitalist policies are often a necessity.

Hedge funds are an increasingly important financial institution. Hedging started by meeting a practical need but soon changed into something much more complex. Hedging is a way of providing security, as in the phrase 'hedging a bet'. For example, an investor concerned that the exchange rate for the pound sterling will fall, can buy the right to sell pounds in three months' time at the present value, so if the currency crashes, losses will be prevented. For a fee, risk is removed. Various forms of right to buy such a right to hedge are bought and sold, including varied financial 'options' and 'derivatives'. Essentially, mathematically complex forms of betting have become an increasingly important global economic activity.

Supporters of the market are confident that the pursuit of financial gain, the accumulation of private property and the race for personal wealth are to be welcomed (Bhagwati 2004; Wolf 2004). They believe that capitalism is the road to prosperity, pleasure, freedom, justice and all that is beneficial. Capitalism, because it is based on market forces, is both natural and good. For the advocates of unrestrained capitalism the only alternative to market forces is government planning and control. They consider intervention inefficient because government planners cannot take into account all the thousands of pieces of information necessary for an economy to function well. In the Soviet Union planning did not meet the needs of consumers and provided no incentive for workers to work hard so as to raise production.

In contrast to bureaucratic planning, the market regulates the economy via forces of demand and supply. Adam Smith, whose book *The Wealth of Nations* launched market-based economics in

1776, believed that these market forces acted like a giant invisible hand managing wealth for the good of the community. If consumers demand goods and are prepared to back up their desire with hard cash, firms will supply their wants so as to make a profit. Competition between firms means that neither consumers nor workers will be exploited. If a firm cuts its wages, workers will sell their labour to a rival and maintain their standard of living. Wage rises can be used to encourage workers to retrain, to work harder and to raise production through greater participation. Likewise, market forces benefit shoppers: if a firm provides shoddy or expensive goods, consumers will go elsewhere. The market is freedom. It is a tool of liberation for workers, who can choose to work for the firm that pays the highest wage.

The market system leads to capitalism because firms have an incentive to invest in new technology to produce cheaper goods to undercut rivals and maintain profits. The market system is based on greed, but greed fuels the common good and drives progress forward as industrialists strive to create new products and new production techniques. Such growth tends to spread prosperity to the entire community via a process of 'trickle down'. Even if a wealthy minority do exist, they have to use their wealth to purchase goods and services from others. In doing so they create jobs and the basis for growing prosperity.

The market is seen as a force for democracy because it breaks up the power of the old feudal elements of society. Kings lose their power and companies have to respect the rest of the community if they wish to gain customers and attract staff. Money is profoundly democratic because whatever the social rank, gender or ethnicity of the person spending it, it still has the same value for firms seeking profit. The notion of private property, a precondition for and goal of the market, makes it difficult for the state to control private citizens.

The pro-capitalist messengers believe that the system brings ever greater benefits. The classic free market is decentralised with economic decisions being taken at a grassroots level. The market also provides a cleaner environment because consumers can purchase greener goods and as levels of prosperity rise societies generally become more environmentally aware. Bjorn Lomborg, the Danish statistician, has argued at great length that information showing declining environmental quality is distorted, and that entering the third millennium, resources such as oil and fish are increasing in quantity while pollution is being defeated by prosperity (Lomborg 2001).

Globalisation brings the benefits of capitalism to all, according to the author Johan Norberg:

> The statistics speak for themselves. Over the past 40 years, average life expectancy in the developing countries has risen from 46 to 64 years. Since 1950, infant mortality has fallen from 18 to 8 per cent. Since 1980 the number of people in absolute poverty was reduced by more than 200 million. The number of states which are democratically governed and respect human rights is increasing all the time. There are still enormous problems in the world, but to anyone who cares to look it is obvious that the world, in most ways, has become a better and a fairer place. (<www.johannorberg.net>)

WHAT'S WRONG WITH CAPITALISM?

Anti-capitalists vigorously challenge the claims of the market utopians such as Lomborg or Norberg. The modern market is dominated by a tiny number of megacorporations who have scant interest in 'market forces', but this is of little concern to advocates of capitalism who have simply invented new economic theories that explain why planning and control by monopolistic multinationals is in the public interest. Thus to keep their power these firms have to constantly develop new products before their patents run out. For example, pharmaceutical companies have to develop new drugs, anticipating the time when patents run out and the original and high-priced drugs are pushed out of the market by cheap substitutes. Other neo-liberals deny that corporations have more power than the thousands of individual firms in competitive markets:

> That isn't true. Corporations can acquire monopoly status in a system of tariffs, licensing and coercion, because then consumers are denied the option of buying from anyone else and potential new businesses are prevented from competing. Capitalism means freedom to pick and choose and to reject the businesses which aren't up to scratch. Corporate liberty in a capitalist economy is the same thing as the waiter's liberty of giving the customer a menu to choose from. And the whole point of free trade is that other waiters – even foreign ones – are allowed to come running up with alternative menus. (<www.johannorberg.net>)

The neo-liberals have been more than happy to surf across their contradictions. Planning by governments or local communities is still condemned by *The Economist* and similar journals as essentially flawed. Most fundamentally, the far from bloodless origins of capitalism are mythologised out of the neo-liberal version of history. Slavery, land enclosure, forced labour, colonialism and most of the accompanying rape and pillage is ignored. Capitalism did not evolve gently but emerged covered in blood. When things fall apart the results are rarely pretty. The capitalist scholars today are also largely silent when it comes to the creation of new markets in far from democratic states such as Chile under General Pinochet and China. Equally, the greenhouse effect, declining fish stocks, the rise of the automobile and the prevalence of low-level nuclear waste suggest that statistics indicating a cleaner environment need questioning.

Challenging the neo-liberal orthodoxy, anti-capitalists point to a range of problems that have grown with globalisation. Poverty is perhaps the most obvious, despite the fact that neo-liberalism should, according to its advocates, deliver high levels of growth that reduce poverty, there is much evidence to suggest that income inequality has grown over recent decades. Indeed, during the 1990s both absolute and relative poverty have increased.

The World Bank (*Economic Outlook* 2000) shows that since 1980 the number of people living on less than $2 per day has risen by almost 50% to 2.8 billion – almost half the world's population. A report from Christian Aid noted that between 1960 and 1997 the gap between the poorest fifth and richest fifth more than doubled, that the top fifth had 86 per cent of the world's wealth, while the lowest fifth had just 1 per cent. The wealth of the world's three wealthiest billionaires is more than that of the GNP of all the least developing countries and 'their 600 million people'. Those who argue that globalisation reduces poverty would do well to study the record of the US, arguably the most globalised nation on earth:

> The gap between rich and poor in America is the widest in 70 years, according to a new study published by the Center for Budget and Policy Priorities. The research, based on newly released figures from the non-partisan Congressional Budget Office, shows that the top 1% of Americans – who earn an average of $862,000 each after tax (or $1.3m before tax) – receive more money than the 110m Americans in the bottom 40% of the income distribution, whose income averages $21,350 each year. The income going to the richest 1% has gone up threefold in real terms in the past twenty years, while the income of the poorest 40% went up by a more modest 11%. (Schifferes 2003)

In the former Soviet Union the creation of a market economy has led to catastrophe. In an article subtitled 'Russia appears to be committing suicide', *The Economist* (2 October) notes that since 1989 the population of the former Soviet states has plunged by several million and is projected to fall from 147 million today to 120 million in 2030. Declining fertility, violence, sexually transmitted diseases, tuberculosis and alcoholism are just symptoms 'of the long, dark night of the Russian soul ushered in by the disorienting collapse of communism'.

There are number of explanations as to why globalisation paradoxically boosts GNP rates and at the same time pushes up poverty. Globalisation allows companies to move easily from country to country, enabling them to pay far less tax to governments, which leads to less redistribution. The monopoly power of drug firms has been a major factor in pushing down life expectancy in Africa. Christian Aid cites Mara Rossi, head of the AIDS department of the Catholic Diocese of Ndola, Zambia, who noted

> The availability of drugs to treat HIV/AIDS is an example of how globalisation fails to benefit some of the world's poorest and most needy people. Because of the monopoly of multinational pharmaceutical companies, drugs are not available to the majority of HIV infected people in Asia and Africa. These drugs must be made accessible in countries such as Zambia. It's no good promising loans to buy anti-retroviral drugs that in the end will increase foreign debt. The majority of AIDS patients in Africa need clean water and food as well as drugs to treat their illness. (Christian Aid 2000)

Neo-liberalism encourages governments to cut welfare programmes in both the south and the north of the globe. Subsidies for cheap food have largely gone, increasing levels of starvation. Privatisation has made it more difficult for the poorest to afford basic utility services such as clean water. Welfare benefits have been made reduced or abolished in parts of the globe including the US. Trade unions are under threat. Typically, Zhang Junjiu, vice chairman of All-China Federation of Trade Unions (ACFTU), has argued that globalisation makes it difficult for trade unions to protect workers pay and conditions. While the Chinese economy grew strongly in 2004, millions were laid off by state enterprises, and multinationals relied on casual workers with low pay. Urban unemployment rose to 8 million. Multinationals can keep moving to countries with low wages, making it difficult for workers in developed countries to maintain employment and for those in poor countries to improve conditions (<www.chinaview.cn 2004–10–10>).

Democracy is another area of concern for the anti-capitalists. While the number of states with nominally democratic systems has increased, globalisation has robbed voters of much of their influence over governments. WTO rules tend to reduce the sovereignty of local and national government by ruling that much legislation produced by states is protectionist and therefore illegitimate. The US government used WTO rules to force EU countries into taking dairy products that contained growth hormones. At present, the WTO is battling to make the EU accept unlabelled GM products, despite the fact that opinion polls suggest that the majority of European citizens wish to be protected from GM. Multinationals who often have more wealth than nations can effectively force countries to reject legislation that may damage corporate interests. Even supporters of capitalism sometimes admit the essentially undemocratic nature of the market. For example, Thomas Friedman, author of *The Lexus and the Olive Tree*, a long hymn to the neo-liberal globalisation, has argued:

> For globalism to work, America can't be afraid to act like the almighty superpower that it is ... The hidden hand of the market will never work without a hidden fist – McDonald's cannot flourish without McDonnell Douglas, the designer of the F-15. And the hidden fist that keeps the world safe for Silicon Valley's technologies is called the United States Army, Air Force, Navy and Marine Corps. (*New York Times*, 28 March 1999)

Poverty is increased and democracy eroded by a process of social dumping or levelling down driven by both the WTO and the multinationals. Countries that reduce governmental controls, taxes and public expenditure attract more investment by international corporations. In the desperate race to attract foreign investment, countries have a huge incentive to sweep away forms of social protection such as trade union rights, maximum working hours and an adequate minimum wage. Despite an ageing population, fewer and fewer workers can gain access to adequate pensions from their employers. In countries such as China and the Philippines blandly named Export Processing Zones (EPZs), have been created where manufacturers can ignore legislation protecting workers, so as to drive pay and conditions down to lower average total costs.

The anti-capitalists believe that the process of neo-liberal globalisation has concentrated wealth and power into the hands of an ever-diminishing minority. This minority is increasingly US based and uses both global institutions and the US to cement its dominance. Thus, the existence of the US as the world's hyperpower is seen as increasingly damaging, allowing a tiny minority of North Americans to shape the world so as to serve their own interests. The growth of capitalism is based on the exploitation of the working class, small farmers and peasants, and it largely excludes women from meaningful participation in political and economic decision-making. Racism is part of the process. All but a tiny minority are defined as 'the other' and seen as a means of creating wealth rather than as human beings with their own ends: creative, social, cultural and ecological. Anti-capitalists also critique the ethos of capitalism, where local diversity in the arts, cuisine and other aspects of life are driven out creating a homogenised global culture. Everywhere individuals drink Coca-Cola, wear Nike and eat McDonald's. The sociologist George Ritzer has created the concept of the macdonaldisation of society to explain how mass production has delivered a world of increasing modular uniformity (Ritzer 1995). Such a capitalist culture breeds alienation, a feeling of homelessness in a world dominated by accountancy, which degrades even those who benefit in material terms from the rule of capital.

Ever-increasing capitalist globalisation damages the environment by lowering standards of protection and by locking us into an escalating system of waste. The world circles to destruction around a mountain of decaying trainers and trashed soft drink cans. The drive for endlessly increasing international trade means that goods are transported ever rising distances, driving up fuel consumption and, in consequence, the greenhouse effect. Higher agricultural exports tend to depress prices because of oversupply and force farmers to exploit ecologically sensitive and essential mangrove swamps and rainforests. Ever increasing economic growth in turn means that more and more scarce resources are demanded, so as to maintain the profit system. Capitalist growth for the whole planet would demand, according to some critics, the resources of four planet Earths, and such resources would have to grow to maintain the capitalist system into the future (Wilson 2002). Neo-liberals argue that the world is getting cleaner, resources are growing rather than shrinking, poverty is disappearing and democracy is on the rise. The evidence is against them on all these counts.

DIVERSITY OR CHAOS: CATALOGUING DIFFERENT ANTI-CAPITALISMS

The demands of the movement seem relatively straightforward. Neo-liberal globalisation is delivering poverty, injustice, authoritarian controls and environmental destruction, so demands our opposition. However, a closer look at the movement indicates intellectual confusion and a chaotic mismatch of contradictory assumptions. While it may be difficult to reach agreement on all issues given the diversity of the groups and networks involved, some of these contradictions seem extreme.

An excellent example is the issue of trade. Groups such as Oxfam believe that the removal of tariffs and other barriers to trade will help developing countries. At present the European Union, the US and Japan heavily subsidise their own farmers and place huge tax on food imports from the rest of the world. A fair trade campaign put together by the NGOs is aimed at removing barriers to trade so countries in the south of the globe can sell more of their agricultural products in the wealthier parts of the world.

Many others in the anti-capitalist movement, including farmers from the south of the globe, believe that free trade, which after all is the aim of the WTO, will actually create greater poverty and drive them away from the land. Free trade means that large-scale Western farmers, particularly in the American midwest, can undercut small developing-country producers and drive them out of business by providing farm products at a fraction of the price. Such fears motivated one Korean beef farmer at Cancun to commit suicide in protest (*Guardian*, 16 September 2003).

How can advocates of free trade and protectionism be part of the same movement? To an extent, the dichotomy is artificial. The US, EU and Japan have embodied the same contradiction ever since GATT was established in 1947. The US government has campaigned strongly for free trade in agriculture when it has benefited and against when it is not in the perceived US interest. For example, the US, under President Clinton, took the EU to court to force them to end support for small-scale banana producers in the Caribbean because this was detrimental to US multinationals like Del Monte who have large banana plantations in South America. Successive US governments have given huge subsidies to American cotton farmers because this is seen as politically expedient. Maybe the anti-capitalists could simply advocate protectionism when it helps the south and promote free trade where it brings benefits? Nonetheless, the trade issue is an excellent illustration of the contradictions that the movement must address if it is to succeed in creating a fairer, greener and more democratic world order.

It is possible to disentangle a series of different, although to some extent overlapping, anti-capitalisms. One group whose work underpins the protest can be termed 'anti-capitalist capitalists' (see Chapter 2). While 'anti-capitalist capitalists' are unlikely to be on the streets at major international protest, they are nonetheless important to the movement. They don't reject the market, greater international trade or economic growth. In the past, they have been prominent supporters of neo-liberalism. As establishment figures who have participated in global economic institutions, they cannot easily be dismissed by advocates of globalisation. George Soros and Joseph Stiglitz are excellent examples. Soros, an international financier who has made millions of dollars from playing the money markets, has come to argue that unrestrained free market forces erode democracy and create social chaos. Stiglitz, who won a Nobel Prize for his development of microeconomic theory, who echoes many of Soros' concerns, is a prominent economist who headed the World Bank and was one of Bill Clinton's key advisers (Stiglitz 2002, 2003).

Others in the movement focus on the destructive role of multinational corporations, arguing that footloose international companies drive down wages, hypnotise us into destructive consumerism and lower environmental standards. Naomi Klein, in *No Logo*, sees globalisation as leading to a race to the bottom, where countries struggle to lower standards so as to attract inward investment (2000a). Multinationals selling brands outsource production to companies that use the cheapest labour. David Korten, author of *When Corporations Ruled the World* (2001), argues that large corporations should be removed and replaced with a local market based on family and community-run business.

It is possible to contrast those NGOs who support further free trade, albeit in a 'fair' context, with those who see trade as damaging. Green localists believe that free trade will impoverish millions of small peasant farmers and accelerate ecological damage. Colin Hines, who co-wrote *The New Protectionists* with Tim Lang (1993) and *Localization* (2000), is representative of such a trend. The new protectionists or localists have also been instrumental in creating the International Forum on Globalisation, a major anti-capitalist think tank and campaigning body. While Hines concurs with many of the concerns of Korten and Klein, his emphasis is on the need to build largely self-sufficient local economies. Perhaps the best-known Green localist is Caroline Lucas, the charismatic Green Party MEP who, with the late Mike Woodin, wrote *Green Alternatives to Globalisation* (2004). The Indian academic Vandana Shiva is another localist. Others such as the journalist George Monbiot have attacked the localists in the movement for ignoring the real benefits of trade and for failing to examine how global economic forces can be democratised (2003b). Chapter 4 deals with green localism.

A section of the anti-capitalist movement focuses on money, banking and debt. The international debt crisis has created the Jubilee movement for debt relief in the south of the globe, while economist James Tobin has suggested that a tax could be levied on speculative flows of currency to create a more stable economic system and to inject some of the money made by financiers back into the real economy. The ATTAC movement, originally formed by journalists from the French newspaper *Le Monde Diplomatique* but now with branches in many countries, has been campaigning with some success for this 'Tobin Tax'. 'Social creditors' and other related 'monetary reformers', inspired by the unorthodox theories of figures like Major Douglas and Silvio Gesell, see finance as an evil and advocate the creation of debt-free money by the community to generate a different kind of world order (Hutchinson et al. 2002; Rowbotham 1998, 2000). The critics of finance capital are discussed in Chapter 5.

Marxists, other socialists and trade unionists have marched at Seattle and have been prominent in other protests against neo-liberal globalisation. Marxist explanations of crisis are particularly important in discussing the approach of socialist opponents of neo-liberal globalisation, including Communist parties and the Fourth International or Socialist Workers Party (Callinicos 2003; Petras and Veltmeyer 2001, 2003; Went 2000). The President of Cuba, Fidel Castro, has produced a fascinating socialist account of global capitalism (Castro 2003). Some Marxists and ex-Marxists have argued that globalisation may lead to a post-capitalist society and the liberation of humanity. Nigel Harris (2003) and Meghnad Desai (2004) both suggest that Marx argued that capitalism, by industrialising the planet, would create the conditions necessary to sustain a fair and prosperous socialist society. Chapter 6 introduces Marxist accounts of globalisation.

The most militant participants in the anti-capitalist protests have been the anarchists, many of whom are non-violent, but there are those, the 'black blocs', who participate in street fighting. The anarchists are inspired by diverse thinkers, but perhaps most prominently by the 'autonomists' such as the academics Harry Cleaver, Michael Hardt and Toni Negri. Like Marx, they argue that globalisation is a product of the most destructive tendencies of capitalism. For them the market is not a means of regulating the economy but a weapon used to imprison workers. They see the workplace as a prison and believe that workers' struggles to escape from the power of capitalism have encouraged firms to relocate globally. In *Empire* Hardt and Negri (2001a) argue that a militant movement, the multitude, can overthrow capitalism and create a new kind of society. Autonomism is placed in a historical tradition of anarchist economic thought ranging from Kropotkin to the workers' communes of the Spanish Civil War. The Marxist and post-modern influences on militant autonomism are also outlined in Chapter 7, with an emphasis on *Empire*.

Ecosocialists such as the US Green presidential challenger Joel Kovel (2002) maintain that the best insights of both Marx and the Greens need to be combined if globalisation is to be understood and resisted. For ecosocialists the basic atoms and molecules of capitalist production conjure up debt, multinational corporations, the dislocations of 'free' trade and all the rest. For the ecosocialists, the idea that capitalism must continue to grow and dominate the planet is alien. Chapter 8 outlines the case for ecosocialism. Finally, Chapter 9 concludes with a look at how an anti-capitalist economy can be built and sustained.

DEBATING APOCALYPSE

Even a brief survey of the main currents of anti-capitalism throws up a number of difficult debates that demand attention. First, is the issue of what can be crudely termed conspiracy or concept. Are economic concepts just window dressing to help legitimise the power of one group over another? While conventional market economists, the media and most politicians argue that there are enduring economic ground rules that provide a guide to constructing a prosperous future, many anti-capitalists suggest that economics is almost entirely irrelevant as an explanation for the workings of the system. The monetary reformers often argue that bankers control the politicians so as to maintain power over the monetary system. The autonomists believe that the economic system is manipulated to control the working class and exploit them. Many of those concerned with trade, whether localists who want more protection or fair traders who want less, believe that bodies like the WTO are motivated not by a concern with comparative advantage and other economic principles, but simply by a wish to benefit the rich and powerful.

Conspiracies make life easy to explain and provide enemies – the bankers, the capitalists, the US – that are easy to attack. There is little doubt that many of our problems result from those with power exploiting those without. Unfortunately, conspiracy does not explain everything. The conspiracy view of economics seems to generate a cartoonish air of unreality. Autonomist Harry Cleaver (2000: 95), to give one example, argued in the 1970s that inflation had been deliberately created by capitalist states to weaken the power of trade unions by reducing the purchasing power of their wages. Yet most commentators agree that deflation where prices fall, rather than inflation where prices rise, is much more damaging to workers because it leads to unemployment. Right-wing politicians like Margaret Thatcher have been obsessed with reducing inflation, an unlikely strategy if inflation really did harm the very poorest as opposed to bankers defending the value of their assets. While conspiracies exist, activists should also be critical of concepts and should beware stereotyping that delivers an enemy who is satisfyingly easy to label, condemn and attack.

The blame game can shade into a form of pseudo or not so pseudo-racism where entire groups are scapegoated for economic ills (Chua 2003). In the United States politician Pat Buchanan has campaigned against the WTO, arguing along with other far-right nationalists that a one-world conspiracy exists to limit local diversity. Banking and capitalism are seen as creating a new world order that benefits only rootless cosmopolitans and wrecks nation states. The far right unites with the far left in its choice of conspiracy enemies (Rupert 2000). Martin Walker, in his study of the far-right British political party, the National Front, described a racist anti-globalism:

Chesterton [the founder of the National Front] combined his anti-Semitism, his anti-Communism, his anti-Americanism and his fervent patriotism and concluded that Jewish Wall Street capitalism was the same thing as Russian Communism. Jewish capital had funded the Bolshevik Revolution of 1917, he believed, and Jewish capital had funded the development and technological base of Soviet Russia. The Moscow-Wall Street axis had its major objective the ruin of the British Empire, the mongrelization of the British race, and eventual world government. The United Nations, NATO and Jewish people were all to be regarded with the deepest suspicion as agents of 'the money power'. (Walker 1977: 29)

A second key issue is that of productivism versus primitivism. Many anti-capitalists would like to see the economy grow essentially for ever. The west provides a development model for the rest of the globe. The problem is that the current workings of the IMF, WTO and other global institutions of economic governance prevent real growth. Yet for other anti-capitalists, inspired by the green critique such as the ecosocialists, economic growth, however measured in a capitalist society, will destroy scarce resources, devastate global ecology and impoverish us in a whole range of ways subtle and not so subtle. The debate about growth throws up profound difficulties, it seems like madness to say that developing countries should not grow; yet capitalist growth for a minority already looks unsustainable given problems such as the greenhouse effect. What would the planet look like if car ownership was as high in mainland China as it is today in New Jersey? Perhaps ways can be found of enjoying life and meeting needs without producing more and more for ever and ever?

A third area concerns strategy. Can the global economic system be changed by gentle reform plans or are the problems identified so profound as to demand sudden and even violent change? Is it possible or desirable to describe a utopia, to paint a picture of a world without capitalism? How can a new kind of society be built that delivers prosperity without creating unsustainable environmental damage or crippling injustice? Changing apparently fixed tracks to the future is not going to be easy. Should anti-capitalists build alternatives or focus on blocking what exists and is cancerous?

These issues run through the entire book and must run beyond it. Suffice to say, we need to take history by the scruff of the neck and debate alternatives that genuinely benefit humanity and other species. The literary theorist Terry Eagleton has argued cogently that the most bizarre utopians are those who predict that capitalism can feed the world and continue into the distant future. The soothsayer 'with his head buried most obdurately in the sand, is the hard-nosed pragmatist who imagines the future will be pretty much like the present only more so [...] Our children are likely to live in interesting times' (*Red Pepper*, February 2004). While Marx famously taught us to doubt everything, we can be certain that another world is both possible and necessary. Getting there remains the question.

2
Vaccinating against Anti-Capitalism: Stiglitz, Soros and Friends

Greenpeace UK

[Joseph Stiglitz] looks like a caricature of a Wicked Capitalist from a Bolshevik propaganda poster circa 1917. You know: the one where a pig-like businessman rests his feet on a perspiring, emaciated worker and spoons caviar into his fleshy gob. Stiglitz is round and portly, with braces to hold up his trousers. He has a big grin, worn on a mouth that looks like it was born to hold a fat cigar. Yet he is one of the most important left-wing economic and political thinkers of our time, and his agenda cuts to the heart of the most urgent moral issue in the world: mass poverty. (Johann Hari, *Independent on Sunday*, 9 November 2003)

Though these banner-wavers hog the headlines and disrupt the streets, they pose no serious threat to the two Bretton Woods institutions [the IMF and the World Bank]. Their goals (such as 'end capitalism') are too absurd; their arguments too incoherent. But this year, more than most, the IMF faces criticism from a more serious source – those inside rather than outside the barricades. A growing chorus of insiders, from staff members (sotto voce) to Wall Street bankers (more loudly), is asking whether the Fund and the rich countries that largely determine its policies know what they are doing. (*The Economist*, 26 September 2001)

Along with the black-clad messengers and NGO activists, some surprisingly sober figures have been prepared to challenge neo-liberal globalisation. The fact that bankers, economists and speculators are questioning the system that made them wealthy clearly disquiets advocates of unfettered capitalism. While some of these 'insiders' criticise the IMF for lack of true zealotry in the capitalist cause, many believe that the globalisation it promotes is socially and economically destructive. Joseph Stiglitz, former Chief Economist of the World Bank, and George Soros, perhaps the world's best-known financier, are the most important. Other 'establishment' figures have echoed their assumptions that the capitalist market needs careful national and international regulation to function sustainably. The late Sir James Goldsmith, the corporate asset-stripper once condemned as personifying capitalism at its worst, attacked free trade and took on GATT, before it was fashionable to do so, during the 1990s (Goldsmith 1994). James Tobin, the economist who argues that speculative flows of capital should be taxed, also springs to mind. The Nobel Prize winner Amartya Sen is also one of a number of economists who have echoed Stiglitz's perspective (Sen 1999). The example of John Gray, a former Thatcherite and contributor to the free market Institute of Economic Affairs, is instructive. His detailed and passionate attack on globalisation from the right is difficult for conservatives to answer (Gray 2002). Drawing upon the Austrian social thinker Karl Polanyi, he argues that neo-liberalism leads to social chaos, smashing the bonds of family and community necessary for a stable human order.

These critics argue that US-style capitalism is far less efficient than European or Asian variants. They believe that the Washington Consensus of unlimited free trade, privatisation and strong deflationary policies actually prevents capitalism from growing and developing countries from becoming financially secure. They echo the key assumption of the economist Keynes, whose policies helped rescue the post-war global economy from recession and mass unemployment, that government intervention actually makes markets work more effectively. Their critique is not dissimilar to that of Hirst and Thompson who argue from a social democratic perspective that capitalism can (and should) be reined in by the nation state (Hirst and Thompson 1999). This chapter focuses on Stiglitz and Soros, examines their challenge to economic orthodoxy and shows how their ideas are derived from John Maynard Keynes' reformist interventionist economic approach developed in the 1930s.

STIGLITZ AND SOROS

Joseph Stiglitz became Chief Economist of the World Bank in 1997. He was also one of President Clinton's key economic advisers and chaired the US Council of Economic Advisers. His ground breaking academic work on asymmetric information, the idea that markets may fail because consumers and producers have imperfect knowledge, won him a Nobel Prize (*Guardian*, 11 October 2001). In 1999 he resigned from the World Bank because he felt that the more powerful IMF was blocking its agenda of reform. In 2001 he published *Globalization and its Discontents*, arguing that neo-liberal globalisation had led to poverty for millions of people and would fail unless thoughtfully reformed. The title echoes Freud's *Civilisation and its Discontents*, an explosive tome that shows how apparent rationality is based upon repression. Stiglitz comes closer to endorsing violence against economic repression than any other commentator outside of autonomist anarchism, bitterly observing, 'For decades, people in the developing world have rioted when the austerity programs imposed on their countries proved to be too harsh ... what is new is the wave of protest in developed countries' (Stiglitz 2002: 3). While the prophets of capitalism ignore or ridicule most of their opponents, they hate Stiglitz with a corrosive passion:

> Mr Stiglitz's prose reads like a draft dictated to a secretary whose mind was apt to wander: readers too will be drifting off a lot. Also, the narrative conveys a whining self-righteousness that is always tiresome and sometimes downright repellent. (*The Economist*, 6 June 2002)

George Soros was raised in poverty, made a fortune and is now best known for using his wealth for ambitious political and social projects. Born in Hungary, his family hid their Jewish origins to avoid extermination by the Nazis and their anti-semitic puppets. In the post-war years Soros found his way to Switzerland, then moved to the UK to study at the London School of Economics (LSE). In 1956 he left for the United States where he managed to make a massive investment fortune. He specialised in arbitrage, the art of skimming off the differential change in value from dealing, especially dealing in currency. He was an early practitioner in the high-risk hedge fund market, an 'investment of $100,000 in Soros's Quantum Fund in 1969 was worth $300 million by 1996' (Hertz 2001: 137). In 1992 he bought billions of dollars worth of foreign currency being sold by the British government to prop up demand for sterling. As the pound slid in value, his currency worth accelerated upwards.

Fiercely hostile to the totalitarianism of both Hitler and Stalin, he embraced the free market philosophy of the Austrian philosopher Karl Popper. Soros established the Open Society Institute, his philanthropic foundation, in 1979, 'to help open up closed societies, help make open societies more viable, and foster a critical mode of thinking' (Soros 1998: 69). Popper argued that socialism led to a closed totalitarian society ruled by experts. Marx, for Popper, is prefigured by Plato who believed in a utopia governed by an elite of philosopher kings. Yet by 1995 Soros had come to believe that unfettered capitalism rather than socialist totalitarianism had become the main threat to freedom. Such sentiments are summed up in the title of his 1998 book, *The Crisis of Global Capitalism: Open Society Endangered* which sees globalisation as a force that must be tamed if a market-based society is to be sustained.

Soros has advanced his ideas practically by funding an interesting range of charitable projects and political campaigns. He sent 400 photocopiers to his native Hungary to promote information access in the pre-internet era. He allegedly helped to topple the President of Georgia in 2004 and poured dollars into anti-Bush campaigning:

> [He] gives away $400m a year through his Foundation and thus subsidizes many of the activist groups, luminaries and publications of the American left, probably dwarfing the sums that once trickled out of Langley or Moscow ... his monetary influence is one of those hushed secrets inside the left usually dismissed as conspiracy-thinking. (Sheasby 2003)

That a self-made capitalist, who has clawed his way to unimaginable wealth using the most abstract and advanced tools of unproductive finance such as derivatives and currency deals, is an opponent of the IMF and George Bush, should give apologists for 'business as usual' pause for critical thought.

FROM KEYNES TO BRETTON WOODS

Soros, Stiglitz and other establishment critics of neo-liberalism draw upon the work of John Maynard Keynes, who believed in the necessity of managing capitalism, both to provide a fair society and to maintain a capitalist system. During the 1930s Europe and North America were plunged into recession. Economies shrank and unemployment figures mushroomed to millions. The resulting turmoil fuelled the political chaos that led to the Second World War. The conventional 'liberal' or 'classical' free market economists believed that the economy worked best without government controls and tended to automatically correct any disequilibria. If demand for goods fell, prices would fall too and eventually shoppers would increase demand as they snapped up bargains. If individuals were unwilling to borrow money, interest rates (the price of money) would fall, and if rates fell low enough, demand for loans would pick up, rescuing the economy. Furthermore, if workers became unemployed they could cut their wages until firms found them cheap enough to employ. These market advocates believed that apparently humane attempts to deal with poverty and unemployment such as state welfare benefits would simply make the recession deeper by discouraging wage-setting. Even socialist politicians such as Hilferding in Germany and Snowdon in Britain accepted this orthodoxy. As the years went by and liberal policies of non-intervention were accompanied by deeper recession, conventional economics became increasingly discredited. The only economies that seemed to work were to be found in Hitler's Germany and Stalin's Russia.

By the late 1930s the Western economies were slowly pulling out of the slump and demand rose with employment as war led to large factory orders for guns, planes and assorted military paraphernalia. Nonetheless, by the 1940s and 1950s the economic orthodoxy was largely abandoned for Keynesianism. Keynes suggested that economics has a psychological element that means if confidence is low, so too is consumption and growth. Prices, wages and interest rates may be 'sticky', by which Keynes meant they would not fall easily, because firms, banks and workers may be reluctant to lower them if they feel that they will still suffer when demand is low. Keynes argued that if people think bad economic news is on the horizon they spend less and the bad economic news becomes a recessionary reality. Businessmen and women are particularly edgy and suffer from a herd mentality, cutting investment when they fear bad economic news. Like deranged beasts they stampede towards slump. The answer is for governments to inject spending in the economy when recession looks likely. In turn, if excessive spending threatens the economy, governments can control it by raising taxes and cutting expenditure.

In July 1944 Keynes acted as the British government's representative to the Bretton Woods Conference in New Hampshire, USA. Bretton Woods aimed to create a new financial architecture and new global institutions to restore economic stability and remove the threat of world recession, after the war had been won. It called for the creation of three key institutions. During the 1940s the General Agreement on Tariffs and Trade (GATT), now known as the WTO, was established to sweep away barriers to trade so as to promote faster economic growth. The International Bank for Reconstruction and Development, commonly known as the World Bank, was set up to lend money to countries, initially for restoration of infrastructures decayed during recession and smashed by war. Its role has increasingly shifted towards funding development projects in the south of the globe. Finally the IMF was created to help countries faced with severe debt problems or balance of payments deficits. Stiglitz sees all three institutions as essentially Keynesian, examples of government intervention, aimed at making the market work and capitalism expand.

AGAINST WASHINGTON

In the same way that revolutionary socialists argue that Stalin betrayed Lenin or Marx, moderate advocates of capitalism like Soros and Stiglitz argue that the IMF et al. have abandoned Keynes' original vision. It isn't that capitalism doesn't work; it is more the case that it hasn't been tried. According to Stiglitz:

> In its original conception, the IMF was based on a recognition that markets often did not work well – that they could result in massive unemployment and might fail to make needed funds available to countries to help restore their economies. The IMF was based on the belief that there was a need for collective action at the global level for economic stability ... Keynes would be rolling over in his grave if he could see what has happened to his child. (*Independent on Sunday*, 9 November 2003)

Since the 1980s the IMF, WTO and World Bank have advocated the so-called Washington Consensus of fiscal austerity (government spending cuts), privatisation and market liberalisation. Swept along by the neo-liberal counter-revolution against Keynesian economics, the consensus argues that for development to occur, barriers to the market should be swept away. The policies that failed in 1930s Europe have been exported to almost the entire globe. The Washington Consensus argues that the poorest countries in the world should cut government spending and increase taxes to reduce indebtedness. The tax burden should, of course, fall on ordinary citizens; taxes on profits would discourage investment and enterprise. State assets should be privatised as thoroughly as possible, while barriers to free trade should be swept away. Export-led growth is also advocated along with the removal of controls on capital. Multinationals are to be welcomed and government regulation slashed to the minimum.

While Soros and Stiglitz are by no means naturally hostile to the US, given their close links with previous American governments, they believe that the Washington Consensus, rather than being based purely on market ideology, is also inspired by the interests of an essentially US corporate elite. The Bretton Woods institutions have massive power to impose their free market medicine because if they refuse to give a country a clean bill of health, foreign capital floods out, leading to economic chaos. If a country rejects free market approaches, money floods out, forcing a rethink. By insisting that barriers to the movement of financial capital are removed the Bretton Woods institutions make it difficult for countries to act independently and they become more closely tied to the whims of global financial markets. Indebted countries that reject the consensus are refused financial stabilisation deals by the IMF and aid from the World Bank. Even countries that are independent of IMF financial aid are influenced by the institution's prescriptions. Typically, British Chancellors of the Exchequer and Japanese finance ministers take close interest in the IMF's annual report of their countries' financial health.

Stiglitz believes that the emphasis on fighting inflation and reducing debt advocated by the IMF can be appropriate in some circumstances. He suggests that some Latin American countries during the 1980s attempted to print money to spend their way out of crisis with predictable results in terms of high inflation: 'Countries cannot persistently run large deficits; and sustained growth is not possible with hyperinflation. Some level of fiscal discipline is required.' Neither does he reject all privitisation: 'Most countries would be better off with governments focussing on providing essential public services rather than running enterprises that would arguably perform better in the private sector, and so privitization often make sense.' Equally, 'When trade liberalization – the lowering of tariffs and elimination of other protectionist measures – is done in the right way', so that inefficient sectors of the economy are removed and replaced with more competitive ones, there can be 'significant efficiency gains' (Stiglitz 2002: 53). Soros argues that in an 'ideal world' the complete removal of capital controls would be beneficial, noting that restrictions to prevent money moving across national borders create 'evasion, corruption and the abuse of power' (Soros 1998: 192). Suggesting that the collapse of the Soviet economy demanded significant change, including major privatisation, Soros notes: 'The fact that radical reforms are often radically misconceived does not obviate the need for radical reforms' (1998: 226).

However, both he and Stiglitz argue that these radical market-based policies have been applied in an inflexible and inappropriate way. Stiglitz argues that the Washington Consensus' obsession with reducing inflation is particularly damaging because it means that some of the poorest countries in the world have to cut spending to prevent prices rising when problems of joblessness and low growth are likely to be far more damaging. In Indonesia, to pick just one example, Stiglitz notes how IMF-inspired cuts to food and fuel subsidies for the poor led to rioting (*Independent on Sunday*, 9 November 2003).

Privatisation breeds corruption when assets are sold off. Even when clean it often enriches an elite of corporate fat cats. Privatisation during a debt crisis when an economy is in chaos can mean that assets are sold at knock-down prices, which may simply mean that they can be bought up by US corporations who become stronger at the expense of developing countries. In Russia, according to Stiglitz, the swift privatisation of state assets led to their purchase by a criminal class who thereby gained massive political power.

Capital liberalisation has reinforced the tendency for democratic decision-making to become subordinated to the demands of financial markets. Soros notes that tax burdens have been shifted from firms and financial operators to citizens increasing inequality:

> Interestingly, the state's share of GNP has not declined perceptibly. What has happened instead is that the taxes on capital and employment have come down while other forms of taxation particularly on consumption have kept increasing. In other words, the burden of taxation has shifted from capital to citizens. That is not exactly what had been promised, but one cannot even speak of unintended consequences because the outcome was exactly as the free-marketers intended. (Soros 1998: 112)

A country implementing policies that the financial markets find distasteful may find that they take their hot money and emerging share market portfolio funds elsewhere, causing slump and currency collapse. As well as tying developing countries to the free market agenda of the Washington Consensus, capital liberalisation means that such states are more susceptible to movements in global currency markets that can cause sudden shocks to fragile economies:

> It has become an article of faith that capital controls should be abolished and the financial markets of individual countries, including banking, opened up to international competition. The IMF has even proposed amending its charter to make these goals more explicit. Yet the experience of the Asian crisis ought to make us pause. The countries that kept their financial markets closed weathered the storm better than those that were open. India was less affected than the Southeast Asian countries; China was better insulated than Korea. (Soros 1998: 192)

Free trade is theoretically beneficial, but opening up an underdeveloped economy to trade has several major drawbacks. It may force down the price of commodities such as sugar or coffee, wrecking the livelihoods of peasant farmers who have little possibility of alternative employment. It can also destroy 'infant industries', new industries that have yet to mature and become efficient and will be killed by unprotected exposure to foreign competition. Stiglitz notes that to achieve growth the successful Asian economies such as Hong Kong, Japan and South Korea initially used selective protectionism to allow their industries to take off.

Soros and Stiglitz feel that the advocates of the Washington Consensus are remote from the problems of the developing world, act arrogantly and are consistently biased to the needs of the rich.

> [M]odern high-tech warfare is designed to remove physical contact: dropping bombs from 50,000 feet ensures that one does not 'feel' what one does. Modern economic management is similar: from one's luxury hotel, one can callously impose policies about which one would think twice if one knew the people whose lives one was destroying. (Stiglitz 2002: 24)

The institutions promoting the Washington Consensus act as if they continue to bear the '[w]hite man's burden', persisting, according to Stiglitz, with the notion that they always know what is best (2002: 25). Stiglitz and Soros argue that the arrogance of the Washington institutions means that developing countries have little say in their own economic development and policies are imposed from above. Such arrogance inevitably breeds discontent, and even where globalisation has the potential to bring benefits, the Washington Consensus has fuelled a hostile counter-movement. Discontent is met by repression: rubber bullets against starving rioters. As Stiglitz observes:

> A common characteristic is: We know best, and the developing countries should do what we tell them to ... They really see themselves as a harsh doctor, giving them the cod liver oil they need, even if they don't want it. The problem, of course, is that quite often the medicine ... kills the patient. (*Independent on Sunday*, 9 November 2003)

It is difficult to think of a single example of a country that has gained from the IMF model of structural adjustment. Botswana is often mentioned, but despite enjoying one of the globe's fastest economic growth rates, the Washington Consensus has not delivered sustainable prosperity:

> The richest twenty per cent of the population earned more than twenty-five times as much as the poorest twenty per cent.[...] Botswana, at twenty-two per cent [population in work], has the world's sixth highest unemployment rate [...] One of the few products of Botswana's increased economic activity which has been widely shared by its poorer inhabitants is AIDS. Women driven into prostitution by poverty are purchased by the truck drivers delivering goods to the elite. (Monbiot 2003b: 214)

Argentina, the Washington Consensus exemplar from South America, plunged into severe recession after following the model rigorously, with resulting mass unemployment, poverty and chaos.

ASYMETRIC INFORMATION AND REFLEXIVITY

While a number of critics wish to maintain a reformed capitalism, Soros and Stiglitz are particularly interesting because they challenge not just the excesses of global neo-liberalism but also some of the foundations of economics. Economists, even many Keynesians, assume that markets generally work, with the actions of consumers and producers leading to efficient outcomes at a micro level. Stiglitz and Soros accept the principle of a market-based society but doubt that the market automatically delivers efficiency. Their critique based on notions of reflexivity and asymmetric information is similar to that of Keynes.

Economists since Alfred Marshall, in the nineteenth century, have argued that human beings are 'rational' in that they seek to maximise their personal benefits and minimise the costs of any transaction. Consumers aim to maximise 'utility' and producers profit. Both groups calculate the best course of action during millions of transactions. The actions of millions of producers and consumers functions as an invisible hand creating choice, prosperity and even justice. The liberalisation suggested by the Washington Consensus is founded on Alfred Marshall's and Adam Smith's assumptions of rationality, calculation and maximising behaviour. Given these foundations, it is safe to assume that the market should be extended as far as possible because it generates efficient outcomes.

Typically, we might argue that if a country removes capital controls, its entry into a global money market will bring benefits. If a country has sound economic policies, money will flow in as investors 'buy' its currency so as to make gains. If a country is running a trade deficit, demand for its currency will fall, because foreigners will demand less of it to buy the country's goods and services. Because demand falls the value of the currency will fall, in turn its exports will become cheaper and its imports more expensive. As more of its exports are sold and fewer imports are bought the deficit will be magicked away. The market is a structural device, a mechanism, for restoring 'equilibrium' or balance.

Yet, as Soros and Stiglitz argue, this notion of the market bears little resemblance to the conditions and complexities of modern economic reality. The money traded for goods is a tiny percentage of speculative currency flows, meaning that currencies are little affected by trade balances and therefore unlikely to float downwards to restore imbalance. With capital liberalisation billions of dollars' worth of currencies flow in and out of economies in seconds. Such flows create waves of chaos rather than restoring equilibrium.

Shares, it is assumed, are bought for profit, so potentially profitable, well-managed companies will enjoy increased demand followed by rising share values. Rising share values will make it easier for such companies to expand. In reality share values can reach mountainous heights before crashing back, as the dot.com bubble of the 1990s illustrated. Share values are often unrelated to company performance. Soros, who has made a billion-dollar fortune from such movements, particularly currency movements, argues that the market is shaped by reflexivity. Economic rationality increasingly depends on our ability to successfully guess the behaviour of other economic actors. Such reflexivity, where individuals reflect on what they think will happen in markets and change their behaviour in response, leads to an increasingly abstract and exaggerated economic system. If shareholders think others are likely to sell their stocks, shareholders sell anticipating that prices will fall – such action leads to a stampede to sell and market instability. Even if dot.coms have little value, the belief that others will buy pushes up share values into a bubble of inflated stock market value. Soros's appreciation of the potentially negative consequences of a market based not on rationality but predictions of mass and often hysterical behaviour is profound:

> The prevailing doctrine on how financial markets operate has not changed. It is assumed that with perfect information markets can take care of themselves; therefore the main task is to make the necessary information available and to avoid any interference with the market mechanism. Imposing market discipline remains the goal.

> We need to broaden the debate. It is time to recognize that financial markets are inherently unstable. Imposing market discipline means imposing instability, and how much instability can society take? (Soros 1998: 175–6)

To understand such instability Soros uses the concept of reflexivity which he traces from Greek drama to the introduction of intersubjectivity into sociology by Alfred Schutz:

> The concept of reflexivity is so basic that it would be hard to believe that I was the first to discover it. The fact is, I am not. Reflexivity is merely a new label for the two-way interaction between thinking and reality that is deeply ingrained in our common sense. (Soros 1998: 10)

Keynes was one of the few academic economists to make large amounts of money from commodity markets! The fact that he, like Soros, had a sharp understanding of reflexivity should be instructive to those who seek to play the markets. Keynes put the concept at the centre of his theoretical system:

> [economics] deals with motives, expectations, psychological uncertainties. One has to be constantly on one's guard against treating the material as constant and homogeneous. It is as though the fall of the apple to the ground depended on the apple's motives, on whether it is worthwhile falling to the ground, and whether the ground wants the apple to fall, and on mistaken calculations on the part of the apple as to how far it was from the centre of the earth. (quoted in Moggridge 1976: 27)

Keynes feared the effect of capital liberalisation as a means of shifting investment from productive activity to a form of gambling:

The social object of skilled investment should be to defeat the dark forces of time and ignorance which envelop our future. The actual, private object of the most skilled investment to-day is 'to beat the gun', as the Americans so well express it, to outwit the crowd, and to pass the bad, or depreciating, half-crown to the other fellow. (Keynes 1960: 155)

Keynes, while no anti-capitalist, believed that extending the market meant extending uncertainties to new areas of human existence with destabilising and potentially damaging consequences. In the third millenium see-sawing currency and share values mean that jobs may be swept away with one spin of the economic roulette wheel.

Stiglitz specifically examines asymmetric information as a form of market failure. He suggests that in the real world information is always imperfect to a lesser or greater extent. Such asymmetry means that markets may not work efficiently and if some actors have access to greater information than others there is the potential for injustice. Assumptions of reflexivity and asymmetric information, ignored by the Washington Consensus, powerfully shape the operation of real markets and have important consequences.

1001 USES FOR A DEAD KARL POLANYI

Virtually all of the critics of neo-liberal globalisation examined in this text make some use of the ideas of Karl Polanyi outlined in his book *The Great Transformation* first published in 1944. Typically Soros observes in his acknowledgements his thanks to 'John Gray [who] made me re-read Karl Polanyi's *Great Transformation*'(Soros 1998: v). Also an exiled Hungarian, writing in the 1940s and 1950s, Polanyi argues that far from being natural markets are of secondary importance in explaining how goods and services are produced and distributed. He suggests that the role played by markets 'was insignificant up to recent times' (Polanyi 1957: 44). Much more important is a notion of human society within which the economy is embedded. He argues that individuals consume luxury goods, not because they directly generate satisfaction and pleasure, but because they confer status. The American economic heretic Thornstein Veblen, famous for his concept of conspicuous consumption, echoes Polanyi's views. He argues that individuals consume luxury goods, not because they directly generate satisfaction and pleasure but because they give individuals status. The Native American 'potlatch' where individuals gathered to smash expensive and rare goods provides another example of such conspicuous consumption (Veblen 1994). The modern 'bling bling' equivalent sees rock stars and hip hop artists smashing up hotel rooms, pouring away bottles of Cristal champagne and crashing expensive cars.

Social factors that glue communities together make the market and other forms of economic activity possible. Without an array of social, rather than state or market institutions, neither the state nor the market could function. We don't generally dump our grandfathers on the streets. Parents feed their children but rarely ask for payment, and examples can be multiplied. For Polanyi the market is based on an ahistorical myth, it is portrayed as universal and inevitable either for ideological reasons or from a failure of imagination. The market is embedded within a host of complex social institutions and practices. Indeed the move towards a society where the market is dominant, *The Great Transformation* of Polanyi's title tends to erode the social institutions that the market depends upon. The ultimate extension of the market threatens the market, destroying the conditions upon which it depends. Childcare and socialisation, household maintenance including cooking and cleaning and a host of other domestic tasks traditionally undertaken by women help to maintain economic activity, as do a range of social obligations such as the activities of postal workers or milkmen/women who look in on the elderly. Soros, utilising Polanyi, argues:

> it seems clear that morality is based on a sense of belonging to a community, be it family, friends, tribe, nation, or humanity. But a market economy does not constitute a community, especially when it operates on a global scale; being employed by a corporation is not the same as belonging to a community. (Soros 1998: 91)

Polanyi's insights suggest that unlimited marketisation is unsustainable. Gray uses Polanyi to sustain an essentially conservative critique of globalisation in his book *False Dawn*. The fruits of globalisation for Gray are family breakdown, drug addiction, debt and an epidemic of alcoholism:

> The Utopia of the global free market has not incurred a human cost in the way that communism did. Yet over time it may come to rival it in the suffering that

it inflicts. Already it has resulted in over a hundred million peasants becoming migrant labourers in China, the exclusion from work and participation in society of tens of millions in the advanced societies, a condition of near-anarchy and rule by organized crime in parts of the post-communist world, and further devastation of the environment. (Gray 2002: 3)

Communitarian advocates of the Blairite Third Way provide another spin on Polanyi, seeking to balance the market with community building, crusades against social exclusion and various partnership schemes.

Radical use of Polanyi is made by autonomist and ecosocialist critics of globalisation, examined in later chapters, such as Hardt and Negri and Kovel. Polanyi's approach suggests that the market is merely one way of dealing with the economic problem and in historical terms a minor one – an insight that, if true, scuppers the ideological pretensions of those who advocate extending the market to virtually every area of human society. The rise of globalisation has implied that no alternative to the market is possible. The economist Amartya Sen, usually seen as a radical voice, typically suggests that banning or bypassing the market is analogous to making conversation illegal or refusing to talk to our friends (Sen 1999: 6). Polanyi suggests that economic alternatives to the market are far from absurd, whereas the introduction of the market is a violent process in at least two ways. First, it involves a battle between social classes: he notes that new poor laws were introduced in Britain in the eighteenth century as part of a battle to replace notions of a 'moral economy' with those of an extended market. Second, such processes are physically violent, with peasants being thrown off the land by processes of enclosure. In this sense the Washington Consensus can be seen as a process not of development but violent expropriation whereby communal resources and informal forms of economic activity are privatised. Armies of migrants facing deprivation provide cheap labour to fuel global corporate profit-seeking.

Soros and Stiglitz, along with other advocates of a gentler capitalist globalisation, use Polanyi's insights to sustain a less fundamental vision. They note that the imperfections of the market, including the fact that it is by necessity embedded in non-economic institutions and practices, demand that globalisation should be introduced gradually, should remain incomplete and should be cemented with a measure of global Keynesianism. Soros and Stiglitz both suggest that a swift march from state planning to a full market economy is likely to be costly because it wrecks social institutions without providing enough time for alternatives to mature. Stiglitz in particular suggests that the gradualist approach to economic reform in China has been more successful than the shock therapy that has left the Russian economy in chaos. He argues that the IMF

> tried to create a shortcut to capitalism, without creating the underlying institutions ... the Russian middle class has been devastated, a system of crony and Mafia capitalism has been created, and the one achievement, the creation of democracy and a free press, seem very fragile. (*Independent on Sunday*, 9 November 2003)

ANTI-EMPIRE

Given the insights of market imperfection outlined above, Stiglitz has suggested that politicians need to behave 'more like scholars' (Stiglitz 2002: x) but observes that 'the opposite happens too often'. Stiglitz and Soros have increasingly focused on the fact that economics has either been used to legitimate American interests or simply junked when it gets in the way of self-interested politicians:

> They talk a free-market ideology but, if you look at their politics in terms of bailouts and protectionism, it is not a free-market policy; if you look at their procurement agenda and what they did with Bechtel in Iraq, it doesn't even look like a fair competition agenda. So you have to sort of suspect an element of ideology but more an element of particular groups seizing control. (*Observer*, 18 May 2003)

Bush, they suggest, has dropped the market approach, and is looking now to heavy-handed state intervention to benefit the hyperwealthy of a hyperpower. Indeed Stiglitz and Soros in their recent writings have moved on to attack Bush's military adventures (Soros 2004; Stiglitz 2003). A number of other voices have echoed the suspicion that globalisation has a specifically American orientation and reflects US corporate and military interests. Will Hutton, former head of the Industrial Society and editor of the *Observer* newspaper, specifically argues that capitalism comes in different varieties and favours Asian or European flavours to those of US capitalism. He suggests that the US system discourages long-term investment and promotes dot.com-style paper gains over strategically focused real growth in assets. Slashed public spending on education and health within the US system weakens the fundamentals of the economy such as a healthy workforce. Equally, the US system breeds systematic and destructive inequality. Despite the rhetoric of pure markets, the government intervenes with measures ranging from subsidies to corporate interests to huge military spending, and not to help the poor or to promote growth but to feed revenue to firms. Hutton argues that the IMF demand for capital liberalisation has made it easier for US financial institutions to grow and made it easier for the US to fund its trade deficit, noting that in 1995 alone 'foreign central banks bought $70 billion of new US treasury securities' (Hutton 2001: 191). The writer Noreena Hertz has looked to socially and environmentally friendly entrepreneurs to provide a more Keynesian and humane form of global capitalism (2001).

Hertz, Hutton, Soros and Stiglitz have increasingly come to see globalisation as an ideological force driven not by market economics but by US demands for hegemony with the economics of the market, providing a gloss of legitimacy to the pursuit of naked power. Typically, Stiglitz notes that for many, globalisation appears to be 'triumphant capitalism, American style' (Stiglitz 2002: 5).

This said, Soros notes that European countries are far from immune when it comes to economic imperialism:

> the French government, for instance, has an even stronger tradition of pushing business interests through political means. The president of an Eastern European country I know was shocked when in a meeting with President Jacques Chirac the French president spent most of their time together pushing him to favour a French buyer in a privatization sale. I shall not even mention arms sales. (Soros 1998: 204)

A genuine consensus for growth and development which advances a true rather than US corporate globalisation has been advocated by Soros and Stiglitz. They believe that the Bretton Woods institutions must be reformed and also support the introduction of the Tobin Tax, named after the economist James Tobin, on capital flows. A percentage tax on capital transactions could raise billions of dollars for development projects and reduce the instability of markets. It is unlikely that universal backing for such a tax would be forthcoming, but studies have shown that even if only a minority of currency transactions were covered it would bring benefits. Tobin believes that his tax could also be levied on share transactions and administered by the IMF to make it stick (Henwood 1998: 319). Henwood, a keen

Tobinist who, like Keynes, knows that financial markets are more about gambling or playing 'snap' than productivity, argues gleefully:

> Few things, aside from the threat of direct appropriation of their property, make Wall Streeters scream more loudly than the assertion that their pursuits are pointless or malignant, and that their activities should be taxed like noxious effluent. Listening to those screams would be another positive benefit of a transactions tax. (Henwood 1998: 319)

Tobin suggested a modest 0.5 per cent tax, and the networks campaigning for its introduction call for a levy as low as 0.2 per cent (see Chapter 5). Soros also advocates the creation of new global credits to finance debt. Stiglitz suggests that the IMF's structural adjustment programmes be linked to social inclusive policies. Above all, the Washington institutions should act in a transparent way and engage in dialogue.

VACCINATING AGAINST ANTI-CAPITALISM

Soros, Stiglitz and associates provide a penetrating critique of the Washington consensus that is driving globalisation. They show how some of the axioms of conventional market economics are flawed, arguing that such concepts, consciously or otherwise, are used to legitimate increasing wealth and power for a corporate elite. Soros summarises, stating: 'the system is deeply flawed. As long as capitalism remains triumphant, the pursuit of money overrides all other social considerations' (1998: 102).

Characteristically, looking at the shock therapy that has wrecked Russian attempts to build a stable society, they praise the more cautious and successful Chinese road to capitalism. While Soros has predicted that globalisation may depose the Chinese Communist Party, he suggests that capital controls allowed them to escape the 1997 Asian crisis that wrecked the economies of their neighbours. Yet such praise suggests the limitations of their approach. Soros and Stiglitz make little comment on the Tiananmen Square massacre, the occupation of Tibet or the Three Gorges dam project which will flood large areas and drive millions of peasants from their land without compensation. Ecological issues are pretty much secondary to them. While advocating transparency, they still believe in a world dominated by a wealthy minority who make key decisions. Indeed, Soros is very keen to use his wealth to increase his own personal political influence. They have no notion that economic growth is unsustainable.

Soros and Stiglitz recognise that market failure is a problem and suggest practical ways of dealing with it. Their vision of an economic alternative to neo-liberalism is neo-liberalism managed a little to make it fairer and more stable; their utopia is Clinton's America, or a less muscular version of Karl Popper's free market, or a more stylish and intelligent version of Blairism. Such visions are likely to look more attractive as US hypercapitalism erodes its own base.

Given their Keynesian roots this approach is hardly surprising. Keynes has been seen as an economic radical because he strenuously criticised many of the assumptions of market-based economics. He also showed an awareness of the subjective human costs of a capitalist economic system. There have been suggestions that it is possible to create a 'green keynesianism' (Elliott and Atkinson 1998). Indeed, Keynes noted:

> The love of money as a possession – as distinguished from the love of money as a means to the enjoyments and realities of life – will be recognised for what it is, a somewhat disgusting morbidity, one of those semi-criminal, semi-pathological propensities which one hands over with a shudder to the specialists in mental disease. All kinds of social customs and economic practices, affecting the distribution of wealth and of economic rewards and penalties, which we now maintain at all costs, however distasteful and unjust they may be in themselves, because they are tremendously useful in promoting the accumulation of capital, we shall then be free, at last, to discard. (Keynes 1972: 329)

He also stated:

> For at least another hundred years we must pretend to ourselves and to everyone that fair is foul and foul is fair; for foul is useful and fair is not. Avarice and usury and precaution must be our gods for a little longer still. For only they can lead us out of the tunnel of economic necessity into daylight. (Keynes 1972: 331)

The Economist noted cynically: 'So prolix was Keynes ... that he is thought to have said everything at least once' (9 October 2003). Keynes was indeed quite happy to promote luxury and waste as ways of sustaining economic growth. He believed that thrift was dysfunctional, but greed was good if it boosted demand and prevented recession:

> Keynes celebrated booms in a manner that would do a Texas populist proud. Shakespeare, said Keynes, died rich, and his days were 'the plamy days of profit' – one of the greatest 'bull' movements ever known until modern days in the United States ... the greater proportion of the world's greatest writers and artists have flourished in the atmosphere of buouyance ... The Shakespeares of the era of junk finance have yet to be discovered, unless Bret Easton Ellis qualifies. (Henwood 1998: 195)

Keynesianism is an ideology that sanctifies shopping and sees reduced consumption as a sin. The pioneering green economist E.F. Schumacher, author of *Small is Beautiful*, bitterly complained:

> Maybe we do not even have to wait for another sixty years until universal plenty will be attained. In any case, the Keynesian message is clear enough: Beware! Ethical considerations are not merely irrelevant, they are an actual hinderance, 'for foul is useful and fair is not'. The time for fairness is not yet. The road to heaven is paved with bad intentions. (Schumacher 1978: 22)

Keynes was well aware of Marx's critique of capitalism. Perhaps more surprisingly he was sympathetic to the monetary reformers like Major Douglas and Gesell (discussed in Chapter 5). Yet Keynes sought not to destroy capitalism or to move beyond it but to sustain it. Indeed, he explicitly argued that in the class war he was on the side of the bourgeois. He developed, using his insights into macroeconomic market failure, a theoretical understanding of how capitalism, that appeared so weak in the 1930s, could be strengthened by selective government intervention. Stiglitz and Soros are in this sense neo-Keynesians, while their criticisms of neo-liberal globalisation are telling, like Keynes it is inaccurate to describe them as anti-capitalists.

Stiglitz is a neo-Keynesian, trying in his academic work to shore up Keynesian macroeconomic analysis, which looks at national economies, with firm microeconomic principles that deal with the basic building blocks of an economy such as the behaviour of firms and consumers. Stiglitz is equally Keynesian in his project to create a more stable and faster growing capitalism. Like many other centre-ground critics the point is not to halt globalisation but to heal it so it can be sustained and grow. The solutions of such mainstream critics of globalisation such as transparency and the Tobin Tax appear to be modest, realistic and just. These capitalist critics of globalisation fear that if the market is extended too quickly or too completely it will collapse. They do not, despite their lip service to Polanyi and talk of asymmetry and reflexivity, follow their doubts and challenge the market in essence. More radical opponents of neo-liberalism, by contrast, suggest that markets are innately undemocratic, that indefinite economic growth is ecologically unsustainable and that the market-based system is tyrannical because it reduces human life to a narrow pursuit of quantitative advantage. As Bob Dylan observed, money doesn't talk, it swears.

By attacking the most obviously repellent features of neo-liberal globalisation, Soros, Stiglitz and friends seek to show how capitalism can be maintained and to channel more radical sentiments into support for a supposedly 'nicer' form of globalisation. They act as a vaccine against the virus of anti-capitalist protest.

3
White Collar Global Crime Syndicate:
Korten, Klein and other Anti-Corporatists

IBM, primarily through its German subsidiary, made Hitler's program of Jewish destruction a technological mission the company pursued with chilling success. IBM Germany, using its own staff and equipment, designed, executed, and supplied the indispensable technologic assistance Hitler's Third Reich needed to accomplish what had never been done before – the automation of human destruction. More than 2,000 such multi-machine sets were dispatched throughout German-dominated Europe. Card sorting operations were established in every major concentration camp. People were moved from place to place, systematically worked to death, and their remains catalogued with icy automation. (Black 2001: 8–9)

To the anti-globalisers, the corporation is a devilish instrument of environmental destruction, class oppression and imperial conquest. But is it also pathologically insane?

That is the provocative conclusion of an award-winning documentary, called 'The Corporation', coming soon to a cinema near you. People on both sides of the globalisation debate should pay attention. Unlike much of the soggy thinking peddled by many anti-globalises, 'The Corporation' is a surprisingly rational and coherent attack on capitalism's most important institution.

Like all psychopaths, the firm is singularly self-interested: its purpose is to create wealth for its shareholders. And, like all psychopaths, the firm is irresponsible, because it puts others at risk to satisfy its profit-maximising goal, harming employees and customers, and damaging the environment. The corporation manipulates everything. It is grandiose, always insisting that it is the best, or number one. It has no empathy, refuses to accept responsibility for its actions and feels no remorse. It relates to others only superficially, via make-believe versions of itself manufactured by public-relations consultants and marketing men. In short, if the metaphor of the firm is a valid one, then the corporation is clinically insane. (*The Economist*, 6 May 2004)

An unseasonable day. I have cycled for hours through streets empty of everybody but the police and knots of protesters, its like a city under siege. May Day 2002, McDonald's, Kings Cross, London. Five thousand anti-capitalists are on the street, bringing traffic to a halt. Home made veggie burgers are handed out to those about to enter the fast food unit. McDonald's is targeted for promoting animal abuse, hostility to unions and a war on high-quality food. In the late 1990s the McLibel trial, the longest libel action in British legal history, took place when the corporation sued a tiny anti-capitalist group for distributing a leaflet entitled 'What's Wrong with McDonald's' (Vidal 1997). Jo Bove, in an episode of Roquefort rebellion, demolished a McDonald's in the south of France in protest at US protectionist measures against French cheese (Herman and Kuper 2003: 57). McDonald's, along with Coca-Cola and Bill Gates' Microsoft, has become a convenient hate symbol.

Corporations have been described as the number one force driving globalisation by a number of authors and many activists. David Korten and Naomi Klein have sold hundreds of thousands of copies of their anti-corporate manifestos *When Corporations Rule the World* (Korten 2001) and *No Logo* (Klein 2001a). Leslie Sklair has developed the concept of a transnational capitalist class, whose wealth and power is derived from control of multinational companies. George Monbiot and Greg Palast in their books *Captive State* (Monbiot 2003a) and *The Best Democracy Money Can Buy* (Palast 2003) suggest that corporations control national governments. Whereas Stiglitz and Soros appear as Clinton or Blair voters who have moved left and Klein is the daughter of US leftists who skipped to Canada during the Vietnam War, Korten looks like a rogue Bush beer-buddy:

I was born in 1937 into a conservative, white, upper-middle-class family and grew up in Longview, Washington, a small timber-industry town of some 25,000 ... [In 1959 as] a very conservative Young Republican, I was deeply fearful of the spread of communism and the threat it posed to the American way of life I held so dear. This fear drew me to take a course on modern revolutions the world over. In one of those rare, deeply life-changing moments, I made a decision. I would devote my life to countering this threat by bringing the knowledge of modern business management and entrepreneurship to those who had not yet benefited from it. (Korten 2001: 13)

Korten, who also served as a captain in the US Air Force in Vietnam, is another example of an individual wedded to capitalist and even conservative values who has been radicalised. He argues that globalisation is designed and driven by the corporations who seek the removal of national barriers to trade. This allows companies to sell to new markets and 'outsource' buying inputs from low-cost, low-wage producers in the poorest countries.

Klein, in contrast, gives the impression of being the prodigal daughter to generations of radicals. A spoilt 'mall brat' at high school, she returned to the fold as a student activist campaigning against sexism, racism and homophobia. She increasingly came to see capitalism rather than political incorrectness as the premier cause of oppression. Klein combines sophisticated cultural politics with a forensic study of marketing behaviour. Klein suggests that the creation of the brand drives outsourcing and leads to the manipulation of consumers. In a post-modern switch, she argues that they sell 'signs' not products. The Nike flash and the McDonald's golden arches have huge symbolic value. This chapter examines the criticisms made of corporations by anti-capitalists, before critically examining Korten, Klein and other anti-corporatists.

THE RISE OF THE CORPORATE CRIMINAL

Korten and Klein are just the best known of many other anti-corporate anti-capitalists who point to the growing power of giant corporations. Much-quoted statistics suggest that in terms of economic activity many corporations are larger than countries. According to the World Bank, transnational corporations control 70 per cent of world trade; the 200 largest control over 50 per cent. Comparing GNP and sales revenue for companies and countries, the United States unsurprisingly comes in at number one, but Exxon Mobil, at number 44 is bigger than Pakistan. General Motors is bigger than New Zealand and Peru (UNCTAD 2002).

Megacorporations, according to Korten and Klein, create a uniform world of fast food outlets, ugly hotel towers, universal brands of margarine and coffee, monoculture computer software, homogeneous Hollywood entertainment and uniformly moulded pop stars. Cultural desiccation, animal abuse, poverty and global warming are all symptoms of a planet run by banal corporate bodies. Others such as the journalist Greg Palast note more sinister accusations. Pharmaceutical corporations have, on occasions, been happy to kill a few of their customers if the cost-benefit calculations warrant such action. Pfizer, a New York-based multinational, manufactured the Bjork-Shiley heart valve:

> At Pfizer's factory in the Caribbean, company inspectors found inferior equipment, which made poor welds. Rather than toss out the bad valves, Pfizer management ordered the defects ground down, weakening the valves further but making them look smooth and perfect. ...
> When the valve's struts break and the heart contracts, it explodes. Two-thirds of the victims die, usually in minutes. (Palast 2003: 228)

It is estimated that 500 individuals died as a result before the US Justice Department took action against the company in 1994. Cigarette firms have long known that they sell a product that kills. In the third millennium, British high streets have become the sites of late-night violence fuelled by a drinking culture, propelled in part by a new generation of teenage-friendly alcohol products peddled by brewers. Ralph Nader, the US Green Party presidential candidate in 1995 and 1999, made his name in the 1960s and 1970s by taking on killer corporations. Most famously, in the 'Unsafe at any speed' case, he revealed that Ford were selling models with petrol tanks at the back of the car which often exploded under crash impact. The company had used cost-benefit analyses to calculate that the money awarded in compensation to accident victims was less than the costs of redesign (Nader 1965).

False accountancy and stock market manipulation have been also widely practiced by transnationals. The collapse of the Enron corporation in 2002 provides one well-documented case, although one suspects there are many more examples where the guilty have escaped unnoticed. Enron, an energy corporation, with reported revenues of $101 million made from selling privatised electricity, used opaque accountancy tricks to make its finances look stronger than they really were: by rewriting its balances so they looked stronger, for example, more funds could be generated from selling new equities to gullible shareholders to maintain expansion. Arthur Andersen, the auditors who checked their fraudulent accounts and passed them despite Enron's numerous instances of financial cheating, collapsed with Enron:

> Enron's accounting trick was to record the value of the sale today of, say, gas, for delivery next year as *revenue* today, but not what it would have to spend to buy the gas. Revenues without costs generate huge profits! Of course, eventually Enron would have to record a cost for the purchase of the electricity. One can in fact continually blow up one's income this way, so long as one is growing; for each year, sales exceed purchase. It is a classic Ponzi scheme, like the chain letter of the past. Such schemes still occasionally occur: people who make money by selling franchises to others, who sell it on to others and on and on. But all such Ponzi schemes eventually come to an end. (Stiglitz 2003: 245)

Enron also created fictitious companies that it sold make-believe gas to. These non-existent sales were recorded as additions to its assets without any balancing liability (Stiglitz 2003: 245).

False accounting, the use of complex financial instruments, political manipulation and smart legal footwork are all instruments used to sustain profit. Dumping is another example; a supermarket will set up in town and sell bread for a fraction of the price of local bakeries. Almost inevitably, such dumping will wipe out the bakeries and a monopoly will result. Bread prices will rise.

Government officials are bribed to give planning permission or look away from pollution and safety abuses. Profits are deposited in offshore bank accounts to avoid paying tax. Employees may be spied on and their emails read to prevent whistleblowing. Both Klein and Korten note that in some parts of the world death squads are used to break strikes. Crimes may take on a political dimension; German corporations and even some North American players bankrolled Hitler (Guérin 1973). IBM is just one of many corporations that made money out of the Holocaust (Black 2001).

While crime is the everyday informal practice of the corporation, the relationship cuts both ways:

Banks and big business are keen to get their hands on the proceeds – laundered – of organised crime. Apart from the traditional activities of drugs, racketeering, kidnappings, gambling, procuring (women and children), smuggling (alcohol, tobacco, medicines), armed robbery, counterfeiting and bogus invoicing, tax evasion and misappropriation of public funds, new markets are also flourishing. These include smuggling illegal labour and refugees, computer piracy, trafficking in works of art and antiquities, in stolen cars and parts, in protected species and human organs, forgery, trafficking in arms, toxic waste and nuclear products, etc. (de Brie 2000)

THE HIDDEN HISTORY OF HUMANITY

Rather than just acting as global grocers or very large versions of the corner shop, Klein, Korten and other critics argue that corporations have real political influence. In the hidden history of humanity, corporations are driving events in their fight for new markets and cheaper sources of raw materials. North America was colonised by corporations such as the Plymouth and Virginia companies, whose existence long precedes the creation of the United States of America. In 1602, the Dutch monarchy provided a charter to the United East India Company for a monopoly over all Dutch trade from South Africa, across the Pacific to South America. The company made treaties, controlled territories and used its own armed forces to maintain dominance. Korten notes that the Company used economic and legal manipulation to enslave producers, for example, banning non-Dutch producers in Indonesia for growing cloves, forcing peasants into poverty and dependence on over-produced rice sold by the company (2001: 60). The British East India Company colonised India and administered the country until 1858. A subcontinent became an instrument for producing profit for one corporation. In the early nineteenth century, the company bought tea from China using opium for exchange. The Chinese resisting the chaos created by hard drug use and confiscated opium from company warehouses in Canton, leading to the Opium Wars of 1839–1842. The British won. The price of victory allowed them to established the right to 'free trade', compensatory payments from the Chinese government and the entitlement of British citizens accused of crimes in China to be tried by British courts (Korten 2001: 61).

Countries become the instruments of corporations. There are numerous examples of national governments intervening, often frankly invading, other states at the bidding of transnationals. In

1954, for instance, US-backed rebels invaded the Central American republic of Guatemala, on behalf of United Fruit Co. The Guatemalan President elected in 1950 had started redistributing land to peasants. United Fruit were asked to surrender some of their estates and were offered compensation based on 'the value set on the property in 1952 for tax purposes "by the owner himself"' (Pearce 1976: 103). Colonel Carlos Castillo Armas, leader of the Guatemalan exiles who undertook the subsequent coup, was trained at the US Command and General Staff School at Fort Leavenworth, Texas. The whole operation was financed, armed and organised by the CIA. The then US Secretary of State, John Foster Dulles, was a major stockholder in United Fruit. Some have quipped that Iraq would not have been invaded if it had grown carrots, but Guatemala was occupied for oranges rather than oil.

Allende's Chilean government was destroyed in a 1973 coup, after it had come into conflict with the ITT communications corporation. The coup was again organised by the CIA, who initiated a truck drivers' strike to destabilise the country. Suspected leftists were massacred in football stadiums, torture was rife and the 'Chicago boys', a group of 'free market' economists loyal to the monetarist Professor Milton Friedman, re-engineered the economy (Petras and Morley 1975).

Foreign policy remains driven by corporate needs into the third millennium, events since the publication of Klein's and Korten's key texts have strengthened their analysis. The Second Gulf War was influenced by corporations such as Halliburton and oil giant Exxon which had strong links with the US administration. Corporations like Exxon have a strong interest in breaking the power of the Organisation of Petroleum Exporting Countries (OPEC). OPEC controls the supply of oil and keeps the price that corporations like Exxon pay relatively high. A non-OPEC Iraq selling cheap oil would help the oil corporations to buy cheaper supplies and push up their profits. In 2002, US-supported right-wingers deposed the Venezuelan President Chavez, whose anti-corporate policies, support for Cuba and patronage of the hard-line Venezuelan secretary of OPEC angered the multinationals. Within a week, pro-Chavez demonstrations placed the populist leader back in power (*The Economist*, 18 April 2002). Examples of foreign policy as a corporate instrument, not just from the US, UK and Holland, but from Spain, Japan or Australia, could be multiplied.

UNNATURAL MONOPOLIES

Criminal activities and coups may be, just perhaps may be, the exception rather than the rule, but there is evidence that the day-to-day activities of multinationals exploit consumers, workers and the environment. Economists have generally assumed that strong competition between firms is beneficial. If there are many different banks, the ones that provide the best deal for customers will survive and the rest will be driven out of existence as savers shift accounts. If there are many producers of chocolate bars, consumers will buy from those that provide the highest quality confectionery at the lowest possible price. Workers can choose the best company with the highest wage, nicest boss and longest tea breaks. Healthy competition maximises the most efficient use of resources because inefficient firms will not be able to sustain the normal profit needed to keep wages sufficiently high to attract skilled workers and prices sufficiently low to maintain customer loyalty. The market tends to create the optimum economic conditions and the market works best the closest it comes to a condition of 'perfect competition' marked by low barriers to entry for new firms and a large number of existing producers who compete sharply on price.

Monopoly, where a single firm sells a good, or monopsony, when one firm or consumer buys a product, are seen within traditional economics as situations that may lead to exploitation and inefficiency. The UK Competition Commission defines a potential monopoly as a firm with 25 per cent market share. Such firms may have the potential to push up prices for consumers and push down the price of raw materials they buy from suppliers. Different sectors of the economy are increasingly being monopolised:

> [A]lmost all primary commodities are each now marketed by fewer than six multi-commodity traders ... The top five companies have 77 per cent of world cereal trade; the biggest three companies in bananas have 80 per cent ...; the biggest three cocoa companies have 83 per cent of world cocoa trade; the biggest four companies have 85 per cent of tea trade; and the biggest four companies have 87 per cent of world trade in tobacco. (Went 2000: 20–1)

Small farmers are forced to cut prices to sell to commodity giants like Cargill. The growth of monopsonistic commodity brokers and huge agribusiness farmers has tended to squeeze out other farmers. According to Korten, between 1935 and 1989, the number of US farmers fell from 6.8 million to under 2.1 million. Small businesses serving local farmers, such as tractor and tool dealers, have gone out of business, causing entire rural communities to disappear (2001: 208). The top ten 'farms' in the US are now agricultural corporations:

Three companies – Iowa Beef Processors (IBP), Cargill and ConAgra – slaughter nearly 80 percent of U.S. beef. One company – Campbell's – controls nearly 70 percent of the U.S. soup market. Four companies – Kelloggs, General Mills, Philip Morris, and Quaker Oats – control nearly 85 percent of the U.S. cold cereal market. Four companies – ConAgra, ADM Milling, Cargill, and Pillsbury – mill nearly 60 percent of U.S. flour. (Korten 2001: 208)

The retail market, which sells food to consumers, used to be a forest of small high street shops but is increasingly an arena of monopoly. In the UK, four supermarkets dominate and are able to push up prices for consumers and exploit farmers. Just two firms, British Sugar and Tate and Lyle, control sugar production. According to Korten, there were 4,100 buyouts or mergers in the US food industry between 1982 and 1990. The largest retail company on the planet is Wal-Mart. In 1999, it gained control of the British supermarket Asda and has been steadily expanding globally (Sklair 2001: 42). In 2003, it sold $256 billion worth of goods, making it the largest firm in the world. Eight out of ten US shoppers use Wal-Mart, it has 3,000 stores in the US and major chains in countries including Canada, China, Japan, Germany and Mexico. Wal-Mart's approach has led to the destruction of local shops and, through ruthless buying policies, has pushed wages down. It increasingly outsources products from the very cheapest Chinese producers, buying $15 billion goods from the country each year (*The Economist*, 17 April 2004). The company has met fierce resistance from unions concerned about low pay and local communities seeking to preserve the environment, but according to *The Economist*, it is fighting back:

With so many eyes watching it, Wal-Mart may have decided that it has to sacrifice a bit of its entrepreneurialism to reduce its legal risks. It recently set up a 'reputation taskforce', introduced new personnel procedures, hired extra lobbyists in Washington, DC, created an 'office of diversity', and launched new public relations and advertising initiatives, dubbed 'good jobs' and 'good works', featuring lots of beaming associates. These are not the actions of a company intending to get smaller. Wal-Mart, already huge, is preparing to get a whole lot bigger. (*The Economist*, 17 April 2004)

While it is rare for a single firm to control a market totally, unofficial cartels, where firms get together to fix prices rather than indulge in unprofitable competition, are both common and hard to detect. Korten uses the term 'managed competition', arguing that transnational corporations increasingly construct alliances and deals that make it difficult to distinguish one company from another. He notes that General Motors owns '37.5 percent of the Japanese auto manufacturer Isuzu'. During the 1990s, he also notes how IBM, Apple and Motorola put together an interfirm alliance to develop computer operation systems. Consumers are given an illusion of competition, when the reality is cooperation to raise profit. Consumer durables such as fridge, freezers, cookers and televisions are produced by five major corporations who control 70 per cent of the world market (Korten 2001: 207). Perfect competition, if it ever existed, is now dead.

GLOBAL GOVERNMENT INC.

Korten suggests that modern corporations are the 'dominant governance institution on the planet' (1998: 60). The Bush Jr cabinet of 2000–04 was, for example, staffed by key corporate figures. Andrew Card, Chief of Staff, was a former chief lobbyist for General Motors; as head of the American Automobile Manufacturers Association, he led their $25 million campaign against stricter fuel emissions standards and the Kyoto Protocol on global warming. General Motors threw a lavish rooftop party when he joined the Bush administration. Gale Norton, Secretary of the Interior, the department in charge of parks and other public lands, was a former oil lobbyist. She headed the Coalition of Republican Environmental Advocates, a group funded by Ford and BP Amoco, which advocated abolishing the Endangered Species Act (Mensler/Corp Watch). Condoleezza Rice, National Security Adviser, sat on the boards of Charles Schwab, Transamerican Corp and Chevron. Chevron christened a 130,000 oil tanker after her. Corporate influence is part of the two party system with firms often donating to both parties, Gore's presidential bid against Bush was bankrolled largely by law firms. The 2004 Democratic presidential candidate John Kerry is notoriously corporate friendly. For example, he used his position on the Senate Finance Subcommittee to support the merger of Fleet Boston Financial with the Bank of America. Fleet has consistently funded his congressional campaigns. The merger, which led to the loss of 2,500 jobs, was strongly opposed by local activists in New England.

In the UK, despite election spending limits, the governing party is usually linked to business interest. Mrs Thatcher was so supportive of McDonald's that she opened their UK headquarters in her parliamentary constituency of Finchley in North London. Her powerful press secretary Bernard Ingham went on to work for the corporation as their head of public relations. John Major's Conservative government of 1992–97 was discredited by corporate-based scandals involving cabinet ministers and backbench MPs who took cash to ask parliamentary questions on behalf of business. Tony Blair's governments have also been mired in allegations of corruption. Labour Party funding has increasingly come from transnationals. Prior to his 1997 general election victory, Blair was flown to a special tropical resort conference by the news magnate Rupert Murdoch. Best known for the genial *The Simpsons*, the Murdoch empire also produces such pro-corporate staples as Fox TV and the *Sun* newspaper. The Murdoch press shifted support from the Conservatives to Labour. The Blair government has since reformed competition and media legislation in ways that benefit Murdoch's News International. After Formula One racing boss Bernie Ecclestone gave large donations to the party, Labour allowed tobacco sponsorship for the sport to continue (Dunleavy et al. 2000: 365).

From the power wielded by Russian oligarchs to the participation of Korean cheabols (corporations), big company influence on national governments, makes a global mockery of democracy. The LSE-based sociologist Leslie Sklair has identified the existence of globalising politicians who work for corporate interests by removing national barriers on trade and investment to benefit the transnationals. These politicians, often trained at neo-liberal university economics departments such as Chicago, Harvard or the MIT, believe that economic prosperity can only be created or maintained by making life easier for transnationals. Representative democracy has effectively become a system of elite pluralism, where rival elite corporations may compete for influence but where others such as trade unionists, environmentalists, ordinary party members or the public have little or no say in the debate. Politics becomes more like business and opposition to capitalism or even just the worst excesses of corporate greed becomes impossible to voice (Sklair 2001).

Korten argues that corporations govern the globe and have created institutions such as the WTO to secure their power. Essentially, there is a shadow global government based upon hidden groups such as the Trilateral Commission and the Bilderberg Group who bring politicians, corporate heads, influential academics and journalists together (Korten 2001: 135; Sklar 1980). Typically, both the leaders of governing parties and those of the opposition in countries like the US, UK and Japan tend to go to Bilderberg events. The famously corporate-friendly British European Commissioner Peter Mandelson is a Bilderberg figure (Ronson 2000: 127). The European Commission drives forward European Union legislation, which must be transformed into law by the individual EU states. The small number of European Commissioners are more powerful than most cabinet members and many Prime Ministers. Unelected, they seem rather to be selected for loyalty to the transnational capitalist class. Mandelson as EU Trade Commissioner provides a pro-business mouthpiece in WTO negotiations.

'Free trade' is, according to Sklair and Korten, driven by corporations. The WTO and trading blocs such as NAFTA allow large corporations access to new markets where they can sell goods to new sets of consumers. In turn, they can relocate production to countries where wages are low and they export without facing barriers such as import taxes (tariffs). It might be thought that nationally based firms would be resistant to allowing access to foreign competitors. Indeed, one potential weakness of anti-corporate accounts of globalisation is the fact that different businesses may have opposing economic/political objectives. Thus in the US, law firms might benefit from stronger rules on corporate behaviour and have therefore been more likely to support the mildly reformist Democrats, who could be prepared to clamp down on the worst excesses of destructive corporations. Chemical and oil corporations have tended to favour the Republicans who are more likely to reduce regulation. However, while disputes may exist, causing the state to act as a committee of corporations or an umpire between corporate interests, Sklair has found that corporations have an almost universal interest in 'free trade'. He notes how the pro-NAFTA lobby included the US Chamber of Commerce, the National Association of Manufacturers, the National Foreign Trade Council, the US Council for International Business, the National Retail Federation, the Business Roundtable and the American Farm Bureau Federation. In the run-up to a Congress vote on NAFTA, the US Chamber of Commerce phoned every congressional representative daily. 'No stone was left unturned. Even Miss Mexico spoke out for NAFTA as she was being crowned Miss Universe!' (Sklair 2001: 102).

The General Agreement on Trade in Services (GATS) extends free trade to 160 areas in the service sector and means that in principle WTO members will have to allow foreign companies to compete in the provision of postal services, telecommunications and healthcare. In preparation for competitive postal services, European Union postal services are being made to cut costs and raise charges to bring in profit. In the UK, thousands of local post offices are likely to close and there is a strong possibility that private competition will lead to 'cherry picking'. Profitable postal services, for instance, those supplying the needs of large commercial interests in major cities, will attract investment, while rural services will close. Already in the UK, the post deliveries have been cut to once a day.

Privatisation leads to 'insourcing' where cheap, often illegal migrant labour is used to cut costs even further. The market is aided by the fact that workers are 'illegalised' when they migrate, so their fear of discovery by the authorities means that they are unlikely to join unions or complain about poor pay. Right-wing media sources, in turn, demonise refugees rather than identifying corporations as a source of low pay and social instability.

Globalising politicians such as Tony Blair have been keen to bring in Private Finance Initiatives (PFI), which allow private corporations to fund and profit from the provision of roads, hospitals and schools, previously provided by the state for the community.

Naomi Klein in *No Logo* shows that firms have been keen to move into new areas of public life to strengthen their brands and exploit new markets. She notes, for example, how education is corporate-dominated. Schools may be sponsored by transnationals, textbooks may contain adverts and university research is ever more dependent on grants from firms. Corporate control of areas of life that were provided by the state or local community has reached absurd lengths. When in 1998 Coca-Cola ran a competition for schools to design a marketing plan for their product, one school, Greenbriar High School, Evans, Georgia, suspended a 19-year old student for wearing a Pepsi T-shirt to the official Coke-day celebrations (Klein 2001b: 95). In 1996 the Centre for the Study of Human Ecology was thrown out of the University of Edinburgh, partly because it was felt to be an anti-corporate institution because of its research into capitalist-driven ecological problems (Monbiot 2003a: 281). The evidence provided by both Klein and Monbiot suggests that universities are increasingly centres for what is best described, with an apology to the oldest profession, as intellectual prostitution.

Corporations are territorially expansive, seeking control over more and more local markets globally. Their ambitions are also intensive, even totalitarian, as they seek to dominate almost every area of social life. Bus shelters and road signs are branded; in Scandinavia telephone calls made cheap by corporate sponsorship are interrupted by adverts. Sporting events like the Olympics are marketing bonanzas for the merchants of fat and fizz. Sklair believes that the power of corporations has created a new transnational capitalist class. He divides this class into four fractions, including (1) transnational corporate executives and their local affiliates, (2) globalising bureaucrats and politicians, (3) globalising professionals and (4) retailers and media communities. All are committed to creating a single world corporate paradise.

Even 'alternative' politicians have been pulled into the transnational capitalist class. The centre-ground Green 2000 faction of the UK Green Party, who sought to make the party more mainstream, created a business-friendly environmental group Forum for the Future, sponsored by oil interests and airlines (Sklair 2001: 211). The German Greens under charismatic leader Joschka Fischer have become a party committed to the market: 'Their ministers are among the more competent ... the party has ditched many leftist positions ... Today, younger Greens are not just environmentalists and socially liberal, but also fiscal conservatives' (*The Economist*, 10 June 2004).

Klein notes that while corporations enjoy a governing role, they are reluctant to pay the taxes necessary for the state to support their position. Transnationals negotiate to move production to free trade zones where they can enjoy tax 'holidays'. Corporate welfare (where governments tax citizens and subsidise companies) is common especially in the US and within the free trade zones.

OUTSOURCING

Klein suggests that corporations have become increasingly virtual, selling not goods but a brand image. Designer labels have become ever more important in the clothing industry and food retailing. Advertising has been used to encourage consumers to buy goods and services they didn't previously need and to allow firms to raise their prices. Klein argues with many post-modernists that the economy is increasingly based on symbolic values rather than material qualities. Firms seek to sell symbols of cultural value to be consumed by individuals keen to assert their value in society through lifestyle consumption. Marketing is used to build brands. Hector Liang, ex-chair of United Biscuits, observed: 'Machines wear out. Cars rust. People die. But what lives on are brands' (Klein 2001a: 196).

Unlike the more extravagant post-modernist accounts, Klein never forgets that goods still have to be made by factory workers. Factory production, though, has been increasingly outsourced. Outsourcing is a process where by corporations act as consumers rather than producers, buying goods from the cheapest supplier and reselling them. Outsourcing has accelerated the creation of ultra-low-wage Export Processing Zones (EPZs), where companies rather than states have jurisdiction and costs can be squeezed in sweatshops. The corporations are ceasing to employ industrial workers; they buy the services of smaller localised manufacturers who compete to push wages and other costs down. Klein notes how Disney spokesman Ken Green responded to questions from the *Catholic Register* about the pay and conditions of the workers who made clothes for the company: 'We don't employ anyone in Haiti ... With the newsprint you use, do you have any idea of the labour conditions involved to produce it?' (Klein 2001a: 198)

Conditions within the EPZs are grim, workers work long hours for low pay, whilst unions are banned and safety is lax. Workers, often young women, have no job security and may be housed in barracks. Police or armed forces may help to maintain discipline. In 2001, according to Klein, approximately 1,000 EPZs existed in 70 countries and employed 27 million workers. The Phillipines, Sri Lanka and Mexico are major centres of EPZs but all are outstripped by China, where some of the worst abuses are apparent. Chinese EPZ workers are estimated to work for around 16 hours a day and are paid an average of just 87 cents an hour:

A 1998 study of brand-name manufacturing in the Chinese special economic zones found that Wal-Mart, Ralph Lauren, Ann Taylor, Esprit, Liz Claiborne, Kmart, Nike, Adidas, J.C. Penney and the Limited were only paying a fraction of that miserable 87 cents – some were paying as little as 13 cents an hour. (Klein 2001a: 212)

Countries that attempt to raise standards may lose business. Economic forces let loose by corporate globalisation maintain poverty. WTO rules make it illegal for states to refuse goods that have been produced by what is virtually slave labour. Klein notes the powerful example of the closure of the only unionised clothing factory in the whole of Guatemala in December 1998. The factory had been unionised after a long and bitter dispute, with wages rising from $56 a week to $71 (2001a: 214). This victory became defeat when the factory was closed and production moved elsewhere. Political violence goes hand in hand with the discipline of the free market. States that resist the corporate agenda face invasion and sanctions, from Chinese opposition to free trade in the nineteenth century or reforming governments in Central or South America more recently. Brutality remains a feature of the workplace:

> In 1993, a Sri Lankan zone worker by the name of Ranjith Mudiyanselage was killed … [after] complaining about a faulty machine that had sliced off a co-worker's finger. Mudiyanselage was abducted on his way out of an inquiry into the incident. His body was found beaten and burning on a pile of old tires outside a local church. The man's legal advisor, who had accompanied him to the inquiry, was murdered in the same way. (Klein 2001a: 214–15)

Outsourcing has led to EPZ-style labour standards in the north of the globe. European food producers forced by supermarket monopolists to push down their costs often have to use illegal foreign labour. Illegal immigrants are in no position to complain about poor conditions, potential injury and long hours. In February 2004, 19 illegal Chinese workers were drowned when they went to gather shellfish in Morecambe Bay in the north of England (*Guardian*, 9 February 2004).

Such exploitation of labour has helped to create a hyperwealthy elite. Korten notes how the $20 million received by basketball star Michael Jordan in 1992 for promoting Nike trainers was more than the entire annual pay roll of the Indonesian factory that manufactured the shoes (Korten 2001: 115). The highest executive package in 1993 was $203.1 million for Disney chair Michael Eisner. Executives are part of Sklair's transnational corporate class that travels by Lear jet, eats in the best restaurants and moves between gated villages, guarded apartments and country dachas:

> Of the many countries I have visited, Pakistan most starkly exemplifies the experience of elites living in enclaves detached from local roots. The country's three modern cities … feature enclaves of five-star hotels, modern shopping malls, and posh residential areas … My hosts [… felt] as much at home in New York or London as in Karachi, Lahore, or Islamabad
>
> Particularly striking, however, was the extent to which – in contrast to their knowledge of or interest in the rest of the world – they had little

knowledge of or interest in what was happening in their own country beyond the borders of their enclave cities. It was as though the rest of Pakistan were an inconsequential foreign country not worthy of notice or mention. (Korten 2001: 117–18)

The environmental ill-effects of corporate rule are perhaps too obvious to discuss. If environmental regulation is reduced, so are average costs, outsourced manufacturers are under unrelenting pressure to cut costs, which means cutting environmental corners. The race for profit can have some surprisingly sinister and unusual effects. Geographer Andrew Goudie blames the replacement of camels with Toyota's four-wheel-drive land cruisers for dust storms that are disrupting the world's weather, stating: 'I am quite serious, you should look at deserts from the air, scarred all over by wheel tracks, people driving indiscriminately over the surface breaking it up. Toyotarisation is a major cause of dust storms' (*Guardian*, 20 August 2004). Dust has been found in the polar icecaps, it darkens the surface and absorbs light, this leads to accelerated melting. Coral reefs are also dying because of the dirt from four-wheel-drives.

ADAM SMITH'S ECOTOPIA

Some variants of anti-capitalist economics are complex. In contrast, anti-corporate anti-capitalism is easily understood. However, Sklair draws on social theory and Klein ideas closely parallel post-modern accounts that suggest that large-scale Fordist production has been replaced by diverse and decentralised manufacture. Post-modernists also argue that culture in the form of the 'brand' has become more important than the physical properties of a good. People buy alternative lifestyles rather than sausages. Klein's account is preferable to that of the broadly post-modern in two ways. First, she does not forget that the branded goods still have to be made by real and exploited people within real and degraded physical environments. Second, she incorporates a political critique. In contrast, the extreme post-modernists find it difficult to argue that any one thing is better than any other. Having swept away foundational truth claims, figures like Baudrillard, who infamously claimed that the First Gulf War did not happen, have no means of voicing opposition to injustice (Baudrillard 1995). Klein is also influenced by a tradition of cultural politics, derived in part from Western Marxists such as Gramsci and Marcuse. Gramsci argued that the ruling class ruled through the creation of ideological hegemony or common sense. Such common sense prevented rebellion. Marcuse argued in books like *One Dimensional Man* that consumer capitalism dulled workers into submission with television and commodities (1964). None of this is so far from Aldous Huxley's prophetic novel *Brave New World* which saw a physical form of cinema, the 'feelies', and a drug, 'soma', used to pacify workers. Both Huxley and the Frankfurt School at their worst tended to cultural pessimism, fearing that all aspects of commercial culture were inferior to traditional high culture. Frankfurt philosopher Adorno, to give an extreme example, believed that jazz music was degenerate compared to Mozart and his peers (Jay 1973: 185). The Frankfurters also believed that a totalitarian society had been created that left little or no room for opposition. In contrast, the post-modern variant of cultural theory has tended to celebrate the subversive nature of all popular culture. Both the Frankfurt School and post-modernists have tended to shift political struggle to the symbolic realm, which is where Klein met their descendants. She notes how in the 1980s she and other young radicals became partisans in the culture wars, arguing that language and access were essential to liberation. Lesbians should be represented on television, and politically incorrect language should be banned from the airwaves. She acknowledges that during the 'culture wars' the need to challenge corporate globalisation was largely forgotten, making it easier for companies to cut workers' pay and shape our subjective desires with confidence.

In *No Logo*, Klein shows that far from living in a totalitarian society, activists can battle the brands and sometimes even win. She is less pessimistic than the Frankfurters but more politically committed in her analysis than the post-modernists. Symbolic politics links to campaigns for better pay and conditions, when, for example, consumers boycott the Nike flash, to fight against the outsourced sweatshops that pay the workers just cents for a pair of new trainers. Klein is refreshingly modest, she explicitly examines recent developments in corporate growth and makes no pretensions to producing a total critique. Her aim in *No Logo* is to catalogue opposition to corporate globalisation.

Korten's theoretical hinterland is frankly embarrassing. While he notes the importance of protest, he has a tendency towards the political equivalent of astrology, making unconvincing claims that the Age of Aquarius is dawning and a change in consciousness will sweep away capitalism. He argues that Western society is based on a dull, quantitative form of materialism, which worships technology.

A new age will see social values based on spirituality with 'Millions of people' awakening 'as if from a deep trance, to the beauty, joy, and meaning of life' (Korten 2001: 340). While social change may require a revolution in ethics, new practices and a critique of many aspects of technology, Korten's assumptions seem too crude to give real hope.

Korten has been termed a 'neo-Smithian' because, somewhat surprisingly, he is inspired by Adam Smith, the founding father of free market economics (Kovel 2002: 162). Smith, far from stating crudely that greed was good, was a moral philosopher, with a distrust of concentrated power. He believed that both the state and corporations tend to abuse their authority and should be replaced by small-scale producers. Indeed, both he and the historical record show that rather than being antagonistic the strong state and the powerful corporations are friends. Corporations have their origin in grants of monopoly power from the state. He believed that the market would take power from both and hand it back to small producers, workers and consumers. McNally argues that both left and right used Smith's ideas and nineteenth-century radicals like William Cobbett might even be termed Smithian socialists (McNally 1993). Korten states that the market is a useful and essentially fair device for producing and distributing goods and services. By popular action to localise production the free market can be restored and mighty corporations made low. He believes that the early American economy based on small firms rooted in local communities provides an economic alternative to globalisation. He argues simply and passionately that capitalism has the same relation to the free market that cancer has to a healthy human body. It can be argued that the relationship between markets and capitalism is rather closer to that of a chicken and an egg than a cancer and a healthy body. Markets seem to have a built in tendency to grow and grow. This tendency leads to the invasion of buying and selling into ever more areas of life; to concentrations of power and wealth; to injustice and ecological destruction. Markets tend to be the little acorns of great corporate oaks. They are the fiscal equivalent of plutonium, best avoided or at least contained if life is to be preserved:

There is evidence that market economies are never fair. Property, as Proudhon famously argued, is theft, and private property is necessary to the market. Usually the act of enclosure that created the property is so distant in history as to be forgotten. This is not the case in North

America. In the US, communal land was simply stolen from Native Americans. There was never a utopia in New England.

Korten is also a populist. Populists in general, whether of the right or left, claim to represent the 'people' against the dominant elite who exploit them (Canovan 1981). Populism is often linked to producerism, which stresses the rights of those who produce goods such as workers, farmers and small business people over the unproductive sections of society who consume their goods. Big business and the banks are favourite targets. Right-wing populists often link in an elite conspiracy to the creation of a communist totalitarian state (Berlet and Lyons 2000).

The nineteenth century saw the emergence of populist parties and movements in America, some of whose key demands were taken up by Democratic and Progressive politicians, resulting in anti-trust laws aimed at destroying monopolies (Ritter 1997). Individuals such as Ralph Nader and the demagogic Michael Moore have continued the populist anti-corporate tradition into the twenty-first century. Populism can, in the hands of Nader and Moore, be a relatively radical force. In any form, though, it tends to replace economic analysis with a focus on the misdeeds of an elite in a world of good guys and bad guys.

Korten's approach, like most populism, is both attractive and a little undernourishing – a kind of fast food alternative economics. Other anti-corporatists such as Klein and Sklair do a more convincing job, with perspectives based on stronger evidence and detailed consideration of cultural and sociological factors; however, there is more to anti-capitalism than hatred of corporation.

4
Small is Beautiful: Green Localism

A few years ago I was eating at a St. Paul, Minnesota, restaurant. After lunch, I picked up a toothpick wrapped in plastic. On the plastic was printed the word *Japan*. Japan has little wood and no oil; nevertheless, it has become efficient enough in our global economy to bring little pieces of wood and barrels of oil to Japan, to wrap the one in the other, and send the manufactured product to Minnesota. This toothpick may have travelled 50,000 miles. But never fear, we are now retaliating in kind. A Hibbing, Minnesota, factory now produces one billion disposable chopsticks a year for sale in Japan. In my mind's eye, I see two ships passing one another in the northern Pacific. One carries little pieces of Minnesota wood bound for Japan; the other carries little pieces of Japanese wood bound for Minnesota. Such is the logic of free trade. (Morris 1996: 222)

Agreements have been made to circumvent National Governments. One of the most significant of these is the General Agreement on Trade in Services (GATS). These services include the commercial aspects of the public services of education, water and health, all potentially very profitable areas. Economic rationalism's aim is to conduct all human activity on the model of buying and selling without constraint in a market place. The market controls all human interaction. (Clare McCarty, July 2003, Australian Green Party election candidate, <www.sa.greens.org.au/speeches/cm_030712>)

'I am not a trade barrier', squeaks the dolphin on an anti-WTO flag carried by green activists at Seattle. Green parties, green direct action networks like Earth First!, environmental pressure groups and animal liberationists have all opposed globalisation on ecological and social grounds. The International Forum on Globalisation (IFG), a body established by Edward Goldsmith, founding editor of the *Ecologist* magazine, did much of the intellectual groundwork for the wider mobilisation against free trade. Goldsmith, a pioneer of green thought since the late 1960s, has developed a devastating critique of economic growth, free trade and conventional development strategies (Goldsmith 1988). Caroline Lucas, a leading member of the UK Green Party, attacks capitalism from a localist slant as ecocidal, exploitative and centralised in her book *Green Alternatives to Globalisation*, written with the late Mike Woodin (Woodin and Lucas 2004). US presidential candidate Ralph Nader has been another important green critic of neo-liberalism (Nader 2002). Green parties worldwide advocate reduced trade. Other authors who support a green localist approach include Colin Hines (2000) and Jerry Mander (Mander and Goldsmith 1996).

Greens are often seen as a movement of the white middle classes, advocating a post-material politics, which is a luxury of the relatively wealthy. However, many green anti-capitalists are active in peasant and radical farmers' movements. At WTO agenda-setting talks in Cancun, Mexico in 2003, Kyung-Hae Lee committed suicide to protest at the damage free trade did to the 120,000 Korean farmers he represented (*Guardian*, 16 September 2003). Mr Lee found that his revenue from beef farming fell by three-quarters after Korea imported cheap agribusiness farmed meat. José Bové in France leads a militant anti-capitalist farmers union, Confédération Paysanne (Herman and Kuper 2003). Radical farmers in the Indian anti-globalisation movement number millions. From Mexico to Korea, farmers and peasants claim that neo-liberalism will flood their countries with cheap crops, privatise land and increase pollution. The Indian ecofeminist Vandana Shiva, arrested on several WTO actions, provides a strong link between radical greens and angry farmers. The subsistence perspective she puts forward in books like *Staying Alive* (1988), argues that peasants, particularly women, carry out the real economic activity. She believes globalisation favours huge agribusinesses and threatens every small producer on the planet.

A minority of environmentalists, as opposed to political greens, are supportive of globalisation, with figures like Paul Hawken (Hawken et al. 1999) suggesting, for example, that *Natural Capitalism* is a possibility. In Europe, where several Green parties have recently participated in coalition government, mild reform rather than ecocentric revolution has been the norm (Papadakis 1998). However, many anti-capitalists are greens. Here the economic ideas underpinning a radical green approach from Sismondi and Ruskin through to Schumacher are explored, whilst localist and subsistence perspectives are placed under the microscope.

GREEN MOVEMENTS AND GREEN ECONOMICS

The global environmental pressure groups like Friends of the Earth and Greenpeace were born in the late 1960s and the first ecological political parties emerged in the 1970s in Australia, Britain, France and New Zealand (Doherty 2002: 122). Awareness of global environmental problems via television and later the internet has been a trigger for green politics. Increasing prosperity has been seen as a source of green politics because it provides individuals with the relative luxury of being able to focus on issues beyond bread and butter (Inglehart 1977). Nonetheless, while Green Parties are relatively new, environmental concern is not. Environmental and animal rights pressure groups are some of the oldest in existence. The Vegetarian Society was established in 1847 and the Open Spaces Society can trace its origins back to the 1850s (Kean 1998). The US Sierra Club dedicated to conserving wilderness was also created in the nineteenth century (Wall 1993). Concern that environmental problems may wreck the economy can be found in ancient Greek society, where Plato drew attention to the effects of soil erosion (Hughes 1994). The earliest UK anti-pollution laws were put on the statute books in the thirteenth century. John Evelyn, in the reign of Charles II, wrote a tract against air pollution and a manifesto for tree conservation (Wall 1993). Green economics also has deep roots. Greens are critical of the notion of economic growth believing that expansion does not necessarily increase human happiness. They also reject anthropocentricism, seeing nature and not just the human part as the measure of all things. Greens stress cooperation rather than competition (Dobson 1991, 2000; Doherty 2002). Greens are also localists who believe that decision-making should be democratised to the grassroots.

One source of green economics is to be found in the nineteenth-century Romantic critique of industrialisation. William Blake famously noted the emergence of 'satanic mills' in England's 'green and pleasant land', Wordsworth and Shelley expressed similar sentiments, which were developed by the Victorian critic John Ruskin who inspired William Morris. Goethe's Romanticism has also been influential. Such concerns were incorporated by urban planners such as Geddes and Mumford in the twentieth century (Gould 1988).

A holistic philosophy that shows how different parts of society and nature are interrelated is taken by greens from the science of ecology, which studies relationships, often invisible without careful study, between different organisms. Holism has spiritual roots drawing upon Eastern philosophies and religions particularly Buddhism and Taoism. The novelist Aldous Huxley developed such insights, as did E.F. Schumacher, the green economist, who wrote *Small is Beautiful* (1978). The Beat poets, especially Gary Synder, drew upon Zen and fed into the 1960s hippie counter-culture, providing a rich soil for the Green parties of the 1970s (Snyder 1974, 1999). Holism remains very important in contemporary green discourse, yet to argue that Asian spirituality gives rise to ecotopia is slightly misleading. China, India and Japan have devastated their environments just as much as the West (Smil 1984; Utsunomiya 1980). Some Zen monks became warmongers in the Second World War (Victoria 1998). The spiritual revolution will not on its own provide an alternative to capitalism. Indeed, Synder, a practitioner of both Zen and green politics, notes: 'sutras were chanted on behalf of the long life of the emperor; the monasteries supported and aided the regime. What it came to most strikingly was the almost complete cooperation of the Buddhist establishment in Japan (with some notable exceptions) with the military efforts of World War II' (Snyder 1999: 98).

A conservative strain runs through some forms of green thought. This is most evident in the work of Edward Goldsmith, who celebrates the stability of tribal societies, the nuclear family and sees functionalism everywhere. For Goldsmith human society is part of a finely balanced nature. An essay entitled 'The Ecology of War' has even argued that war, well localised and small-scale, is beneficial to society (in Goldsmith 1988). Ironically, the subsistence ecofeminists while critical of male dominance stress that traditional peasant societies are socially and ecologically sustainable. Like socialism and spirituality, such functionalism is not swallowed whole by modern greens. Indeed, the Green Party of England and Wales was created by former members of the Conservative Party including Goldsmith but has since moved to the left (Wall 1994). By the 1980s ecological political parties had constructed a wider agenda which was well summarised by the four values espoused by the German Greens when they entered parliament in 1983: ecology, social justice, grassroots democracy and peace (German Green Party 1983). The German, French and Austrian Greens came out of the social movements against nuclear power and weapons (Poguntke 1993). As Green parties have grown, they have been able to win seats in parliaments and local councils in ever larger numbers. One of the reasons for their success, especially in Europe, has been the movement of traditional socialist parties like the German Social Democrats and British Labour Party to the right. The socialist parties have come to adopt variants of a 'Third Way' ideology, which has committed them to the market because they perceive globalisation to be an inevitable process demanding ever greater competitiveness. The resulting wage cuts, bouts of privatisation and loss of services have meant that some trade union activists have been drawn to the Greens. Clinton's New Democrat approach led to Ralph Nader running as a high-profile Green presidential candidate (Nader 2002). In New Zealand, a Labour Party commitment to neo-liberal economics helped the Greens to grow rapidly. However, where Greens have been most successful, they have often joined coalitions with the former left parties who have embraced globalisation. The New Zealand Greens forced a general election because they refused to condone the government's support for GM crops coming into the country (*The Economist*, 1 August 2002). In contrast, in Germany, the Greens have supported neo-liberal economics, including public spending and welfare cuts (Lees 2002). Green economics, like the other variants of anti-capitalist and indeed capitalist thought discussed here, swims in the sea of history and cannot be seen as a set of pure moral principles or scientific axioms. Social forces have helped shape green ideology and the most radical greens have had to challenge more centre ground members in a series of ideological contests (Wall 1994).

AGAINST GROWTH

Perhaps the most subversive and unusual element of green anti-capitalism is opposition to economic growth (Goldsmith 1972; Porritt 1984; Trainer 1985). In the early 1970s, scientists became concerned that ever-increasing economic growth would damage the environment (Meadows 1974). The idea that human societies should produce more goods and services every year is, as we noted in Chapter 1, environmentally suspect. Scarce resources such as oil will eventually be exhausted, although it is difficult to calculate when. In the search for new resources vital ecosystems are disrupted. To produce more goods, more energy has to be produced which leads to an increase in greenhouse gases, or, if the nuclear route is taken, to problems of radioactive waste. If we consume more goods this creates jobs and enhances profits but leads to ever larger mountains of rubbish that have to be disposed of by dumping or poisonous incineration:

> The more people consume, the better it is. It's not so much a question of consumer durables as of durable consumers. And in order to achieve this, consumers must be manipulated into the smoothest possible cycle of acquisition and disposal, into a uniform, superficial understanding of personal and social requirements. Consumption becomes an end in itself. Even when the market reaches saturation, the process doesn't stop; for the only way to beat a glut is to turn everybody into gluttons. (Porritt 1984: 47)

There are many arguments that can be marshalled to suggest that economic expansion can be ecologically sustainable. Growth can be delinked from energy use and waste (Weizsacker et al. 1997). Conservation measures and the application of new technology mean that more goods can be produced per kilowatt. Indeed, in recent years GDP, the most common measure of economic output, has been growing faster than energy use. As societies become wealthier more services rather than physical goods are consumed, a tendency which also has the potential to reduce pollution. Because of green and environmental movement pressure, more ecologically sustainable practices are being used to maintain growth. In Germany, in particular, the practice of ecological modernism, which uses high technology to try to sustain both the environment and economic expansion, has become important (Mol and Spaarrgaren 2000). Solar, wind and other low-pollution, low-impact renewable energy sources have been advancing (Elliot 2003). Recycling has become a necessity and there is now a strong zero-waste movement (Greenpeace 2001). More people in Western societies eat organic food or are vegetarian, practices that reduce waste because they need less energy input without artificial fertilisers and pesticides. Many of the fears that Greens linked to economic growth seem to have been either exaggerated or are non-existent. Oil did not, as some commentators suggest, run out in 1979! The move to a high-tech information economy has also been seen as a way of increasing economic value without increasing the output of pollution.

Yet as we have noted, environmental problems remain severe and remain linked to growth. The burning of fossil fuels seems to be causing a greenhouse effect, which may already be causing problems in terms of species loss, the migration of diseases and pests to new areas of the world, desertification and extreme weather patterns (Firor and Jacobsen 2002). The sun may be shining outside my home as I write with temperatures above those of my childhood in the 1970s. I may be happy to contemplate my vines and consider buying an olive tree, yet I fear damage from the ever stronger storms that hit my home with increasing frequency year on year.

The information-based economy may seem virtual but, as Naomi Klein exhaustively demonstrates, branded goods still have to be produced and computers made by exploited workers (2001a). Computer manufacture and disposal are sources of pollution and resource use. Some services have little physical impact but the huge global growth in tourism is accelerating air travel, which has become the fastest-growing source of greenhouse gases. Cars are far cleaner, but pollution from cars is rising because the number of miles they are used for is rising sharply in many parts of the world. The fundamental problem with globalisation from a green point of view is that it leads to ever greater economic activity. Such activity demands more production, more consumption and ever increasing waste. Edward Goldsmith provides an instructive apocryphal story of two friends who both inherit a 10,000-acre tract of forest. Friend one leaves his 10,000 acres in its pristine state. Friend two sells the trees to McMillan Bloedel Corporation who cuts them all down, sells the mineral rights and the topsoil, fills the resulting dank hole with toxic waste, and constructs a shopping mall and theme park. Friend one is labelled as a waster, friend two boosts GNP by millions of dollars, runs for office and becomes a senator (Mander and Goldsmith 1996: 15).

Woodin and Lucas point out that globalisation by accelerating growth is speeding the greenhouse effect, with parts per million by volume (ppmv) of greenhouse gases now standing at 370 ppmv, a peak which is 30% higher than the previous high over 10,000 years ago in the last interglacial period. They state that consumption of fresh water is doubling every twenty years, 12% of all bird species and a quarter of all mammal species are threatened with extinction (Woodin and Lucas 2004: 33).

Greens in the south of the globe are, despite lower levels of material development, critical of conventionally measured growth. The Iranian Green Party typically notes:

> Since economies grow while ecosystems do not, a growing economy is a threat to the long-term health and well being of a society. In fact, in industrialized countries, large corporations seeking increased revenues are often the main perpetrators of environmental destruction. Although Iranian economic growth is less than growth in industrialized countries, Iran is still faced with difficult problems because of its fundamentalist regime. In fact, in addition to environmental destruction caused by profit seeking corporations, the ineffectiveness and corruption of the reactionary Islamic regime has caused much of the ecological devastation plaguing Iran today. (<www.iran-e-sabz.org/program/program>)

ECONOMICS AS ALIENATION

Greens also argue that economic growth cheapens human existence. Areas of life that are not directly productive in an economic sense come to be valued less and less. Indeed, it is only what can be calculated, bought and sold that truly has worth:

> Economics ... suddenly becomes the most important subject of all. Economic policies absorb almost the entire attention of government, and at the same time become ever more impotent. The simplest things, which only fifty years ago one could do without difficulty, cannot get done any more. The richer a society, the more impossible it becomes to do worthwhile things without immediate pay-off. [Economics] tends to absorb the whole of ethics and take precedence over all other human considerations. Now, quite clearly, this is a pathological development. (Schumacher 1978: 67)

The pressure to be competitive individually or collectively driven by globalisation is particularly damaging. Workers are expected to put in ever longer hours. Universities must concentrate on promoting skills that lead to further economic growth. Status is measured by wealth that drives even the 'haves' to spend longer working and consuming. Far from maximising 'utility' or benefit for individuals, neo-liberalism increases levels of personal stress (Toke 2000). Economic rationality based on quantitative measure treats anything that cannot easily be measured and sold with contempt. An Australian Green noted:

> Like George Orwell's term 'Newspeak', Neo-Liberal speak usually denotes the opposite of the truth. The long line of such economic rationalist coinages includes: 'the level playing field' that is always on a slope, 'industry parks' that never see a flower, 'world's best practice' unprovable, empty rhetoric but, rather like the Freemason's handshake, indicates they're in the Economic Rationalists' club. (Clare McCarty, July 2003, Australian Green Party election candidate. <www.sa.greens.org.au/speeches/cm_030712>)

Toke has also shown how, in the UK, governments keen to raise economic productivity have forced schools to compete with each other, with demands for growth rather than human need determining the direction that education takes (2000).

All needs in a capitalist society are transformed into the need for commodities. To be a good parent, one should work long hours to afford more 'things' for the babies. To be fulfilled sexually requires a huge and diverse industry. The body, created by unhealthy food and a sedentary car-based lifestyle, has become a new focus of capitalist growth with billions spent on new diets (Fromm 1979). Ted Trainer notes in *Abandon Affluence!* that 'Acquiring things is important to many of us today because there is not much else that yields interest and a sense of progress and satisfaction in life' (quoted in Dobson 1991: 85).

Economic growth does not even remove poverty: the richest generally see the biggest gains and the poorest are usually separated from resources that they previously had access to. In the nineteenth century, surveying the chaos created by the Industrial Revolution, Sismondi echoed the green critique of growth and wider economics. In 1819 Sismondi identified England as the home of economics, a nation obsessed with global competition where wealth paradoxically breeds poverty, dissatisfaction and crisis:

> England has given birth to the most celebrated Political Economists: the science is cultivated even at this time with increased ardour ... Universal competition or the effort always to produce more and always cheaper, has long been the system in England, a system which I have attacked as dangerous. This system has used production by manufacture to advance with gigantic steps, but it has from time to time precipatated the manufactures into frightful distress ... In this astonishing country, which seems to be subject to a great experiment for the instruction of the rest of the world, I have seen production increasing, whilst enjoyments were diminishing. The mass of the nation here, no less than philosophers, seems to forget that the increase of

wealth is not the end in political economy, but its instrument in procuring the happiness of all. I sought for this happiness in every class and I could nowhere find it. ... Has not England, by forgetting men for things, sacrificed the end to the means. (quoted in Luxemburg 1971: 175–7)

Economists would argue that England after the disruption of industrialisation benefited from prosperity, yet they seem to suggest that disruption should constantly occur so as to fuel ever more prosperity. Such a system, as Sismondi observed, turns humanity (and nature) which are 'ends' merely into 'means' for an alien economic system. GNP, competitiveness and production are in the saddle and ride humanity.

The Victorian social critic John Ruskin, in a statement that rings true a century after he penned it, noted:

the real science of political economy, which has yet to be distinguished from the bastard science, as medicine from witchcraft, and astronomy from astrology, is that which teaches nations to desire and labour for the things that lead to life: and which teaches them to scorn and destroy the things that lead to destruction. (quoted in Boyle 2002: 13)

Like Sismondi and Ruskin, Schumacher in his green economics primer *Small is Beautiful* stressed that economics should be a means of making human beings happier and serving ethical needs:

This is standing the truth on its head by considering goods as more important than people and consumption as more important than creative activity. It means shifting the emphasis from the worker to the product of work, that is, from the human to the sub-human, a surrender to the forces of evil. (Schumacher 1978: 54)

BAD TRADE

Greens have increasingly turned their attention to trade. Economists have argued that trade is beneficial because of gains from comparative advantage, competitive pressure, economics of scale and technology transfer. Competitive pressure means that by opening a country up to trade, domestic producers lose any monopoly status they had and are forced to become more cost efficient. Comparative advantage, a notion developed by Adam Smith and refined by Ricardo, occurs when countries specialise in the goods or services they are best at producing and exchange them for others. Economies of scale occur when increased production by a firm leads to lower average costs. A firm with a national market typically might sell to 30 million consumers, with a continental market the firm gains access to 300 million, with a global market perhaps more than a billion. Increased production allows expensive machinery to be used more efficiently, bulk buying of parts and raw materials can be enhanced and specialised staff recruited. These and a host of other savings lower costs. Trade also should create development via technology transfer from richer skilled nations to the rest of the planet.

Greens are sceptical:

> Trade is rarely conducted between equal partners. In Smith and Ricardo's theory, trading nations are assumed to be equal partners making rational decisions based on objective assessments of the factors of production each has available to it through accidents of history, climate and geography. No weight is given to the power imbalances that exist between traders and producers and between different nations. Throughout the history of international trade, 'comparative advantages' have been created artificially and protected fiercely. Whether through gunboat 'diplomacy', colonisation, slavery, land enclosures, or protective subsidies, dominant trading nations have for centuries expropriated and jealously guarded the factors of production and market access they need to establish 'comparative advantages' over would-be competitors. (Woodin and Lucas 2004: 7)

Competition usually leads to a race to the bottom with companies forced to cut wages, working conditions and environmental protection to minimise costs. Korten has noted how competition may ultimately lead to a contradictory state of monopoly as global corporations emerge and eliminate domestic firms (2001: 206–7). They can then raise prices and punish consumers, but are less interested in using their margins to benefit workers or the environment.

WTO rules on patents are aimed at preventing poorer countries from copying products from Europe and North America, so they actually prevent technology transfer. Most notoriously, patent controls, relaxed only after huge international protest, were used to prevent South Africa developing cheap versions of the anti-AIDS/HIV drugs it needed. Technological transfers can, on the other hand, spread toxic or socially disabling practices from one part of the globe. Economies of scale may be significant but diseconomies can also occur. Schumacher noted:

> I was brought up on the theory of 'economies of scale' – that with industries and firms, just as with nations, there is an irresistible trend, dictated by modern technology, for units to become ever bigger ... [Yet] Small scale organisation allows for greater flexibility and human communication, in short decentralised economic activity allows for 'the convenience, humanity, and manageability of smallness.' (1978: 62–3)

Trade, when successful in conventional terms, accelerates economic activity that damages the environment:

> By now, it should be clear that our environment is becoming ever less capable of sustaining the growing impact of our economic activities. Everywhere our forest are over logged, our agricultural lands over cropped, our grasslands overgrazed, our wetlands over drained, our groundwater's overtapped, our seas over fished, and nearly all our terrestrial and marine environment is over polluted with chemical and radioactive poisons ... In such conditions, there can only be one way of maintaining the habitability of our planet, and that is to set out to reduce the impact. Unfortunately, the overriding goal of just about every government in the world is to maximise this impact through economic globalization. (Mander and Goldsmith 1996:79)

GREEN ALTERNATIVES TO GLOBALISATION

Mike Woodin and Caroline Lucas argue that opposition to globalisation is not enough, coherent economic alternatives have to be outlined together with a series of measures to move from our present society to an alternative future. They build on the approach of Colin Hines, author of *Localization: A Global Manifesto* (2000). Globalisation for all three authors is largely politically driven. Drawing on the analysis presented by anti-corporate anti-capitalists (see Chapter 3), they suggest that globalisation has been advanced to meet the needs of an elite. Globalisation is not an irreversible or automatic process, it is politically driven and can be rolled back or radically transformed. Thus they feel it is quite wrong for politicians such as Tony Blair to argue that policies such a privatisation and support for multinationals are inevitable because they are a product of globalisation.

Globalisation is ecologically damaging and therefore the ecological crisis that centrally motivates Greens can only be solved by reversing it. However, economic security is vital to ecological reforms:

Why, for example, should a young man who earns the minimum wage in a dead-end job be expected to fret about the social and environmental consequences of his choice of mode of transport when there is no decent public transport for him to use and when, at every turn, the message is reinforced that the possession of sufficient wealth to purchase the latest car is the measure of man? Equally, why should we expect the poorest countries to cut greenhouse gas emissions when the richest nations blatantly shirk their disproportionately greater responsibility to do the same? (Woodin and Lucas 2004: xix)

An economically secure society would also be more likely to respect nature if decisions were made democratically, according to Woodin and Lucas. This is one of the reasons why they oppose globalisation, because it is difficult to give people a real say if decisions are taken on a planetary scale. While some issues, such as cuts in greenhouse gas emissions, inevitably have to be decided globally, most should be taken as locally as possible to enhance democratic participation. Bodies such as the WTO are more influenced by corporate pressure than the wishes of any imagined global community.

Woodin and Lucas distinguish between green and socialist anti-globalists, suggesting that the left largely ignore ecological issues. They also argue that Green political approaches are not the same as environmentalism, which fails to provide a radical alternative to existing policies. Greens, in turn, while valuing the local, reject atavistic, expansionist nationalism and embrace an internationalist politics. In the UK the Greens have made alliances with both Plaid Cymru, the Party of Wales and more enduringly, Mebyon Kernow, the Party of the 'Sons of Cornwall'.

Woodin and Lucas stress the links between globalisation, privatisation and poverty. They note how the IMF's Structural Adjustment Programmes insist that to achieve financial help countries must sell publicly owned resources including power supplies, telecommunications and even transport infrastructure. The stability pact of the European Union, insists that countries in the euro currency area limit government spending. Even without these institutional pressures, the need for foreign direct investment from multinationals encourages states to cut spending on public spending and the environment, so as to reduce corporation tax and attract firms (Woodin and Lucas 2004: 58). Senegal, seen as an IMF success, slashed government spending and increased growth rates but saw unemployment rise from 25 per cent to 44 per cent between 1991 and

1996 (Woodin and Lucas 2004: 57). Transnational corporations may dominate the globe but they produce relatively few jobs given their desire to downsize and outsource. The 200 largest global corporations employ just 0.75 per cent of the world's workforce (Woodin and Lucas 2004: 73).

The ecological ill-effects of globalisation are emphasised with reference to food. Peasants are being squeezed out by 'free trade', local diversity in diet is eroded and in the great food swap, identical commodities move thousands of miles across the globe wasting energy and pushing up the production of greenhouse gases. Supermarkets are damaging to farmers, consumers, workers and the environment (Woodin and Lucas 2004: 155–6). European, North American and Japanese agricultural production is protected, while southern countries are forced by global bodies to open up their markets, often with disastrous results:

> the IMF bulldozed Haiti into liberalising its rice markets. It was flooded with cheap US imports and local production collapsed, destroying tens of thousands of rural livelihoods. A decade ago Haiti was self-sufficient in rice; today it spends half of its export earnings importing rice from the US. (Woodin and Lucas 2004: 147)

They outlined the absurdity of trade like for like which seems to make a nonsense of comparative advantage and specialisation:

> In 1998, Britain imported 61,400 tonnes of poultry meat from the Netherlands and exported 33,100 tonnes of poultry meat to the Netherlands … it imported 240,000 tonnes of pork and 125,000 tonnes of lamb, while it exported 195,000 tonnes of pork and 102,000 tonnes of lamb. In 1997, the UK imported 126m litres of milk and exported 270m litres of milk … In 1999, the EU imported 44,000 tonnes of meat from Argentina, 11,000 tonnes from Botswana, 40,000 tonnes from Poland and over 70,000 tonnes form Brazil … meat exports from the EU to the rest of the world totalled 874,211. (Woodin and Lucas 2004: 148)

The food industry promotes obesity and is often hugely abusive to animals, transported ever increasing distances and factory farmed under appalling conditions to push unit costs down.

Woodin and Lucas argue that change must occur, arguing that the present trajectory of the global economy damages its citizens, other species and the natural environment that sustains life. The solution is to introduce local currencies (a theme discussed critically in our next chapter) and to rewrite the multilateral rule book of institutions such as the WTO, the IMF, the World Bank and the EU to promote local economic development. Localisation does not mean complete self-sufficiency or the rejection of trade if it brings real gains. However, social and environmental concerns mean that it is often better to produce goods locally rather than exporting them from many thousands of miles away. Hines concisely defines localisation:

> The alternative is that everything that could be produced within a nation or region should be. Long-distance trade is then reduced to supplying what could not come from within one country or geographical groupings of countries. This would allow an increase in local control of the economy and the potential for it being shared out more fairly, locally. Technology and information would be encouraged to flow, when and where they could strengthen local economies. Under these circumstances, beggar-your-neighbour globalization gives way to the potentially more cooperative better-your-neighbour localization. (Hines 2000: viii)

The localists have been challenged by a number of writers including the journalist and green supporter George Monbiot, who argues that localisation would prevent development and would put countries in the south at some disadvantage (2003b). Other commentators reflect such views that globalisation can be greened or reformed. The German Greens argue for 'green globalisation' and believe that institutions such as the European Union can be used to limit the environmental consequences of globalisation. Monbiot argues that trade should be made fairer. Globalisation has both benefits and costs but demands regulation. Monbiot believes that global institutions such as the IMF and WTO could be used to benefit the poorest, if they were made subordinate to a new world parliament with representatives elected from the entire world. The localists respond that they are not fundamentalists and believe that trade should occur where vital. They argue that trade is too unpredictable to be the sole source of development, that unrestricted trade means that 'infant industries' will fail to grow, and point to falling incomes as trade increases for the bulk of peasant-based producers even in tiger economies like China (Woodin and Lucas 2004: 100). They also challenge Monbiot's plans for a world parliament as naive, pointing out that even if the political will could be conjured up to create it, constituencies with 10 million voters apiece would eliminate the possibility of meaningful participation (Woodin and Lucas 2004: 89).

SUBSISTENCE PERSPECTIVES

Ecofeminists have also developed a fundamental critique of economics in general and globalisation in particular. Vandana Shiva, the Indian physicist, is very much at the forefront of the anti-globalisation movement. Her subsistence perspective turns economic wisdom on its head, not merely criticising economic growth but arguing that growth fuels poverty. Where Soros, Stiglitz and the NGOs call for reform, to achieve speedier development, she and her colleagues see the development process as one of enclosure. Economic 'development' occurs when ordinary people are forced from the land and made to take part in market economic activity. They lose their freedom, health and their standard of living falls as they are denied access to economic resources such as common land used for grazing animals. Forests that produce fuel, food and medicine are enclosed, literally and legally. As private property they can be used to grow crops for export; exports can be measured in monetary terms and lead to economic growth, despite rising real poverty (Shiva 2000).

GNP fails to measure what is economically important. From the subsistence perspective, what matters is the domestic work of women, which, like the backs of elephants in certain cosmologies, supports the weight of the universe. The bulk of important work, such as gathering firewood, growing crops, herding animals, cooking meals, repairs and caring, has been completed in most societies in most parts of the world for most of human history by women. The male, who makes politics, drinks and gambles, has long been redundant in the world of subsistence.

The subsistence greens like Shiva attack the predominantly male economic community for having no insight into real economic activity. They see globalisation as a means of waging war on the poor by driving peasants from the land. The political economy espoused by Shiva echoes the complaints of the Zapatistas who, as we noted in Chapter 1. launched a revolution because they feared the effects of the NAFTA. Peasant opposition to globalisation is both more radical and more conservative than other strains of anti-capitalism. These are people who quite like mobile phones and the internet but are very keen to be left alone to live in an informal village economy. They believe in a revolution that rejects almost all aspects of economics, practical and conceptual, so they can live in conditions that are often seen as 'primitive'.

GM crops and other high-tech solutions to the problem of hunger are a particular source of anger to the hungry. Numerous studies have suggested not that there is an absolute shortage of food in the world but that distribution is a problem. Free trade is one means of making life difficult for peasant farmers because their crops may be more expensive than the products of large-scale agribusiness. They cannot sell their surpluses and find it more difficult to maintain independence. Agribusiness and big landowners gain most from new technologies and can out-compete small peasants. Modern agriculture demands neat rows of single crops for the export-led growth advocated by globalists. Monoculture is more vulnerable to pests so needs more pesticides. It leads to declining soil fertility, so needs more fertilisers. It prevents the growth of local crops for local use. The alternative is multicropping garden-style diversity producing the foods, medicine, building materials, fuel and many other 'products' needed by ordinary people. Shiva observed during her 2000 BBC Reith lecture on globalisation:

> A study in eastern Nigeria found that home gardens occupying only 2 per cent of a household's farmland accounted for half of the farm's total output. In Indonesia 20 per cent of household income and 40 per cent of domestic food supplies, come from the home gardens managed by women.
>
> Research done by FAO has shown that small biodiverse farms can produce thousands of times more food than large, industrial monocultures. And diversity in addition to giving more food is the best strategy for preventing drought and desertification.
>
> What the world needs to feed a growing population sustainably is biodiversity intensification, not the chemical intensification or the intensification of genetic engineering. While women and small peasants feed the world through biodiversity we are repeatedly told that without genetic engineering and globalisation of agriculture the world will starve. In spite of all empirical evidence showing that genetic engineering does not produce more food and in fact often leads to a yield decline, it is constantly promoted as the only alternative available for feeding the hungry. (<news. bbc.co.uk/hi/english/static/events/reith_2000/lecture5>)

The examples Shiva gives can be multiplied. For example, Bettina Maag illustrates how the Tamang of Central Nepal has a tree-based commons economy:

A Tamang, when asked about the use of the forest, will immediately answer 'the forest gives us timber, fuel wood and fodder.' Indeed, a wide spectrum of tree species found in the Tamang region is used to satisfy various local needs. Almost every species is in some way incorporated in the farming system' (Maag 1997: 114).

Whereas Korten loves New England in the post-revolutionary era after the defeat of the British, Shiva and friends look to strong women who have lived through empires. Such women ignored the imperial warlords, kings, khans and generals, while simply getting on with pig breeding. The subsistence ecofeminists' utopia is the eternal margin forgotten by the men at the top. Maria Mies, a German subsistence green, recalls how her mother survived the immediate aftermath of the Second World War nurturing piglets so that the family would have something for winter. Many of her neighbours in despair at the devastation suffered in defeat, found domestic farming tasks hard to face and consequently suffered privation (Bennholdt-Thomsen and Mies 1999: 9).

Subsistence greens can give an almost infinite number of examples of networks of women peasant producers actively resisting the march of modern economics. In Germany, they point to self-help socialist cooperatives that grow food. In Japan, there are the Yabo farmers, who live in cities and often work in high-tech sectors like IT, and many of them are single parents. Hostile to neo-liberalism, they compost kitchen waste, cooperate to grow food in urban areas such as Tokyo and divide their crops. They are not totally self-sufficient, but grow up to 100% of the vegetables and 70% of the rice they need. (Bennholdt-Thomsen and Mies 1999: 137). Shiva claims that:

Indian women have been in the forefront of ecological struggles to conserve forest, land and water. They have challenged the western concept of nature as an object of exploitation and have protected her as Prakriti, the living force that supports life. They have challenged the western concept of economics. (quoted in Dobson 1991: 50)

The Indian novelist Arundhati Roy, although less starry-eyed about the joys of feminist peasant life than Shiva, has looked at how huge dams like that in Naramada displace millions of people from villages flooded after their construction. The dams also prevent fertile mud from being deposited on river banks, farmed for thousands of years, causing further displacement, further poverty and major environmental problems (Roy 1999, 2002). The lowest caste dalits suffer while the huge energy corporations including Enron profit (Roy 2001). Subsistence greens argue that neo-liberal globalisation leads to poverty, trade to reduced choice and growth to eco-catastrophe. Subsistence greens are angry about neo-liberalism, Shiva notes:

> So no matter where you look, the World Bank is basically taking away the resources of the people, putting it in the hands of global capital, destroying the livehoods of people in the name of efficiency and forcing destitution on millions and billions of people. Its policies are nothing short of genocide.
>
> Of course the World Bank and the IMF officials visit the Third World, but they do not know the realities because all they look at is the returns on investment calculations that they have already made in Washington before they made their trips. (Interview in Indy Media, <archives.lists.indymedia. org/imc-houston/2001-January/000353>)

BEYOND GREEN ANTI-CAPITALISM

The green critique at its most radical goes further than anti-corporate anti-capitalism by stating that economics is a system that tends to dominate and distort human values. The greens, especially at their most crazily radical, unpick economics bit by bit. The starting definition of economics found in any textbook is that it is 'a study of how scarce resources are used to meet unlimited human wants', and is a definition that Greens find alarming. While resources may be limited and demand careful nurturing, the notion that human wants are infinite is seen as both unproven and a source of danger. Economists' concern with unlimited wants suggests that economic growth must continue. Greens would argue that instead the economic system in its reliance on economic growth makes us want more and more. A modern capitalist economy is based on the systematic construction of dissatisfaction through branding, advertising and a range of ever more imaginative marketing techniques. One thinks of the Tibetan Buddhist realm of the 'hungry ghosts', where dissatisfied spirits wander, trying unsuccessfully to feed their infinite appetites.

Some green localists such as Hines argue, in essence, that if the economy were decentralised democracy, ecological sustainability and justice would automatically follow. This is an assertion that is difficult to sustain. In addition, elements of the green critique can shade into a rather crude conservative functionalism. Subsistence anti-capitalists like Shiva seem to suggest that pre-industrial societies were fairer and functioned naturally in comparison to the chaos of globalisation. It's worth considering the title of Achebe's splendid Nigerian novel, *Things Fall Apart*, (1971). The African society in *Things Fall Apart* is tragically ripped apart by the arrival of globalising English colonialists. The Christian Church infiltrates and destroys reverence for the pagan gods of the forest, especially the powerful snake deity. However, the society that fell apart was also based on hierarchy, the domination of women by men, torture and pervasive violence. Small may be necessary but it is not enough.

Many greens have linked localism to explicitly socialist sentiment. The British Green Party has increasingly been recognised even by critics such as the Marxist John Rees as part of the left:

> Since the late 1980s the British Greens have established a small but real constituency in British politics, partly among those concerned with environmental issues, partly among people of a broadly left wing disposition who could no longer stomach Labour. Well-known activists such as Caroline Lucas, re-elected in June as MEP for the South East, are rightly respected, in particular because of their ability to relate environmentalism to the broader anti-capitalist agenda. Unlike their French and German counterparts, the British Greens have not participated in the social-liberal coalitions or supported imperialist wars. They are part of the radical left broadly defined. (Rees 2001: 13)

The green critique has been combined, by some, with socialist theory to create an ecosocialist alternative to neo-liberalism (Chapter 8). Other greens have turned to various forms of monetary reform, seeking to understand how money and especially the creation of debt fuels capitalism, economic growth and globalisation. Such money-centred anti-capitalism is the subject of our next chapter.

5

Planet Earth Money Martyred:
Social Credit and Monetary Reform

Anti-globalists see the 'Washington consensus' as a conspiracy to enrich bankers. They are not entirely wrong. (*The Economist*, 26 September 2001)

The Jubilee movement established to resist the global debt crisis and ATTAC, an NGO campaigning for a tax on international currency exchange, are the most visible signs of a movement suspicious of money. Many activists agree that the 'finance industry lies at the heart of globalisation' (Hutchinson et al. 2002: 5). The Washington Consensus examined in Chapter 2 is a banker's consensus driven by the need to pay back debt at all costs. Free trade allows payments to bankers to be generated, government spending must be cut to reduce debt, while privatisation allows global financiers to pick up bargains. Capital liberalisation, which removes all barriers to the circulation of currency between countries, means that money can be sucked out of a country if it pursues radical policies or otherwise displeases the markets. A total of 95 per cent of capital movements between countries are speculative. A mere 5 per cent of the dollars, yen, euros and other national currencies that cross borders do so to pay for trade or to fund physical investment in factories. The rest is exchanged at ever faster rates to make money out of money – selling for example, yen to buy dollars in the hope of generating a profit. The rather abstract nature of finance has led to calls for reform. Debt drives environmental damage – peasants may be forced to cut down forests, to displace rare mountain gorillas and drain fish-filled lakes, so they can sell commodities to pay off interest. Monetary reformer Frances Hutchinson observes that 'the anti-globalization and environmental movement did not start with Rachel Carson, still less with Seattle', and goes on to describe a pedigree flowing back to the eighteenth-century Scottish banker John Law, biblical notions of jubilee, US populism and Douglas Social Credit (*Social Creditor* June 2002: 1). Monetary reformers argue that elite bankers who lend it out and collect the interest essentially create money out of thin air. Debt is often described as the primary source of social injustice. The solution involves not just debt forgiveness but the creation of debt-free money by states or local communities. This chapter outlines the case against the World Bank and the IMF, outlines the nature of ATTAC and finally examines the radical message of monetary reform.

IMF APOCALYPSE

The IMF, which lends money to nations with severe debt problems, was created to maintain the stability of the global financial architecture as part of the Bretton Woods process in the 1940s. In return for economic assistance, as we noted in Chapter 2, it has insisted on controversial Structural Adjustment Programmes (SAPs) that lead to enhanced poverty. Michel Chossudovsky, a Canadian economist, has argued that both the IMF and the World Bank have helped to create chaos in the former Yugoslavia, reduced Russia to 'Third World' status and contributed to devastating poverty in nations including Rwanda and Somalia (Chossudovsky 1997). While Stiglitz and Soros tend to argue that the Washington consensus, at least before the arrival of President Bush Jr has been a product of economic dogmatism rather than malice, Chossudovsky is one of many critics who see it as a weapon used to maintain super-imperialism.

In the 1980s, an international debt crisis erupted making as many as 100 states insolvent (George 1990). In the 1970s, developing countries had been encouraged to borrow the excess cash that oil-rich states had deposited in European and American banks. The huge 1973 rise in oil prices meant that states such as Saudi Arabia had spare cash and nowhere to place it but foreign banks. Banks found it difficult to find customers to lend the oil dollars to because rising petrol prices had pushed down economic activity in Europe, North America and other wealthy states. Excess cash meant that borrowing was cheap, and African, Asian and South American leaders were encouraged to borrow to recycle bank assets and maintain bank profitability. By the 1980s, commodity prices such as coffee were on the slide and interest rates rose sharply, debts became difficult to pay, forcing states to approach the IMF for aid. In return for debt help, the IMF insisted on a series of SAP 'conditionalities'. In theory, SAP 'conditionalities' are sets of sound economic principles that a debtor must follow to help resolve crisis. They resemble an agreement by an alcoholic to throw away the whisky and to keep off the vodka in return for professional help. Some see SAPS as tough but fair and economically sound. In fact, as Stiglitz and Soros remind us, they may make the patient sicker, creating poverty that is likely to swell rather than subdue debt.

Chossudovsky argues that SAPs, by insisting that governments privatise large parts of their economies, allow largely US-based multinationals to increase their ownership of foreign assets. Export-led growth, demanded by the SAPs, creates oversupply of commodities such as coffee, which further depresses prices and benefits relatively rich consuming countries rather than producers. Spending cuts create political instability, and in the case of Yugoslavia, allegedly led to the disintegration of states (Chossudovsky 1997).

SAPs have included devaluation of national currencies to enable export-led growth by making products sold on the world market cheaper. Yet such devaluation has made it even cheaper for foreign corporations to buy up assets at knockdown prices. Devaluation by reducing currency value has made it expensive for citizens to buy even basic foodstuffs and has fuelled inflation. As we noted in Chapter 2, inflation is the number one enemy for the Washington Consensus, whose proponents then insist on further cuts in government spending to keep prices from rising. IMF policies have led to the collapse of the Somalian economy, creating famine and vicious civil war. In particular, currency devaluation pushed down revenue from crops and pushed up prices for fuel, fertiliser and other farm inputs (Chossudovsky 1997: 102).

Chossudovsky provides many case study examples of his basic thesis that the IMF is an instrument of US foreign policy. In Vietnam the US re-ran the war they lost militarily in the 1970s, gaining financial victory during the 1980s:

> The social consequences of structural adjustment applied in Vietnam since the mid-1980s are devastating. Health clinics and hospitals have closed down, local-level famines have erupted, affecting up to a quarter of the country's population, and three quarters of a million children have dropped

out of the school system. There has been a resurgence of infectious diseases with a tripling of recorded malaria deaths during the first four years of the reforms. Five thousand (out of a total of 12,000) state enterprises have been driven into bankruptcy, more than a million workers and some 200,000 public employees, including tens of thousands of teachers and health workers, have been laid off.

A secret agreement reached in Paris in 1993, which in many regards was tantamount to forcing Vietnam 'to compensate Washington' for the costs of the war, required Hanoi to recognise the debts of the defunct Saigon regime ... as a condition for the granting of fresh credits ... The achievements of past struggles and the aspirations of an entire nation are undone and erased. (Chossudovsky 1997: 147)

A free market discourse is used to legitimate the policy goals of an elite. The IMF along with the World Bank are 'regulatory bodies' that intervene to control the global economy through 'a worldwide process of debt collection' (Chossudovsky 1997: 15). According to Chossudovsky, the Washington Consensus pushes down wages, which benefits transnational corporations but tends to lead to global economic decline because falling wages rob workers of the purchasing power to keep shopping. In response the financial rulers of our planet are to encourage super-consumption by a global elite, to avoid economic depression. Typically, President George Bush has successfully introduced huge tax cuts for the super-rich, ironically causing US government debt to mushroom.

FINANCING ENCLOSURE AND ECOCIDE

Stiglitz acted as Vice President and Chief Economist for the International Bank for Reconstruction and Development, more commonly known as the World Bank. The World Bank has been targeted by environmentalists and social justice campaigners for funding huge dams and other projects that have dispossessed millions of people and devastated local ecosystems (Caulfield 1997; Rich 1994). The World Bank aims to lend money to development projects across the globe to create economic growth in the poorest nations. It has been widely criticised for focusing on projects that wreck the environment and promote enclosure (Rich 1994). Active in over 100 countries, the Bank is an enormous force. The Bank is the number one financier of the big dams that Roy and Shiva attack so vehemently (see Chapter 4). In its 60-year history it has funded at least 552 dams at a cost in 2004 currency of $86 billion (the Yacyret Dam, Argentina/ Paraguay, alone involved $6 billion lost to corruption) and at least 10 million people evicted from their homes. The Bank has spent $26.5 billion on fossil fuel projects such as coal- and oil-fired power stations since 1992 (<www.irn.org/programs/finance>).

In 1992 World Bank Chief Economist Larry Summers scandalised the world when a memo he wrote, insisting that the developing world was underpolluted and it would make economic sense for African countries to receive more toxic waste, was leaked by *The Economist*. His economic logic, in orthodox neo-liberal terms, was clear. Individuals in African states had a far lower income than those in wealthier parts of the world, so death or injury would be less costly in terms of lost income. In response the *Financial Times*, a newspaper not known for its radical credentials, ran a piece under the title 'Save Planet Earth from Economists' (George and Sabelli 1994: 98–100).

The Bank has also been criticised for supporting dictatorships and colonial powers. One of its earliest loans in 1947 allowed the Dutch government to launch a war against Indonesian nationalists who were attempting to gain independence (Rich 1994: 69). Between 1976 and 1986, the bank lent Indonesia $630 million to resettle millions of their poor to Borneo, Irian Jaya (the occupied western half of Papua New Guinea) and Sumatra. Six million people were moved into areas that were often pristine rainforest. Deforestation proceeded at a rate of 10,000 square miles a year. Environmental problems ranged from acidification of soils to plagues of insects. The Indonesian military dictatorship massacred several million socialists in the 1970s and were keen to use resettlement as a means of reducing discontent by funnelling the poor into wild areas occupied by the state (Rich 1994: 37).

Between 1981 and 1983, the Bank lent $443.4 to Brazil's North West Region Development project. Brazil was then a military dictatorship and the money was used to build highways to open up the rainforest. Rainforest destruction, desertification from inappropriate crop growing and the spreading of disease to unprotected native populations were some of the results. The Bank also helped finance the use of 3,000 tons of DDT, banned in most industrialised countries, to deal with the spread of malaria (Rich 1994: 28). Lending to Brazil rose from nothing in the early 1960s when it had an elected government to $73 million on average a year after the 1964 military coup to nearly $0.5 billion during the 1970s. The elected socialist government of Chile received nothing, but Pinochet's free market dictatorship, which overthrow it violently, was rewarded with solid credit. Despite the fact that China in 2004 had $470 billion in foreign exchange reserves, the Bank has been keen to support its pro-market policies with apparently unnecessary lending. China's appalling human rights record is of no importance in Bank considerations (*The Economist*, 22 July 2004). In *Faith and Credit* (1994), Susan George and Fabrizio Sabelli have described the bank as a religious body, the Church of the Washington Consensus. It has 300 full-time public relations employees selling the message (*The Economist*, 22 July 2004).

Protests have forced some change in Bank policies. For example, in 2003 it cut funding to the Cambodian Forestry programme after it was found that the government had inflated the amount of rainforest left in the country, allowed companies illegal logging access and barred conservationists (Bretton Woods Project, 16 January 2004). However, 2004 also saw the Bank return to funding big dam projects and deciding to fund Cambodia despite a lack of progress over forestry policy.

An endorsement from the World Bank encourages other lenders and donors to provide support. Credit rating agencies Moody's or Standard & Poor assess the financial worth of entire countries, mainly based on IMF and World Bank data. Those states that break the neo-liberal rules see their ratings plummet and cash flowing out. Development is based on enclosing the commons, enclosure that demands military force and repression. The World Bank continues to finance globalisation in the third millennium, a process that seeks to integrate the poor violently into a market economy.

ON THE ATTAC

Without the Bretton Woods institutions global financial forces would still, according to many commentators, threaten justice, ecology and democracy. Trillions of dollars of currency, as we have noted, at several points in this text flow at ever faster rates across the globe on a daily basis. While such cash is largely speculative (used to make money out of money) rather than invested physically, outflows of 'hot money' can lead to falling exchange rates and possible economic collapse. Currency speculation provides an example of the basic economic law that there is an inverse relationship between ones contribution to society and monetary reward. In *The Bonfire of the Vanities*, Tom Wolfe's central character, a bond trader, is at a loss to explain his job to his daughter, for bonds we may read currency or shares or hedge funds or any other way of making money from buying and selling financial instruments to scrap off tiny margins of gain:

'Daddy, what is it that you do?' And the Master of the Universe is lost for words – how indeed would you describe bond dealing to a seven-year-old? And his wife jumps in and says, 'Well, darling, just imagine that a bond is a slice of cake, and you didn't bake the cake, but every time you hand somebody a slice of cake a tiny little bit comes off, like a little crumb, and you can keep that.' (Wolfe 1988: 260)

The growth of 'unproductive' speculative cashflows increasingly distorts the 'normal' workings of capitalism. Speculative flows have tended to intensify economic crisis, for example, leading to the near collapse of the Asian 'tiger' economies in 1997.

In response to the Asian crisis the editor of *Le Monde Diplomatic* Ignacio Ramonet wrote an article entitled 'Disarm the Markets' and launched the Association for the Taxation of Transactions and for Aid to Citizens (ATTAC) in 1997 (Patomaki 2001: 180). Its main demand is the creation of a Tobin Tax, named after the economist who came up with the idea, of a 0.5 per cent charge on speculative currency transactions. This would reduce speculation and thus create greater currency stability, making the destruction of national economies less likely in times of economic instability. By discouraging speculation the tax would make it easier for national economies to resist global market forces. The tax would also raise billions of dollars that could be used to relieve hunger, fund environmental protection and perhaps finance the United Nations or other instruments capable of creating a more democratic form of global governance.

ATTAC has been most active in France, where it has 24,000 individual members and the support of 1,000 separate organisations (Patomaki 2001: 181). ATTAC has branches in countries from Austria to Portugal in Europe, in North America, Asia and Western African states like Senegal and Mali. It has been active in anti-globalisation demonstrations but has also worked through parliaments. In 2004, the Belgium government voted for the tax (*Guardian*, 5 July 2004). A European Parliament vote instigated by ATTAC was lost with just six votes – British Labour MEPs keen to maintain the position of the city of London as a financial centre and to support US interests narrowly defeated the motion (Patomaki 2001: 178).

While there are a number of technical problems with the tax, it should be difficult for speculators to avoid it by shifting countries.

After all, the bulk of transactions are made in just four currencies: the dollar, the euro, the pound sterling and the yen, and most transactions take place in just ten key countries. However, persuading the US to introduce the tax given the continuing strength of the Washington Consensus on Capitol Hill amongst both Republicans and Democrats is an obvious stumbling block. While many radicals from the Green Party to socialists in the Fourth International support the tax, it is clearly at best a way of reducing speculative flows just a little rather than a means of creating economic transformation. The Finnish economist Heikki Patomaki, who has produced the most extensive and sophisticated account of the tax as a means of 'throwing sand in the wheels' of the global market, admits:

> Nobody should be led into the false belief that the Tobin tax – or another regulation mechanism for the financial system – would solve all the world's problems ... More thorough reforms are needed to make the global economy socially responsible and democratic. (Patomaki 2001: 221)

MONETARY REFORM

Rather than blaming merely the Washington Consensus or speculative flows of hot money, the most radical monetary reformers believe that the very existence of debt-creating banks is the source of global chaos. Canadian John McMurtry, author of *The Cancer Stage of Capitalism*, argues fiercely that:

> There is no fraud in history that remotely approaches the monopoly expropriation by private banks of the public powers of money creation and dissolution. Its invisible chains bind and imprison the lives and life economies of people across continents. (McMurtry 2002: 130)

McMurtry's vigorous attack on the banks is largely inspired by the work of Major Douglas, 'labelled as a "crank" by every newspaper that banks advertised in or lent to' (McMurtry 2002: 127). Major Clifford Douglas, a Scottish engineer, writing in the aftermath of the First World War, argued that debt-based money created by banks is the root of most evil. Critics of globalisation, including McMurtry, Herman Daly, Richard Douthwaite and David Korten, acknowledge the value of Douglas' social credit philosophy (Rowbotham 1998).

Most money even in Douglas' day was no longer created by governments but by private banks who then lent the money to governments who paid for it using taxation. Douglas saw money as socially constructed and of symbolic value only. Despite its lack of 'reality', money, rather than being a neutral fluid that allowed economic development to take place, could distort production, distribution and consumption. Banks created credit, increasing the money supply, to maintain economic activity. Yet credit created by bankers has to be paid back, according to monetary reformers enslaving both producers and consumers with debt; 97 per cent of the money supply in the UK at present is made up of debt money that must be paid back with interest:

> Most people, when they are told this, dismiss the claims utterly and in their minds clearly regard you as politically disturbed person; a sad case of mental fixation, perhaps unable to cope with the demands and opportunities of the modern world. This is really quite understandable. The natural assumption is that there must be more to this matter. If banks and building societies do indeed create money, there must be a rationale behind the decision to leave the creation and supply of money to them. It defies belief that such an extraordinary arrangement should exist without there being a good reason for it, but it is true. (Rowbotham 1998: 5–6)

Banks create money and lend to borrowers who then spend it into circulation. The economist John Kenneth Galbraith noted that this is 'a method so simple the mind is repelled' (cited in Rowbotham 1998: 10–11). Modern money is electronic and virtual, it only has value because we believe it has value.

Douglas believed that social credit, quite literally debt free money, created by the community could be used to reward all citizens with an income. He believed that the real riches of society were based on cultural inheritance built up by society by generations of creativity. Such cultural inheritance was for Douglas a forgotten and all-important factor of production. Wealth is generated by ideas, which give rise to technological innovation. Rather than being the unique product of particular inventive individuals, such cultural wealth is produced by the community, which should be rewarded for its collective intellectual labour with a national dividend (Hutchinson and Burkitt 1997: 59–60).

Douglas was an economic utopian:

> The strength of the appeal, which Major Douglas makes to his followers, is that his theories promise something for nothing. Consumers are to receive credits;

dividends are to be issued to all; taxation will become unnecessary and no one will be called upon to pay the cost. (Hiskett and Franklin 1939: 163)

Keynes famously described him as 'a private' rather than a general in an army of economic radicals challenging the bankrupt orthodoxy of liberal thought (Bell 1993: 163). Nonetheless, Keynes felt that he was a more important economic commentator than Marx because he suggested that credit could be used to prevent recession. Douglas' social credit enjoyed some support and interest in the 1930s. A Social Credit Party was established in the Canadian province of Alberta and won a stunning victory in the 1935 provincial elections (Macpherson 1953; Stingel 2000). Social credit has also been politically significant in Australia and New Zealand. Indeed, the New Zealand Labour Party is said to have won a general election on a social credit programme (Hutchinson and Burkitt 1997: 147). Working-class activists in the Coventry League of the Unemployed and the Kibbo Kift Kin, a bizarrely named socialist scouting body, came together to found the Social Credit Greenshirts (Drakeford 1997).

Social creditors contend that ecologically destructive economic growth is explained by the creation of debt money that forces us to produce and consume more and more. Douglas noted in the 1930s that:

Industry has run riot over the countryside. A population, which has been educated in the fixed idea that the chief, if not the only, objective of life is well named 'business,' whose politicians and preachers exhort their audiences to fresh efforts for the capture of markets and the provision of still more business, cannot be blamed if, as opportunity occurs, it still further sacrifices the amenities of the countryside to the building of more blast-furnaces and chemical works. (Douglas 1979: 107)

Douglas powerfully criticised the notion that human wants were unlimited and growth must therefore continue infinitely. He saw wants as constructed by forces of finance to maintain accumulation. He also believed that 'the genuine consumptive capacity of the individual is limited, [therefore] we must recognize that the world, whether consciously or not, is working towards the Leisure State' (Douglas 1979: 110). In Douglas' alternative future, business

would of necessity cease to be the major interest of life and would, as has happened to so many biological activities, be relegated to a position of minor importance, to be replaced, no doubt, by some form of activity of which we are not yet fully cognizant. (Douglas 1979: 110)

Supporters have argued that social credit produced by the community rather than banks could be used to fund expensive policies without massive tax rises. Alternative energy systems, home insulation, recycling schemes, land reclamation and measures to end poverty could be funded by debt-free money produced by the community (Price 1981).

Both Douglas and modern social creditors such as Hutchinson believe that a national dividend, a form of guaranteed income, could be introduced. This would decommodify labour, encouraging individuals to workshare and allowing unpaid creative and necessary social labour to be undertaken. Jobs that were unnecessary and ecologically destructive could be swept away, thus removing the opportunity cost of environmental destruction as the price of job preservation. The building blocks of conventional economics, infinite wants, scarce resources and opportunity cost would be removed by the Douglas revolution. Scarcity is a particular target of Douglas's ire:

The world is obsessed, or possessed, by a scarcity complex. While at the date of writing Great Britain is preparing for another war, she still has a million unemployed, farms going out of cultivation and agricultural products being destroyed because they cannot be sold, publicists still inform us on the one hand that the situation is due to over-production, and on the other hand that sacrifices must be made by everyone, that we must all work harder, consume less, and produce more. (Douglas 1979: 89).

Social credit, for advocates, seems an obvious solution to the global debt crisis and provides a way of tempering globalisation. Globalisation is seen as a product of demands for increased free trade as nations struggle to export surplus goods that are unsold because of the chronic loss of purchasing power (Rowbotham 2000).

Douglas, never an easy man, according to biographers, seems to have become increasingly ill and embittered after the 1930s. His ideas became marginal even amongst those who challenged the economic orthodoxy. Depressingly, Douglas was, even for a rather intolerant age, astonishingly anti-semitic. Prone to conspiracy thinking, he celebrated the 1940s by becoming an early advocate of Holocaust revisionism, suggesting that Jewish financial forces were behind the Second World War (Stingel 2000). The social credit movement shrank and split into various warring factions and it was not until the 1990s that his ideas re-emerged. Sadly Douglas support groups have often functioned as a rather bizarre dating club where greens and leftists have been able to partner neo-nazis and anti-semites (Wall 2003).

Opposition to finance capitalism of course goes far wider than Douglas. Critics of usury look to Aristotle, the Bible and the Talmud. Frances Hutchinson, Mary Mellor and Wendy Olson flag up the importance of John Law, an eighteenth-century Scottish banker who fled to France after a legal scandal (Hutchinson et al. 2002: 57–60). He invented a form of paper money for the French government to help them overcome financial crisis. Regrettably investors lost faith in paper and bankruptcy resulted. A very great range of monetary experiments accompanied the American Revolution. Way back in 1731 Benjamin Franklin, amongst his other hobbies, used to print money (Boyle 2002: 25). In the 1780s, Franklin and other American revolutionaries advocated not just taxation with representation but believed that national sovereignty was based on the ability for states to create their own credit. There is a long pedigree of opposition to the banks by small farmers and workers in the US populist movement (Ritter 1997).

President Abraham Lincoln, finding that the banks would only lend his government funds to fight the civil war at high interest rates, issued his own currency, the greenback. This was spent into existence, much to the annoyance of the bankers (Greco 2001: 43). Some argue that his assassination was part of a bankers' plot to preserve their power. Lincoln was, in the words of one populist pamphlet, 'money martyred' (Search 1977).

Monetary reform was significant at the birth of socialism. The utopian socialist Robert Owen, for example, advocated the creation of labour notes to replace bank money. The anarchist Proudhon in the 1840s saw banks as a source of injustice and backed the creation of labour credits to make way for a socialist system (McNally 1993). Arthur Kitson, an inventor and industrialist active in the early twentieth century, also campaigned on the injustice of debt money, which he claimed was produced by self-enriching bankers (Hutchinson et al. 2002: 158). Frederick Soddy, a Nobel Prize winning chemist who wrote on ecological issues and feared the effects of economic growth, saw bankers as a force for evil because they rather than productive groups governed the economy. Gesell, a Swiss Austrian, called for the principle of demurrage – essentially a negative interest scheme, where money would progressively lose its value if not spent, designed to promote economic activity. Like Douglas, Keynes lavishly praised him (Boyle 2002: 233). There are perhaps hundreds of monetary reform theorists who agree that it is wrong for banks to hold a monopoly of credit (Boyle 2002; Lietaer 2001).

LETS AND LOCAL CURRENCIES

Monetary reform ideas were put into action in the small Austrian town of Worgl in the 1930s, where the local mayor Michael Unterguggenberger created demurrage money to move their community out of recession (Boyle 2002: 236). Local factories had closed during the 1930s economic crisis and the local council had found it difficult to raise local tax. The council issued 30,000 Austrian schillings. These currency notes fell by 1 per cent every month, so recipients had an incentive to spend them as fast as possible. The currency was also known as 'stamp scrip' because unless it was stamped by the authorities to show the decline in value, it would not be accepted and would become worthless. The currency circulated quickly, taxes were raised, unemployment fell and Worgl prospered until the Austrian National Bank stepped in to close the system down.

Inspired in part by such ideas, thousands of local monetary experiments have been launched around the globe. Micro-credit, where development networks allow local community enterprises to borrow on favourable terms, is another (Hulme and Mosley 1996). 'Time dollars' from Ithaca in the US allow citizens to swap labour and have been recognised by government agencies (Greco 2001). The fastest growing have been Local Exchange and Trading Systems (LETS) invented by the Canadian activist Michael Linton (Greco 2001: 89). Since the 1980s, they have become increasingly common, using commuter software to construct local barter schemes where individuals trade services such as plumbing and babysitting (Douthwaite 2000). The New Economics Foundation has argued with some technical flourish that rather than being dependent on bankers and global finance, governments could create their own money and control their own economic destiny (Huber and Robertson 2000).

The former banker Bernard Lietaer has drawn attention to a variety of new locally created currencies, which he sees as the basis for a future of 'sustainable abundance'. He is particularly enthusiastic about the example of municipal rubbish-based currency in the Brazilian city of Curitiba. When a new mayor, Jaime Lerner, was elected in 1971, he found that the town was out of cash and the rubbish was piling up in the streets, so anyone who brought their glass, paper, plastics or vegetable waste for recycling was rewarded with a bus token. The tokens evolved into an alternative local currency and the town took off. The average citizen earns three times the Brazilian minimum wage and according to Lietaer, Curitiba has been able to 'join First World living standards within one generation' (2001: 201). Mike Woodin and Caroline Lucas suggest a local currency could be introduced for London, using computer technology. Local currencies are seen as a way of encouraging local economic activity so as to act as a barrier to globalisation (Woodin and Lucas 2004: 194).

SOCIAL CREDIT ANTI-CAPITALISM

The ideas of monetary reformers with their schemes to print money and create a new economic order cannot be dismissed entirely. Money, far from being 'real', is clearly socially created. Making this point in an otherwise strongly critical account of Douglas social credit, Hiskett and Franklin note that:

> The attempt, which is sometimes made, by orthodox defenders of the banking system, to show that banks do no more than lend the money, which is deposited with them, is based on a specious argument, which tries to prove too much. The indisputable fact is that, by action of the banks, £1,000 of new cash, deposited with the banking system, is built up into a total of £10,000 deposits by the addition of £9,000 of credit money. (1939: 105)

Their account is slightly out of date. Today, banks feel little need to maintain reserves of currency and continue to build up mountains of debt-based cash. Yet although money is 'virtual', the message of the monetary reformers may not quite provide a panacea. Conventional critics of monetary reform argue that money creation can be ineffective or inflationary. More radical voices suggest that the development of debt free money may not be as crucial to creating an ecologically sound and social justice economy as the reformers suggest.

One issue is 'neutrality'. Most conventional economists argue that money is neutral, this means that money should not be confused with real wealth. By producing more money we cannot really make people richer: if the New Zealand government doubled the amount of money in the economy this would not automatically double the quantity of goods and services in the New Zealand economy. Instead the price of goods and services would tend to increase.

Keynes argued that money was not entirely neutral, if there were unemployed resources in an economy, for example, if workers were unemployed and land 'idle', an increase in the money supply might be accompanied by growth. However, he believed that consumer and especially business confidence were far greater influences on 'real' economic activity. Simply printing money does not create wealth as some monetary reformers seem to suggest. Money, even if it is made in a debt-free form, will fuel either growth or inflation. If the community 'prints' more money and spare productive capacity is present, more goods will be produced, creating more economic growth which is potentially destructive from a green perspective.

Money is socially constructed and has no objective source of value other than collective sentiment. If banks simply produced unlimited amounts of money at the stroke of a pen, their legitimacy would fall and their deposits would cease to be seen as 'good.' If governments or the community were simply to supply more money, public confidence in the currency might fall. If confidence in a currency is low, it falls in value and may be unacceptable. This explains the value of the dollar. The political and military power of the US creates confidence in the dollar which is seen as a 'hard currency', so in many parts of the world US currency rather than the local currency is used. Military and political stagnation with rising debt pushes the dollar down. Thus socially constructed money is still likely to follow Gresham's law that accepted credit will be pushed out by that with less perceived legitimacy – good money is driven out by bad. To make money work appropriate rituals have to be performed. Equally, bankers cannot be seen as the source of *all* evils, as wicked magicians who commit the evil of usury to gain dominance over creation. If people believe that money has value then it has value! If authorities have power, money works perhaps to give them more power, but merely to construct money is not enough. Currently, only a minority use the local currency and LETS schemes and they are very much at the fringes of society. But then it might be argued that all the anti-capitalist alternatives discussed in this title are marginal and a hard fight will be needed to take them centre stage.

Radicals as well as defenders of the economic orthodoxy also criticise the monetary approach. Monetary reformers argue that debt money is the root of all evil. Yet all forms of money have ill-effects on society. Money has long been a source of destruction and it's largely pointless to distinguish between good (debt free) and bad (banker created) cash (Buchan 1997). In a money-based economy an individual has to have money to exchange for goods and services to survive. This means that one has to constantly find new ways of acquiring money, leading to waste and dissatisfaction. To survive I need to sell more books. Therefore, if more people borrow my books from friends or libraries I find it more difficult to survive. Money discourages us from creating an economy based on what is useful and instead creates new needs. The need to constantly buy and sell to survive leads to human alienation and ecological destruction. The prophetic Czech American anarchist Fredy Perlman argued:

> As soon as men accept money as an equivalent for life, the sale of living activity becomes a condition for their physical and social survival. Life is exchanged for survival. Creation and production come to mean sold activity. A man's activity is 'productive,' useful to society, only when it is sold activity. And the man himself is a productive member of society only if the activities of his daily life are sold activities. As soon as people accept the terms of this exchange, daily activity takes the form of universal prostitution. (Perlman 1992: 36)

James Buchan, a former *Financial Times* journalist, argues that all money has destructive consequences because it promotes quantity over quality and makes everything from emotional responses to wildlife potentially purchasable. Hegel, Marx and the Romantic poets suggest that money is dangerous:

> the habit of calculating and making comparisons in money diminishes much that is strange and precious in creation, indeed abolishes quality itself as a mental category by which to understand reality; displaces trust in people by trust in money, and thus poisons the relations between human beings and atomises society; and submerges being in possessing. (Buchan 1997: 271)

Money is rather addictive, Buchan describes it as 'frozen desire', and it fuels addictive compulsive behaviour. Hegel famously stated that the spirit of money was the life of that which is dead moving within itself (*ein sich in sich bewegendes Leben des Toten*) (Avineri 1972: 35). Capitalism is about more than finance. David Harvey, for example, argues that a capitalist economy tends towards crisis for a variety of reasons including the mismatch between consumption and investment (1999). He believes that credit creation allows firms to invest in factories and machinery, despite a lack of demand for their goods in the short run. Debt rather than driving the system instead functions to smooth out mismatches between supply and demand. Rather than being the 'heart' of the system, it is the 'liver' or 'kidney', an essential but not the essence of the economic body. While Harvey acknowledges that debt creation ultimately leads to greater potential for crisis, he suggests it should be seen as part of the system not its principle driving force.

The Curibita example shows that local currency experiments can aid ecological rather than greed-centred economies, but Lietaer overstates his case. Monetary reformers argue that if banking was reformed, capitalism would no longer be destructive or perhaps would not exist at all. This seems a little simplistic both in terms of explaining the forces that drive capitalism and the forms of injustice it creates in the world. Marxists, in providing an alternative account of capitalism, have argued that the problems we face have rather deeper roots. Marxism, evaluated in the next chapter, has its own strengths and weaknesses in explaining the process of globalisation and looking to alternatives.

6
Imperialism Unlimited: Marxisms

Captain Samaritano had an almost maternal affection for the manatees, because they seemed to him like ladies damned by some extravagant love, and he believed the truth of the legend that they were the only females in the animal kingdom that had no mates. He had always opposed shooting at them from the ship, which was the custom despite the laws prohibiting it. Once, a hunter from North Carolina, his papers in order, had disobeyed him, and with a well-aimed bullet from his Springfield rifle had shattered the head of a manatee mother whose baby became frantic with grief as it wailed over the fallen body. The Captain had the orphan brought on board so that he could care for it, and left the hunter behind on the deserted bank, next to the corpse of the murdered mother. He spent six months in prison as the result of diplomatic protests and almost lost his navigator's licence, but he came out prepared to do it again, as often as the need arose. Still, that had been a historic episode: the orphaned manatee, which grew up and lived for many years in the rare-animal zoo in San Nicolas de las Barrancas, was the last of its kind seen along the river.

'Each time I pass that bank,' he said, 'I pray to God that the gringo will board my ship so that I can leave him behind all over again.' (Marquez 1989: 331–2)

The capitalist epoch will come to be seen as one in which we relied on incredibly crude economic mechanisms called 'markets.' Markets are like machines for coordinating and relaying information, but they are only effective in relaying limited kinds of information in very circuitous ways. Markets are often thought to be highly efficient, but in the future they will be seen as highly inefficient and costly. Markets not only fail to take account of social and environmental costs, but they also generate instability, insecurity, inequality, antisocial egotism, frenetic lifestyles, cultural impoverishment, beggar-thy-neighbour greed and oppression of difference. (Albritton 1999: 180)

Che is iconic. Red flags, clenched fists and tabloid leftist newspapers can still be found. Slowly at first, speedier after Seattle, Marxists and an array of socialists have joined the anti-globalisation movement. The threat posed to working conditions by the WTO has been one trigger leading to a revitalisation of the Old Left, with disparate strands united in opposition to the neo-liberal agenda. Unions in the US were key players in the anti-WTO protests. In the UK, the Socialist Workers Party has worked with moderate greens such as the journalist George Monbiot to build 'Globalise Resistance'. In France, the Fourth International, heirs to Trotsky, have been involved in ATTAC, the NGO promoting the Tobin Tax. Kurdish Maoists are highly active in anti-capitalist protest across Europe. Sem Terra, the landless movement of Brazil and part of Peoples Global Action, are apparently influenced by Marxism (Callinicos 2003: 84–5). At Prague, anti-IMF actions included 'a Communist demo organised by the ex-government of Czechoslovakia' (Anon. 2000: 3).

Almost all Marxists argue that capitalism is not just corporations or banks but a system. Capitalism is innately destructive. It cannot be reformed but must be smashed. They agree, however, on little else. Marxist parties and groups are usually disciplined and centralised in contrast to the loose anti-capitalist networks. They are numerous and divided by obscure differences of dogma. In England and Wales there may be as many as 40 Marxist political parties, with a combined membership probably smaller than the single 6,000-strong Green Party. There are two Communist parties; a New Communist Party; several Marxist-Leninist Communist parties who follow Mao; the Socialist Party of Great Britain, so old (founded in 1904) that it predates the Labour Party; dozens of Trotskyite groups; new socialist alliance parties such as Respect and the Red Party. The UK is not uniquely fertile: Argentina has over 20 Marxist Parties including the Socialist Workers Front, the Socialist Workers Movement and the Socialist Workers Union. There are many more self-proclaimed Marxists active outside party politics.

Marxist approaches to globalisation are difficult to explain for several reasons. First, however carefully one reads Marx, his ideas remain frustratingly unfinished. Much of what he wrote in the nineteenth century is surprisingly robust. Marx can be amusing, exciting to read and is generally more subtle than many Marxists and critics admit. His core arguments, that capitalism is unjust, tends to keep expanding, and leads to alienation and to the growth of monopoly, are at least clear. Yet some of the most important links between his ideas were never made. So for instance he argues that profits tend to fall and that capitalism is prone to recession, but he 'did not develop a complete theory of crisis' (Went 2000: 65).

Second, attempts to fill in the gaps and popularise Marx have often made matters worse. Engels, his co-author, tried to reconstruct much of what Marx wrote after his death in 1883. Scraps of paper and crossed-out paragraphs were put together to finish the volumes of *Capital*, his masterwork. One gets the impression that much of *Theories of Surplus Value* was scratched onto cigar packets left under his bed. Presenting Marx's ideas so they would appeal politically to the working class, Engels emphasised the elements of Marx's thought that suggested that capitalism was doomed and communism was inevitable. The Second International Marxism of the late nineteenth and early twentieth centuries enhanced the view that Marxism was a form of scientific socialism, a political version of physics based on laws of historical progress:

> What distinguished Marxism in this context was its rare ability to link revolutionary fervour and desire for change with a historical perspective and a claim to be scientific. Almost inevitably, therefore, the inherited ideas were simplified, rigidified, ossified. Marxism became a matter of simple faith for its millions of adherents. (McLellan 1980a: 2)

Marx, whatever his faults as an individual and a thinker, has often been ill-served by his disciples. The establishment of Communist parties under Lenin and then Stalin turned Marxism into a dry dogma, a religion. The almost universally dismal political practices of far-left parties in the twentieth century, from Cambodia to Camden, have produced cartoon Marxisms, largely devoid of intellectual content.

Third, the dogmatism of the Marxist Parties led to a split between academic and activist Marxism. While some important Marxist intellectuals such as Gramsci and Althusser have been members of the Communist Party, or other far-left parties, or politically active in different ways, many more have enjoyed little or no real as opposed to theoretical participation. Academic Marxism has become a minor industry producing conference papers, books and doctorates. While there is nothing wrong with this and advances have been made, much theorising has been obscure and devoid of political implication. Some of the more obscure variants of Marxism with the least apparent connection to practice, such as the Japanese Uno School, are extremely important in providing detailed and sophisticated accounts of how modern capitalism works. While we may agree with Uno theorists that anti-capitalists 'must not shy away from using abstract theory to make sense of the world', there is a danger that academicisation may hide the contributions Marxism can make to real-life struggle (Albritton 1999: 181).

Fourth, Marxism has become a tree with a thousand branches. Lenin invented the concept of the Communist Party, having split his Bolsheviks from the Mensheviks. Some pre-Leninist Marxist parties like the DeLeonists exist as tiny political fossils, even today. Trotsky divided from Stalin to create the Fourth International; this has splintered many times and today one tiny group has launched a movement for a Fifth International. Mao also separated from the Stalinist orthodoxy. Fidel Castro, while a leader of an 'orthodox' Leninist party once linked to Moscow, has broadly combined guerrilla warfare strategy, Third World nationalism and most recently environmentalism in his Cuban version. Euro-communism, an exception to revolutionary hostility to capitalism, has been a distinct strategy of Communist parties keen to prosper in parliamentary systems. Intellectual divisions include Western Marxism (a diverse and untidy tradition including the Frankfurt School), analytical Marxism, several varieties of post-Marxism, regulation theory, critical realist Marxist, and so on. Marxist doctrine as developed by Marxist parties has sometimes functioned as a tactical weapon against others on the far left rather than a serious guide to action. Marxist parties may maintain their distinct identities in a small but crowded field through differences of ideology.

Finally, Marx's own, often splendid, deep and provocatively rude writings, have a rich and complex philosophical basis, making them difficult to understand fully. While it draws upon Hegel, Feuerbach, Kant and Spinoza, Marx's approach often seems, although there are no direct links, to owe something to William Blake or Taoism

(McLellan 1980: 101). Marx read Kopel's biography of the Buddha but his method was drawn from German philosophy and the classics (Sheasby 2004). His PhD examined the philosophical differences between Democritus and Epicurus and he was a member of the Young Hegelian circle. Without appreciating the paradoxical feel of his ideas little progress can be made in understanding them. Typically, the *Communist Manifesto* (co-written with Engels) contains statements that are both pro- and anti-capitalist. Thus some familiarity with Marx's broad method of thinking which draws upon contradiction to think creatively about society is necessary to understand his ideas.

For the reasons outlined above any serious review of Marxist anti-capitalism will be something of a roller-coaster ride. The Marxism that effortlessly linked exploitation, class struggle, capitalist crisis and communist victory is no more. Marx's ideas are best understood if one understands the man himself and his social context, an easy and pleasurable task which can be approached by reading any of several excellent biographies, especially Francis Wheen's amusing recent work (2000).

Alex Callinicos, a leader of Britain's largest far-left group the Socialist Workers Party (SWP), has produced *An Anti-Capitalist Manifesto* (2003) which provides an example of how Marxist political groups have tried to understand globalisation and interact with the wider anti-capitalist movement. Robert Went has attempted to apply the analysis of Ernest Mandel, the Belgian economist and member of Trotsky's Fourth International, to such questions in *Globalization* (Went 2000). *Another World is Possible* by David McNally, a Canadian Marxist, focuses on commons and enclosure (2002). James Petras and Henry Veltmeyer, supportive of the revolutionary movements in South America including the Mexican Zapatistas, the Argentinean Picquertos and Marxist guerrilla groups, argue that globalisation is simply imperialism renamed (Petras and Veltmeyer 2001, 2003). Some Marxists have argued that globalisation is a positive development and will create the necessary preconditions for a socialist society. Such individuals are obviously not active in the anti-globalisation movement but the suggestion that their ideas can be drawn directly from Marx's own writings means that their views must be examined. Meghnad Desai's important book *Marx's Revenge* is representative of such an approach, although it would probably be inaccurate to label Desai as a Marxist (Desai 2004). Fidel Castro, President of Cuba, combines the contradictory strands of Marx's own writings to show that the development of a global market has both costs and benefits. His ideas can be read in *On Imperialist Globalization: Two Speeches* (2003). In this chapter, a brief summary of Marx's economic analysis and method is offered. Marxist accounts of imperialism are introduced, and the Marxist accounts of globalisation described above are explored and a critique is developed.

MARXIST ECONOMICS: THE UTTER BASICS

History is the history of class struggle declare Marx and Engels in the *Communist Manifesto*, later arguing that capitalists exploit the labour power of workers. A worker makes, say, ten mopeds in a day and the capitalist takes seven of these. A worker produces, say, 100 DVD players in a day but receives only a fraction of their worth in wages, equivalent to perhaps the value of 30 DVD players. The rest of the value goes into profit, that is, to the capitalist owner of the company. To simplify, slightly, we have a system of economic theft. Workers can go on strike and use various means to achieve a 'fair day's pay for a fair day's work', but will always be exploited in a capitalist system because the capitalist will take some of what they produce and control how they work:

> People overwhelmingly prefer to cling to precarious conditions as farmers, fishers, hunters and the like rather than sell their human capacities to a buyer. It is only when there is literally no other way to survive – when, in short, all other economic options have been taken away from them – that people reluctantly accept a life as wage-labourers. (McNally 2002: 65)

Individuals have to be forced to work for capitalists by separating them from their own means of production. If people have their own land to grow food or their own tools to produce goods, they will be reluctant to work for the capitalist. We have to be forced to work through violent processes that generally involve taking away communal land and other shared resources. This process is discussed in more detail in the next chapter and has been noted by the subsistence greens examined in Chapter 4.

Goods (and services) have both use value and exchange value. Use value is determined by the usefulness of a product, yet capitalists are not primarily motivated by use. Instead, they seek to increase exchange value. Exchange value is the amount of money (or goods/services) a product can be exchanged for. The market is based on 'inherently unequal relations of exchange between large property owners and those who are propertyless. If the latter risk hunger and deprivation in the event that they cannot find a buyer for their labour, they are at a structural disadvantage' (McNally 2002: 61). Capitalists are compelled to maximise profit by exploiting labour power to multiple exchange values. Workers can be made to work harder or longer. Exchange values have to be 'realised' by selling goods and services so 'use' values cannot be entirely ignored, since consumers will be unwilling to buy useless objects. However, capitalism puts enormous energy into marketing, to make us find the 'useless' 'useful' in order to keep consumption levels up. The problem of how 'use' relates to 'exchange' is examined in Chapter 8.

The surplus value which capitalists extract from workers in exchange for wages is the basis of profit and such profit is extracted from the workers. Profit is reinvested in capital, that is, machines and other means of production to raise productivity. Capitalists may or may not be 'bad' people but are forced by competition to increase profit levels by exploiting workers. This is because a company that does not invest in the most efficient machinery will find that its costs tend to be higher than rival firms. A firm must invest in order to survive turning money into capital and back again into money. The lazy or humane capitalist fails in the race and is put out of business. 'A benevolent capitalist who paid his workers wages that broadly corresponded to the amount of value they created would soon find himself out of business' (Callinicos 2003: 37).

The capitalist firm must keep on growing or it will die because it will be overtaken by other businesses. While competition is unlikely to be eliminated, the advantage given by economies of scale mean that smaller companies are likely to be replaced by larger. The development of global markets and the emergence of giant multinationals, which Schumacher condemns, are clearly explained by Marxist analysis:

> Constant efforts to cut costs are forced on capitalists by competition, the primary driving force in capitalism. Any new method of production which reduces costs (a technical improvement, or an 'improvement' in labour discipline) will bring extra profits to those who introduce it quickly, before the general price level has been forced down. Once it is generally adopted, competition forces prices down in line with costs, wiping out any remaining high cost producers. Marx assumed (in general rightly) that large scale-production is more efficient than small-scale. Competition therefore forces capitalists to accumulate and reinvest as much as possible in order to produce on a large scale. Marx called growth through reinvestment of

profits, *concentration of capital*. Bigger firms will be better able to survive, especially in slumps, and will be able to buy out smaller firms. The growth of the scale of production by amalgamation of capitals is called *centralization of capital*. (Brewer 1990: 33)

Although Marx, like most economists of his day, thought in terms of private ownership by entrepreneurs, public ownership by shareowners will encourage even a monopoly to keep growing. Shareholders will demand high share values and/or higher dividends and will dump firms that do not grow. Marx, as Callinicos notes, provides a structural theory of accumulation, capitalists exploit the creativity of workers, skim off profits and reinvest in new capital, not because they believe in a particular set of values, as David Korten and many Greens suggest, but just to survive in business (Callinicos 2003: 37).

Economics is a field of conflict with workers fighting to improve pay and conditions and firms attempting to maximise profit. Technological, cultural and social changes are the only constants of capitalism. Capitalism is like a bicycle. A bicycle tends to fall over if one ceases peddling; capitalism tends to collapse if it fails to grow. Although it might be said that capitalism demands, unlike a bicycle, that we peddle faster and faster for ever. It can be distinguished from other forms of society 'by dynamism and by instability' (Callinicos 2003: 37). Thus capitalism is crisis-ridden. Marx argued that labour power is the source of exchange value and profit. Machines gradually replace workers and as the proportion of labour in the production process falls, so, other things being equal, does profit. In Marx's analysis if all value comes from labour, if less labour is used to produce goods, less value will be generated when such goods are sold. While this may seem a little obscure, simple supply and demand analysis gives us the same result. As workers are replaced by machines, oversupply pushes up the quantity of goods produced and leads to falling profit. Crisis is not fatal, at least not immediately. Marx identified a whole host of processes from selling more goods (small profit margins multiplied by greater sales maintain profit) to exploiting workers more intensively, which tend to conserve the capitalist 'mode of production'. While Marx, in several passages, stated that crises would intensify, careful study of his work suggests that this is not necessarily the case (Desai 2004).

Marxists have long argued as to the exact nature of the tendency for profit to fall and the crisis identified by Marx (Went 2000: 65). Many

Marxists have argued for an underconsumptionist view, suggesting that consumption will fail to keep up with production, leading to falling prices, negative profits and killer slumps. Others stress overaccumulation, noting that supply will rise too fast to sustain profit. These two views are essentially one. Other contradictions include the possible mismatch between different 'departments' (more or less 'consumption' and 'investment' in machinery) of the economy, thus capital may increase faster than demand for goods and services again feeding into slump. Autonomist Marxists stress the essential conflict between workers, who want to hold on to more of their labour power and capitalists who wish to steal it away (Cleaver 2000). For ecosocialists the basic contradiction between use values and exchange values is the mother of all other contradictions and crises (Kovel 2002).

As capitalism develops, ways around contradictions tend to be found but they tend to lead to new contradictions. For example, the growth of vast financial markets producing credit, which horrifies social creditors, allows consumption to expand to maintain profitable demand. Accelerating debt expands consumption and allows exchange values to be realised. The mismatches in the economy can be bridged by borrowing (Harvey 1999). However, this leads to new contradictions. While the problems of capitalism cannot be blamed on the banks, debt creation certainly leads to new problems.

Contradictions and conflicts, whether class-based, environmental or economic, to the extent that can be separated, lead to change. Marx argued that capitalism by massively increasing the means of production and forging working-class opposition tends to create communism. Marxist politics tries to activate these tendencies. Ultimately, accelerating change may lead to a communist society, where the market is replaced by conscious human planning. Abstract economic 'laws' and the 'needs' of an elite are replaced by a society based on human need. This process is a revolution both because it is likely to demand violent change and because it leads to a break between one kind of society and another. Capitalism in its search for profits is the force that promotes globalisation but will mutate into communism.

Marx drew upon a rich heritage of thought, which is often forgotten by anti-capitalist activists today. Hegel, Kant and Spinoza informed his thought. From Feuerbach he gained the notion of 'fetishism', a process where we give something invented by the human imagination, artificial but effective power over us. Gods and goddesses invented by human beings rule over us. Objects are given power and return to shape our desires. Commodities, goods we make, are given energy and become our masters. Capitalism is a process of 'fetishism' where by an economic system constructed collectively by the actions of millions of human beings, comes to dominate human beings (Kolakowski 1988: 276). Desai notes how Marx's 'training in Hegelian philosophy equipped him [to deal with economic questions] at a level of depth and generality which was totally alien to the British way of doing political economy. He used the method of immanent criticism. This meant mastering the classical political economy completely, accepting its logic but then proposing a better political economy as a critique from within which to point up and resolve the internal contradictions' (Desai 2004: 55). Hegel specifically equipped Marx with the dialectic. The dialectic comes from the Greeks and is akin to dialogue, the interplay between two forces that transforms both ... like conversation or cooking or sex.

Reality is a process of constant revolution. Identity is relational; we have identity in relation to that which is different. Change occurs when relationships are rearranged. Phenomenon is a product of self-contradiction and such contradiction leads to change. Contradiction is all; Marx characteristically notes the contradiction between 'progress' and exploitation. Concepts enslave workers, machines crush their individuality in the pursuit of surplus value:

> all means for the development of production undergo a dialectical inversion so that they become means of domination and exploitation of the producers; they distort the worker into a fragment of a man, they degrade him to the level of an appendage of a machine, they destroy the actual content of his labour by turning it into a torment; they alienate from him the intellectual potentialities of the labour process in the same proportion as science is incorporated in it as an independent power; they deform the conditions under which he works, subject him during the labour process to a despotism the more hateful for its meanness; they transform his life-time into working-time, and drag his wife and child beneath the wheels of the juggernaut of capital. (Marx 1979: 799)

MARXIST THEORIES OF IMPERIALISM

Marx wrote little directly on processes of colonialism; he never used the term 'imperialism', let alone 'globalisation' (Brewer 1990: 25). His main efforts in *Capital* went, despite much historical digression and polemic, into describing an abstract model of the 'pure' capitalist society. What he did write on the creation of global markets through foreign colonialism, is, unsurprisingly, contradictory. He argued that the British acted to oppress Ireland, Ireland was Britain's first colony and efforts to bring capitalist development to Ireland had been deliberately aborted by the Brits (Brewer 1990: 48). Irish Republicans have found it easy to drop the Catholic Easter Rising theology and adopt a Marxist label where necessary. For Ireland, we could swap Iraq or Vietnam and no great theory would be required. Such analysis is based on nationalism as much as economic analysis and would reflect the very straightforward view that imperialism is based on the exploitation of the weak by the strong.

In contrast, Marx argued that British colonialism in India was progressive in the long term. The British brought capitalism to India, and this was a violent process but one which created the preconditions for real economic growth and expansion. The dilemma with Marxist accounts from Marx onwards is that they provide a mixed message: imperialism, capitalism and globalisation are both good and bad. Marx noted that the British had transformed land ownership, created a free press and introduced 'the electric telegraph'. The British bourgeoisie (capitalist class) would ultimately have to be thrown out, but their attempt to draw the country into a global market was necessary:

> Has the bourgeoisie ever done more? Has it ever effected a progress without dragging individuals and peoples through blood and dirt and misery and degradation? The Indians will not reap the fruits of the new elements of society scattered among them by the British bourgeoisie till in Great Britain itself the ruling classes shall have been supplanted by the industrial proletariat or till the Hindoos themselves shall have grown strong enough to throw off the English yoke. (quoted in Brewer 1990: 55)

Clearly, the view of a purely exploitative relationship would end the need for further speculation: what is the point of developing a sophisticated theoretical account of one group kicking another and stealing their stuff? The more theoretical account, in turn, puts Marxists in the pro-globalisation camp, stressing that the growth of global markets is a precondition for socialism (Desai 2004: 154).

The first Marxist to challenge and develop Marx's views on imperialism was Rosa Luxemburg. A Polish revolutionary, killed after the abortive Spartacist Uprising, she believed that capitalism suffered from a potential crisis of underconsumption. Exploitation of the working class meant that consumers, who derived their income mainly from work, did not have enough purchasing power to buy the products manufactured by capitalism. This mismatch between production and consumption could be overcome by selling to new markets outside the capitalist system. Imperialism used military force to gain control of territories outside of capitalism whose populations would buy excess goods. Her approach fits the facts of the Opium Wars, where Britain went to war to force the Chinese to accept imports of the drug. Her views parallel the accounts of social credit/monetary reformers who see excess production as a motive for enhanced trade. John Hobson, a non-Marxist critic of imperialism, held broadly similar views. Imperial expansion might also provide a source of cheap raw materials and labour. Luxemburg notes the importance of creating a reserve army of spare labour, a theme previously explored by Marx, to keep wages low in the capitalist heartlands (Luxemburg 1971).

Luxemburg, who bitterly attacked the processes leading to the enclosure of the commons and saw little of intrinsic value in capitalism, argued that the full creation of a global market would lead to the collapse of capitalism because it would cease to have outside markets in which to sell excess goods. Critics have suggested that excess production can be mopped up by capitalist investment in new means of production, by credit creation or state consumption, especially on weapons. However, whatever other conclusions can be drawn from Luxemburg, expansion of capitalism globally is strongly motivated by demands for new markets, cheap raw materials and new sources of potential labour power.

The 'classic' Marxist account of imperialism was developed out of the insights of Hobson and Luxemburg by Hilferding, Bukharin and Lenin. Lenin's pamphlet *Imperialism: The Highest State of Capitalism* (Lenin 1982) is the most readable description. All three argued that capitalism had shifted into a new epoch of imperialism. The union of financial interests and manufactures in finance capital marked this. Finance capital, a term coined by Hilferding, a German socialist, has nothing to do with monetary reform or a world run by bankers. Bankers and industrialists get together and cooperate in new corporations. Finance capital leads to monopolies that dominate their respective national economies. The monopolists, to cut a long story short, control governments and launch wars to capture new territories. Territorial expansion provides markets, raw materials and cheap labour. The First World War can be seen as an imperialist war with German, British and Russian empires competing for domination.

Imperialism was 'the highest state of capitalism', Lenin argued, because the 'anarchy' of the market was largely replaced by the planned decision-making of huge corporations. Since the 'classic' account of imperialism, matters have become muddily confused for a number of reasons. Imperialism, as described by Lenin and co., did not lead to the replacement of capitalism by communism. Fordism and post-Fordism are generally seen as new stages of capitalism and there may be many more stages to go before socialism is achieved. The multi-imperialism of the European powers was replaced by a globe divided between the Cold War powers. Since the Cold War, the US has emerged as the global hyperpower.

In a loose sense, we can talk of American imperialism. There are many examples of US intervention in virtually every continent that is motivated by the needs of US corporations. Conflict in the former Yugoslavia can be seen as benefiting German firms at the expense of Russian companies. Wars for oil are imperialist and the Gulf Wars pitted US imperialism against the needs and desires of French firms.

Imperialism in the everyday sense is exploitation. However, in Marxist accounts, including those of Bukharin, Lenin and Luxemburg, far from leading to poverty, it brings capitalism to new parts of the globe. While this is a violent process and may increase inequality, it raises the productive forces, which creates 'growth'. The idea that imperialism leads to underdevelopment is alien to the Marxist tradition. Continuing and even increasing poverty in the south of the globe cannot easily be explained by a Marxist approach. Imperialism has been analysed by a series of dependency theorists who argue that through processes of 'unfair' trade, such poverty will remain. These reverse the Marxist conception of imperialism, but this is generally forgotten. Many Marxist tinged approaches seem to owe more to dependency theories and various forms of nationalism (Brewer 1990; Desai 2004; Warren 1980). American imperialism has long been the target of South American populist leaders such as Chavez, the Venezuelan President. It is no bad thing that such figures as Chavez criticise globalisation or GM crops and work to better the lot of the poor. In 2004 *The Economist* (16 October) noted that 'Supporters of Venezuela's president, Hugo Chavez, pulled down Caracas's statue of Christopher Columbus to celebrate the anniversary of his landing in the Americas. Mr Chavez has renamed it "Indian Resistance Day".'

However, anti-imperialism has become yet another form of the evil bastard approach to political economy. The view that the Americans dominate the world, so if we sweep away US power we can achieve a just world, is a view that is too crude to sustain and has little or nothing to do with Marxism. Dutch or Indonesian capitalism would still be capitalism.

MARXIST APPROACHES TO GLOBALISATION

Some Marxists and writers influenced by a Marxist tradition argue that the creation of a global market is necessary for the creation of a Communist society. This approach can be justified by examining Marx's work, particularly the *Communist Manifesto*. In the 1980s Bill Warren's book *Imperialism – Pioneer of Socialism* inspired controversy with this view (Warren 1980). During the 1990s the now extinct Revolutionary Communist Party fronted by the academic Frank Furedi argued in its glossy journal *Living Marxism*, that the technological advances created by capitalism such as GM crops were necessary for a socialist society. The group collapsed and its main figures became keen advocates of the free market and various forms of right-wing productivist politics. The former editor of *International Socialist*, Nigel Harris, has moved from a Marxism that celebrates capitalist growth to straightforward belief in the market (2003). Desai too argues that Marx was right to celebrate the growth created by capitalism but wrong to expect a socialist future beyond it; indeed, Desai argues that a careful reading of Marx's mature work suggests that capitalism can be sustained for ever (2004).

Globalisation creates massive technological development and raises the productive forces; this means that communism can be created on the basis of surplus rather than shortage. The exhaustion of new markets will lead to economic crisis, which will fuel demands for a socialist planned economy. Globalisation/imperialism/capitalism will sweep away old forms of injustice such as feudalism and destroy superstition and traditional beliefs standing in the way of 'progress'. The growth of a global market will create a global working class which has both the means and the motive to destroy capitalism. The planning undertaken by huge multinational corporations can be viewed as the basis for socialist planning. Such a pro-globalisation Marxism is explained with the greatest sophistication by Meghnad Desai, a British Labour Party member and former Marxist. *The Communist Manifesto* contains several passages endorsing the revolutionary effect of capitalism in sweeping away traditional localist economies, celebrated by the likes of Vandana Shiva and the greens today:

> The bourgeoisie has, through its exploitation of the world market, given a cosmopolitan character to production and consumption in every country. To the great chagrin of reactionaries, it has drawn from under the feet of industry the national ground on which it stood. All old-established national industries have been destroyed or are daily being destroyed. They are dislodged by new industries, whose introduction becomes a life and death question for all civilized nations, by industries that no longer work up indigenous raw material, but raw material drawn from the remotest zones; industries whose products are consumed, not only at home, but in every quarter of the globe. In place of the old wants, satisfied by the production of the country, we find new wants, requiring for their satisfaction the products of distant lands and climes. In place of the old local and national seclusion and self-sufficiency, we have in every direction, universal inter-dependence of nations. And as in material, so also in intellectual production. The intellectual creations of individual nations become common property. National one-sidedness and narrow-mindedness become more and more impossible, and from the numerous national and local literatures, there arises a world literature.
>
> The bourgeoisie, by the rapid improvement of all instruments of production, by the immensely facilitated means of communication, draws all, even the most barbarian, nations into civilization. The cheap prices of commodities are the heavy artillery with which it batters down all Chinese walls, with which it forces the barbarians' intensely obstinate hatred of foreigners to capitulate. It compels all nations, on pain of extinction, to adopt the bourgeois mode of production ... (Marx and Engels 1985: 83–4)

This pro-globalisation strand of Marx's thought is largely ignored by Marxists who seek to work with the anti-neo-liberal globalisation movement; it would be difficult to sell socialist newspapers to demonstrators with banner headlines of 'Defend the WTO – forward to Socialism'. One common theme from Marxists in the movement is the idea that globalisation has not really occurred or is just a cover for imperialism, defined as a political process closely linking economic and military power.

James Petras and Henry Veltmeyer in *Globalisation Unmasked* argue that the capitalist world, far from entering a new era, is essentially the same. They specifically enumerate a range of groups who can be brought together to fight neo-liberalism. As well as the traditional working class, the unemployed and indigenous people are also important. Globalisation is just an ideological excuse for maintaining a market economic system and strengthening US control. Chris Harman from the Socialist Workers Party has drawn on the accounts of sceptics such as Paul Hirst and Graeme Thompson to show that the world is far less economically integrated than is normally supposed (Hirst and Thompson 1999). However, he suggests the capitalist economic system has long made it difficult for national governments to pursue truly independent policies. In the 1930s, the first British Labour government was forced to drop radical redistributive policies because of the perceived need to retain the Gold Standard. The Gold Standard fixed the value of the pound to gold and was thought necessary to maintain Britain's economic standing in a global system. Imperialism remains and such imperialism is largely American (Harman 2000a; Wood 2003b).

Other Marxists are less willing to dismiss globalisation as simply American imperialism but are keen to use the basics of a Marxist approach to win over anti-capitalists to a more radical opposition. All Marxists reject the idea that one aspect of capitalism such as banking or the corporations can be tackled to create a fairer society. Everything must go, David McNally notes:

> It is the nature of capitalism to degrade, dehumanise, and oppress – to commodify everything and to exploit all but the tiny minority who control the world's wealth. Rather than accidental, a perverse distortion of an otherwise fair system, this drive to commodify and exploit is the very nature of the beast. (McNally 2002: 273)

Alex Callinicos of the Socialist Workers Party argues in *An Anti-Capitalist Manifesto* (2003) that neo-liberal globalisation can only be explained by Marxism. He argues that to achieve non-capitalist society loose anti-capitalists will have to engage more fully with trade unionists. This is an uncontroversial view amongst Marxists and many non-socialists in the broad movement against neo-liberal globalisation.

Robert Went, from a Fourth International perspective, gives a good example of how trade unions can globalise their actions for better pay and conditions in his book *Globalization*:

> When Ford factory workers in Cuatitlan, north of Mexico City, struck in 1994 against layoffs and for better working conditions, members of United Auto Workers in a US Ford factory sent money to support the action. Their reasoning was: if the Mexicans win, that's good for us as well as them because

Ford won't be so quick to (threaten to) move production to Mexico. There are many other such possibilities for intensive contacts and common actions by unions in different countries. (Went 2000: 126–7)

Both Callinicos and Went come up with a list of 'transitional demands'. This concept developed by Trotsky refers to a set of 'reasonable' policies, acceptable to a broad front of radicals, that, if implemented, would tend to tip the capitalist system into crisis and towards a socialist system. Much of what they outline would be acceptable to Soros, Stiglitz, Hertz and other capitalist critics of the excesses of neo-liberalism. Went calls for regulation of the financial sector, noting 'all small steps in this direction', including a Tobin Tax, 'are worthy of support' (Went 2000: 123). Third World debt should be cancelled and 'fair prices' paid for Third World products. Export-led growth should be replaced with 'organising of production to meet local and regional needs'. Indeed, Went has some sympathy for a localist approach, noting (unusually for a Marxist) the paradox of irrational trade: 'there are flowers grown in Israel, flown to the international flower auction in Holland, and bought there for sale the next day in Israel – where they have to be flown back' (Went 2000: 182). Workers should control work; 'giving a high priority to everyone's personal development and work satisfaction so as to make optimal use of the now largely unused creativity, knowledge and insights of the people who do the work' (Went 2000: 124). Work sharing and support for domestic labour such as caring are also important alongside 'a global minimum income for everyone' (Went 2000: 125). Went also talks of a global approach to environmental problems, calling for a maximum amount of car production per year. 'Economic growth will not be an end in itself within such an alternative logic, but will be subordinated to the planned satisfaction of the needs of the world's total current and future population' (Went 2000: 124).

Callinicos' set of 'indicative' demands is almost identical, although he explicitly mentions strong redistributive taxation, a reversal of privatisation, stronger civil liberties and demands for disarmament. Both Callinicos and Went argue that neo-liberal globalisation has already been slowed by protest and can be transformed through further militancy. They argue that nation states still have much power and can be pushed into action by radical street based pressure from greens, NGOs, unions and others. Yet while they present many of the same demands as more moderate critics of capitalism, they seek to destroy the present economic system, not merely to make it a little fairer or environmentally sustainable:

> It is clearly possible to throw a certain amount of sand in the machinery of globalization. However important such small changes and improvements can be – and they are in themselves very worthy of support – only symptoms are being combated and not the disease as the fundamental characteristics and laws of motion of the world capitalist system remain unaffected. It is not possible with the existing economic logic, in which profit maximisation comes first, to solve the most important problems that humanity faces. Under capitalism the individual interests of speculators, employers or investors determine what they do. The partial rationality of their actions clashes with the general social interest of present and future generations. (Went 2000: 121–2)

Callinicos notes that reforms will always lead to political difficulties. Reforms may clean up capitalism enough to allow it to survive a little longer. Those who seek a different kind of economy and society can end up being incorporated in existing power structures, doing the dirty work of the system. However, to reject all reforms and hold out for revolution would be insanely sectarian. Transitional demands provide a partial way out of this dilemma because they tend to work against the logic of the present economic system:

> For example, to introduce universal direct income at a relatively generous level would severely compromise the present workings of the labour market, and thereby remove one of the essential conditions of capitalist exploitation. They are what Trotsky called transitional demands, reforms that emerge from the realities of existing struggles but whose implementation in the current context would challenge capitalist economic relations. (Callinicos 2003: 140)

CASTRO ON GLOBALISATION

Other Marxists have given more thought to practical change and have stressed the ecological dimensions of opposition to globalisation. Of these, perhaps the most important is Cuban President Fidel Castro. Indeed, Fidel Castro is the nearest the Marxists have to a Stiglitz, Soros, Korten or Klein. Castro also deals with contradictory Marxist approaches to globalisation rather more honestly than other commentators; the fact that Marx is on record with pro-globalisation statements is largely ignored by Callinicos, McNally and Went.

Castro argues that while US imperialism directly threatens Cuba, globalisation cannot be reduced to the needs of specifically US corporations. He believes that globalisation is a cultural phenomenon with language, literature and music becoming worldwide in scale. There is even existing socialist globalisation with Cuba sending doctors and teachers to Africa, South America and other parts of the globe. The country has developed particularly warm links with Venezuela's populist leader Hugo Chavez. Of course, nations with similar political objectives have maintained alliances throughout history, but Castro produces evidence that a new globalisation from below and from the poor/oppressed is already apparent. Technological development is another reason why globalisation is in principle beneficial and cannot be reversed.

Castro rejects the view that globalisation is a product of a plot by a small elite; instead, the *Communist Manifesto* indicates that it is born out of a broad historical process (Castro 2003: 9). However, Castro then notes the world is dominated by a particular form of neo-liberal globalisation, which even capitalists admit is destructive. He is particularly amused that a capitalist multi-millionaire like Soros is so critical of neo-liberalism:

> neo-liberal globalization wants to turn all countries, especially all our countries, into private property ... They want to turn the world into a huge free-trade zone, it might be more clearly understood this way because, what is a free-trade zone? It is a place with special characteristics where taxes are not paid; where raw materials, spare parts and components are brought in and assembled or various goods produced, especially in labour intensive sectors. At times, they pay not more than 5 per cent of the salary they must pay in their own countries and the only thing they leave us with are these meagre salaries. (Castro 2003: 13)

Progress, Castro argues, echoing Marx's dialectical account, creates its own discontents:

> Labour productivity and the most sophisticated equipment born out of human talent multiply material wealth as well as poverty and layoffs, what good are they to mankind. Perhaps to help reduce working hours, have more time for resting, leisure, sports, cultural and scientific upgrading? That is impossible because the sacred market laws and competition patterns – increasingly more

imaginary than real – in a world of transnationals and megamergers do not allow it all. Anyway, who are competing and against whom? Monopoly- and merger-orientated giants against giants. (Castro 2003: 15)

While nearly all Marxists now pay lip service to environmental sustainability, Castro is explicit in his suggestion that unlimited economic growth is unacceptable. Rather than seeking to raise the productive forces in a crudely quantitative ways, Castro argues that there are ecological limits to growth. He echoes the approach of Caroline Lucas, Mike Woodin or other greens, stating that needs must be met for people on a planetary basis rather than providing luxury goods:

> The consumption pattern they are imposing on the world is sheer madness, chaotic and absurd.
>
> It is not that I think the world should become a monastery. However, I do believe that the planet has no other choice but to define which are going to be the consumption standards or patterns, both attainable and obtainable, which mankind should be educated. (Castro 2003: 18)

Castro's ideology in the 2000s combines organic agriculture with *Capital*:

> By creating unsustainable consumer patterns in industrialized countries and sowing impossible dreams throughout the rest of the world, the developed capitalist system has caused great injury to mankind. It has poisoned the atmosphere and depleted its enormous non-renewable natural resources, which mankind will need in the future. Please, do not believe that I am thinking of an idealistic, impossible, absurd world; I am merely trying to imagine what a real world and a happier person could be like. It would not be necessary to mention a commodity, it suffices to mention a concept: inequality has made more than 80 per cent of the people on the planet unhappy, and this is no more than a concept. (Castro 2003: 18)

Castro has been leader of a state that has survived constant attacks from the US and managed to make considerable progress in health care and education. Castro is extremely proud of the fact that Cuba has a high level of Olympic gold medal winners per capita and that literacy levels and infant mortality figures are better than parts of the US. Cuba has also made major progress in moving to organic agriculture. The British NHS has sought to learn from Cuban medical care. Cuba has benefited in many ways from relative isolation, a case study in the real advantages of 'localisation'. Although desperately poor in comparison to Western countries, Cuba is relatively prosperous next to neighbouring Haiti. However, Cuba remains a one-party state (although of course the record of the US as a two-party system is hardly an ideal model of even liberal democracy) and civil liberties, while better than many Caribbean states, are hardly stunning. The relative success of Cuban anti-capitalism demands support but does not necessarily provide a model that can be exported on a global scale.

MARX BEYOND MARX

It would be possible to move through many more Marxist manifestos; however, the arguments surveyed briefly above are broadly representative. Capitalism is a total system, which cannot be reformed. Globalisation is variously rejected as a mask for imperialism, embraced as paving the way to communism or seen as a contradictory phenomenon both hostile to life but capable of being turned into something different. Marxists are also orientated to struggle rather than seeking reforms to mend the system.

There are a whole series of problems with the Marxisms on offer. Russia under Stalin or China under Mao are hardly paradigms of freedom and all-round human creative development. Marx is in some senses a prophet of globalisation, technological development, the exploitation of nature and the advance of the market. Many of Marx's suggestions have come to nothing. The revolutions in his name in China, Cuba, Vietnam, with the partial exception of Russia, while not without their heroic moments, have been from peasants compressed by enclosure rather than workers in capitalist states. However, the sophistication and complexity of Marx's thought provides a rare élan absent in much of anti-capitalist literature, yet the nuances of his ideas seem absent from many contemporary Marxist approaches. Marxism today, if represented by the far-left parties, seems to consist of bad attitudes to bad things. The contemporary Marxists, while loudly against injustice, often seem distant from Marx's doctrine. Marxist partisans simply echo much of the critique of Korten, Klein, the greens and NGOs but with a little more vehemence.

Most Marxist parties take a Leninist line that stresses the need to construct a disciplined centralised party to lead 'The Revolution'. Also many, but not all, Marxists have promoted a productivist politics that celebrates the expansion of the economy. Anarchists and greens have criticised both tendencies. Some within the direct action movement have accused Marxist parties of 'vampirism' and of trying to use the anti-capitalist movement as a means of recruiting new members:

> Seeing a growing anti-capitalist movement, they saw an opportunity to fill the other half of the equation – sure, we're all anti this, that and the other, but what are we for? The SWP's answer to this is that we should be building a centralised, hierarchical party, making it as big as possible and then hopefully taking over the state in the name of the working class. Once we've done that we can centrally plan the economy (i.e. work) and expand production (i.e. industry). This is so far from the free, equal and ecological community most of us want it's amazing the SWP felt able to act the way they have. (Anon. 2001c: 134).

New kinds of Marxism have evolved that seek to go beyond Marx or to emphasise a greener and more anarchic bearded prophet. The traditional planned economy churning out tractors, bread queues, nuclear submarines and desiccated central Asian lakes provides an unsustainable alternative to the chaos of capitalism. Attempts to 'green' Marxism are clearly necessary. Some progress has been made in this direction by a minority including Castro, but the ecosocialists examined in Chapter 8 argue that socialism must be transformed if it is to sustain the earth.

Autonomist Marxists have cross-fertilised anarchist and socialist ideas. Harry Cleaver, a leading US autonomist, noted that 'several generations of Marxists have given us the habit of perceiving the mechanism of domination. What we need now is to use Marx to help us discover the mechanisms of liberation' (Cleaver 1991: xx). Autonomism, while a Marxism, claims to be based on an anarchic perspective stressing the creativity of grassroots struggles. Autonomism, particularly in the form presented in Hardt and Negri's *Empire*, has also attempted to develop a more sophisticated understanding of global sovereignty rather than the rather problematic accounts of 'classic' 'Marxist' imperialism. Autonomism is described in the next chapter.

7
The Tribe of Moles:
Autonomism, Anarchism and Empire

resistance.org

Old Mick was a veteran squatter, rebel and thief. His most successful heist was the reclaiming of his life from those bosses and jailers who think they own us. For decades he lived in the gaps. No one made him into a wageslave. No dropout, he fought. He was no saint, but if ever there was a temporary autonomous zone, Mick was it.

His funeral was one of the best 'actions' I have ever been on. Mick wanted to burn in Lyminge Forest, a larger part of which was saved from destruction by direct action. Funeral pyres are illegal, death rights have to be sanctioned by the state. Mick wasn't going to take that, neither were his mates [...] Ten foot the pyre of 'stolen' wood rose, Mick's coffin astride. Night came. Fireworks shot into the sky. Crackling fire, we saw Mick's bones burn, back to the earth. For hours he burnt. (Anon. 2003:100)

We asked for information on marriages. Although the comrades naturally favoured free love, the people enjoyed lawful marriage because a marriage ceremony in these peaceful villages is a festive occasion, celebrated with great gusto by the whole community. On the other hand, legal marriage does violate libertarian principles.

Our comrades met this problem by going through all the legal procedures and then rendering the marriage legally meaningless by destroying the documentary proof of marriage, as if no marriage had taken place. (Leval 1990a:155)

Anti-capitalism protest is marked by black flags as well as red and grows from loose networks rather than being organised by a central body. Anti-capitalists are more likely to label themselves as anarchists than socialists, greens, social creditors or followers of George Soros. Anarchism, far from just being about bad attitude, draws on an intellectual tradition. In the nineteenth century, anarchist movements inspired by the writings of Mikhail Bakunin, Peter Kropotkin and Emma Goldman dominated radical politics in much of Spain, Italy and southern France (Woodcock 1963). Now, after a century in the shadow of socialism, anarchism once again draws the numbers to demonstrations. Paradoxically one of the primary intellectual sources for today's anarchists is autonomism, a body of theory that claims to be 'communist' and which is informed by Marxist theory. The anti-capitalist magazine *Aufheben* noted:

> For many of those dissatisfied with the versions of Marxism and anarchism available to them in the UK, the notions of 'autonomy' and 'autonomist' have positive associations. For example, the recent 'anti-capitalist' mobilizations of J18 and Seattle both drew on themes and language associated with *autonomia*, such as autonomous struggles and diversity. (<www.geocities. com/*Aufheben2*/auf_11_operaismo.html>)

Autonomism, which developed in Italy during the 1960s and 1970s, starts from the principle that the working class should resist capitalism independently, that is, autonomously from political parties and trade unions (Dyer-Witheford 1999; Wright 2002). *Empire* by Toni Negri, a former political prisoner/Italian philosopher, and Michael Hardt, a US literary theorist, provides a detailed explanation of globalisation from a broadly autonomist perspective (Hardt and Negri 2001a). *Empire* has been a minor literary sensation, although it is probably, given the complexity of its ideas, more bought than read. Nonetheless, *Empire*, and the autonomism that it draws upon, are important strains of anti-capitalist thought. For autonomists the working class consists not just of factory workers but of all who serve and are exploited by capital. Society has become the social factory; housework helps support capitalism; students by developing the power of intellectual labour are also part of the working class, and so on (Wright 2002: 37). So although autonomism originated as a form of 'workerism', it has perhaps been the current of anti-capitalist theory that is happiest to see social movements and counter-cultures as the cutting edge of resistance. The expression 'tribe of moles' was coined to identify the varied subversives who fight capitalism from the margins of the social factory. Such diverse forms of militant resistance from DIY culture to squatting, spontaneous strikes, and Earth First! are generated by members of the tribe:

> One early characterization of this new subjectivity (which is actually seen as a diversity of subjectivities) was given by Sergio Bologna in the 1970s who identified a new 'tribe of moles' – a loose tribe of highly mobile drop-outs, part-time workers, part-time students, participants in the underground economy, creators of temporary and ever-changing autonomous zones of social life that force a fragmentation of and crisis in the mass-worker organisation of the social factory. (Cleaver 2003: 49)

Marx identified the international working class with the mole: emerging into open struggle when it could but digging subversively between bouts of open conflict. 'Well grubbed, old mole', he might shout from his desk after reading a *Times* account of strike or rebellion (Hardt and Negri 2001a: 57).

Autonomism originated when a group of socialist intellectuals and union activists established the journal *Quaderni Rossi* ('Red Notes') in October 1961. They drew hope from a wildcat (unofficial) strike at Fiat, which saw militant workers not only reject union advice but also march upon and occupy the offices of the UIL, one of the three big national unions (Fuller 2001: 65). *Quaderni Rossi* argued that the Communist Party and other far-left parties and unions had brokered a compromise between workers and capitalists that was preventing, temporarily at least, the construction of a socialist alternative. The Fiat action, in contrast, showed that the Italian working class could create its own political space outside of these institutions and build a culture of resistance. Despite bouts of intellectual obscurity and arrogance, autonomism has generally tried to learn from and be led by the working class rather than to tell the workers how to revolt.

Even at its strongest during the 1970s, Autonomia Operaia ('Workers' Autonomy') was never a party or a single organisation. Within a particular city, several autonomist cells might exist, often divided bitterly over matters of philosophy, strategy and political organisation (Wright 2002: 152; Dyer-Witheford 1999). Spring 1977 saw a peak in factory-based protest and action in the universities by autonomists followed by shocking state repression. Although the Communist Party sought to create a historical compromise coalition government with the centre right Christian Democrats (DC), during the last years of the 1970s naked class warfare broke out in Italy. Aldo Moro, the DC leader, was kidnapped and murdered by the Red Brigade, a shadowy far-left terrorist group. The autonomists were attacked by the Italian state. Negri was arrested and accused of masterminding the kidnapping, and he later fled to France and accepted political asylum. During these years a 'shoot to kill' anti-terrorist law led to the deaths of 150 people, and in 1980 it was estimated that there were 3,500 political prisoners in Italy (Plant 1992: 129). The movement was shredded by repression (Bull 2003: 83). The autonomists were never pacifists and their ideas inspire the most militant of contemporary anti-capitalists: the 'black bloc' who are happiest smashing windows and fighting with police.

In both Italy and France, autonomist-influenced gangs were dubbed 'metropolitan Indians' by the press because they painted their faces and wore feathers. The 'Indians' variously broke into shops and stole or 'expropriated' ostentatiously useless goods, dined in expensive restaurants without paying, blockaded leftist party congresses and indulged in other guerrilla tactics (Plant 1992: 129; Wright 2002: 197). In Denmark, Germany and Switzerland the Autonomen, a loose network of radical squatters, anarchists and anti-fascists, influenced by autonomism, have been a feature of the political landscape since the 1970s (Katsiaficas 1997). Autonomists have long acted against neo-liberal globalisation:

September 1988, when the Autonomen prepared demonstrations against the conventions of the World Bank and the International Monetary Fund in Berlin. Thousands of militant demonstrators tried to stop the top finance ministers of 150 countries and over ten thousand world bankers from planning their future exploits ... For their part, the Green Party and its affliates attempted to defuse the planned confrontation by calling for a convention of their own to discuss the possibility of an 'alternative world banking system' unlike the Greens, the radical Autonomen would have little to do with banks – alternative or not – or any kind of system. The type of world they seek to create and to live in is as far removed as possible from money, centralization, government, and ownership in all their forms. (Katsiaficas 1997: 12)

The Zapatista movement in Mexico shows autonomist affinities and has networked with autonomist figures such as Harry Cleaver, a Texan professor who wrote *Reading Capital Politically* (2000) (Hardt and Negri 2001a: 55; Holloway and Pelaez 1998). Autonomists have also fed into academic discourse, contributing to journals such as *Capital and Class* and *Rethinking Marxism*. Political shoplifting remains in their repertoire of action:

> A group of 200 leftwing protesters wearing balaclavas, carnival masks and bandanas over their faces, went on a 'proletariat shopping spree' in a Rome hypermarket at the weekend, carrying off goods and handing them out.
>
> They swarmed into the Panorama hypermarket on the outskirts of the Italian capital on Saturday shouting 'free shopping for all'.
>
> After failing to negotiate a 70% discount with the supermarket's manager, the group barged loaded trolleys past cashiers and distributed the goods to a crowd outside.
>
> Police chose not to intervene but later claimed to have identified 87 members of the group, who now face legal action.
>
> The 'proletariat shoppers', included a Communist town councillor, Nunzio d'Erme, and the spokesperson of I Disobbedienti (formerly the Tute Bianche), Luca Casarini, who led violent G8 anti-globalisation protests in Genova in 2001. (*Guardian*, 8 November 2004)

Autonomists are Marxists, but not exclusively so. Michael Hardt has suggested that drawing upon one thinker 'rather than a set of methods, principles, and ideas always runs the risk of precluding innovation and creating a new dogmatism' (Hardt 2004: 170). He and Negri prefer the label 'communist' to 'Marxist', arguing that 'Spinoza was a communist thinker long before Marx' (Hardt 2004: 170). Autonomism fuses, roughly speaking, Marxism, anarchism and post-modernity. It's Marxism stresses working-class resistance rather than structural laws as the driving force of economic development. While Hardt and Negri refuse to be labelled as anarchists, 'their view of the state is recognizably an anarchist one' (Rustin 2003: 3). Finally, Hardt and Negri in particular look to a number of thinkers usually seen as post-modernists, such as Deleuze and Foucault (Callinicos 2001; Read 2003). The philosopher Spinoza provided Hardt and Negri with the concept of the multitude, their particular version of the revolutionary class. The power of the multitude is latinised as *potentia* (Ryan 1991: 216). These three sources of thought seem almost entirely contradictory: what can anarchist Marxist post-modern theory be other than mud? But all three fields of thought point towards a relatively simple and surprisingly coherent conception of economics. The innate creative energy of life fizzes through us all and this energy means that capitalism can be resisted, reshaped and ultimately abolished (Hardt and Negri 2001a: 358). The multitude is the angry and determined tribe of moles.

ANARCHIST MARXISM

Autonomism grew, as we have seen, out of Marxism. Even *Empire*, as we shall discuss later, reads like an over-the-top post-modern version of *Capital*. Unlike most variants of Marxism, discussed in the last chapter, the autonomism stresses the power of the working class rather than the workings of capitalism. Drawing upon the first chapter of Marx's *Capital*, the autonomists argue that capitalism is driven by the need both to exploit and to control the working class (Cleaver 2000). Thus autonomism is a form of 'subjective' rather than 'objective' Marxism. Autonomists argue that ordinary people, rather than being the puppets of the capitalist system, jerked up and down by its mechanisms as it lurches through crisis, instead force capitalism to change. Such power is not the power that can only create a revolution in the future, when the productive forces are 'ripe', but is a power that workers exercise on a day-to-day basis. Tronti has noted:

> We too have worked with a concept that puts capitalist development first, and the workers second. This is a mistake. And now we have to turn the problem on its head, reverse the polarity, and start again from the beginning: and that beginning is the class struggle of the working class. (Dyer-Witheford 1999: 65)

Nearly everything planned by capitalists, who include both factory bosses and government ministers, is concerned with keeping the tribe of moles from grubbing up the foundations of the system. Technological change occurs because capitalism requires new ways of keeping workers under control. Government policies are introduced to prevent rebellion by ordinary people. Globalisation, as we shall see, is used as a weapon in the struggle against the powerful and ever adaptable tribe of moles. The autonomists are intoxicated by Marx's observation that it 'would be possible to write a whole history of the inventions made since 1830 for the sole purpose of providing capital with weapons against working class revolt' (Dyer-Witheford 1999: 3). Autonomists share with Harry Braverman, and perhaps Marx, given the previous quotation, the assumption that new technologies are introduced not directly to increase productivity but to deskill the working class, so that they can be controlled more easily (Braverman 1974). As the working class finds new forms of resistance, the capitalists must develop new means of retaining control. The Mayday Monopoly group, who created the anti-capitalist day of action in London, based on the 'Monopoly' board game, view the replacement of rail, as the favoured form of mass transport, by road as 'mainly a political decision. Rail workers had a reputation for militancy, and it was thought that road transport was immune from industrial action' (Anon. 1999b: 10). Cleaver has argued that the Green Revolution, which brought high-yield crops and fertilisers to Asian countries, was aimed at destroying strong village-based communities to reduce the possibility of guerrilla resistance to capitalist development (Cleaver 1981).

Class struggle moves through cycles of class recomposition and decomposition. When the working class recomposes it becomes stronger and more militant, ready to throw off its chains and cease to be a class at all. Resistance to capitalism accompanies recomposition. To survive, capital needs to create class decomposition so as to disperse working-class power (Cleaver 2003).

The tendency for profits to fall is directly a product of working-class resistance, which raises wages and lowers working hours as militancy succeeds. The autonomist analysis is, ironically, similar to the supply-side economics of free marketeers like Milton Friedman and right-wing politicians such as General Pinochet, Ronald Reagan and Margaret Thatcher. Every aspect of economic debate from the existence of inflation to the movement of foreign direct investment is a result of the conflict between workers and capital.

The struggle of Vietnamese peasants in their war against the US forced up US arms spending and virtually bankrupted the US in the early 1970s. The expansion in the US money supply fuelled inflation and wrecked the Bretton Woods system of currencies fixed to the dollar. Interestingly, the autonomists here ignore the role of the Vietcong, the Vietnamese Communist Party. As we have seen, the activities of Communist parties are seen by the autonomists as preventing the spontaneous struggle of the multitude.

In short, crisis is created by working-class action. At both a factory floor and state level, new structures are created to prevent the collapse of capitalism. In explaining political economy the autonomists draw upon the insights of regulation theory. Regulation theory, developed by French theorists, suggests that a particular form of management is needed within particular states in particular periods to preserve capitalism. Autonomists argue that Keynesianism, as applied in Western Europe and North America between the 1940s and 1973, provides a good example. Rather than being seen as an alternative form of economic analysis to free market classicalism, it was a political means of controlling working-class revolt. Because of the growth of working-class militancy a welfare state had to be created to prevent all-out revolution and the collapse of capitalism. The working class, not Keynes, created Keynesian economics. When Keynesianism failed, new strategies had to be found. Monetarism is normally seen as an abstract economic theory that explains how increases in the money supply lead to rising inflation. Monetarist-inspired government spending cuts and attacks on union power were part of a political fight. Alan Budd, one of Mrs Thatcher's advisers, stated that her economic policies were designed to weaken the working class: 'What was engineered in Marxist terms – was a crisis in capitalism which re-created a reserve army of labour, and has allowed the capitalist to make high profits ever since' (quoted in Harvey 1999: xv).

Autonomists argue that emerging capitalism first faced the professional worker. This worker is highly skilled and operates complex and difficult machinery; one thinks of print workers who set type by hand before the introduction of computer technology. Such workers are in a strong position to push up wages and conditions, and given their power may see no necessity for capitalist management.

To defeat the professional worker new forms of machinery were introduced to mass produce not just goods but individuals. The mass worker is created by this new state of capitalism. The mass worker is shorn of skills and can be more easily controlled as she or he is forced to work at the rhythm of the conveyor belt. Thus 'Fordism' is a response to the professional worker, a response that came to be linked to Keynesianism and a global economy based on the dollar:

This meant that production-line type work was introduced, removing the need for many highly skilled workers or any direct connection to what was being produced. Productivity and production were increased by stepping up the exploitation of the workforce, allowing both wages and profits to rise, thus creating the demand to absorb the increase in production. Fordism was a system based upon mass production and mass consumption. It was premised on an implicit trade-off between increased alienation and boredom at work and increased consumption during 'leisure' or 'free' time – dissatisfaction turned into demand. The ever-increasing rate of exploitation, consequently, expanded the total amount of capital in circulation and made possible the growth of finance capital and the boom in credit and lending. (Anon. 1999b: 38)

Workers in the post-Second World War Fordist era accepted a 'social wage' in the form of a pension and other state benefits in return for higher productivity. However:

Things start to come apart. In the inhuman conditions of the assembly-line factory, the productivity deal always rested on a delicate balancing of capitalist profits and worker anger ... Mass workers increasingly refuse to restrain wage demands within limits functional to capitalist growth or to tolerate conditions accepted by their unions. Management responds to wage pressures with attempts to intensify the pace and intensity of work, thereby precipitating further resistance. A wave of wildcat strikes, slowdowns, sabotage, and absenteeism – which the autonomists christen 'the refusal of work' – sweeps across Europe and North America, ... rendering factories from Detroit to Turin to Dagenham virtually unmanageable. (Dyer-Witheford 1999: 75)

Thus the deal broke down in the 1970s, causing economic and political crisis with strikes, sabotage and 'sickies' taking their toll on productivity. The workers recomposed as a class, so capital had to promote class decomposition, a process that created a globalised, information-based, post-modern economy. Keynesian economics is replaced by free market substitutes, factories close in those areas of the globe with greater militancy and new technologies are used to make workers easier to dismiss and control.

In this post-Fordist era the tendency for society to become a social factory, with profit generated in diverse locations, accelerates. Production becomes increasingly decentralised and virtual. Academic, communicative and caring professions become economically vital. By splitting workers away from the factories and reconstituting society on a for-profit basis, control is reasserted. Yet from student unrest to unofficial strikes in call centres, from anti-road protests to the on-street movement against globalisation, the working class/multitude has shown its power (*potentia*) again.

Notions of the social factory have given rise to a distinctive feminist current in autonomist theory. Feminist autonomists have emphasised that capitalism has long depended on the unpaid domestic labour of women to support male factory workers, socialise children and to undertake other forms of 'affective' production to maintain the system. According to Maria Dalla Costa women directly produce surplus value as housewives (Wright 2002: 134); autonomist feminists have inspired the Wages for Housework campaign. Globalisation has led to the increased use of women as poorly-paid producers of goods in Export Processing Zones.

Negri in his reading of Marx associates such forms of exploitation with the notion of 'formal' and 'real' subsumption of labour. Formal subsumption occurs prior to the creation of capitalism and in its early stages. Marx links the early stages of formal subsumption to 'primitive accumulation', where individuals can survive outside of the market economy by growing food, using common land to graze animals and squatting. They don't want to work in the factories because they have their 'means of production' to keep them fed. Workers have to be forced to become workers by separating them from their ability to be economically independent. Land is enclosed with fences and the peasants are turned into homeless wanderers who can be incorporated into the factory system. Marx provides many examples. For instance, in Scotland in the eighteenth century:

> the Gaels were both driven from the land and forbidden to emigrate, with a view to driving them forcibly to Glasgow and other manufacturing towns. As an example of the method used in the nineteenth century, the 'clearings' made by the Duchess of Sutherland will suffice here. This person, who had been well instructed in economics, resolved, when she succeeded to the headship of the clan, to undertake a radical economic cure, and to turn the whole county of Sutherland, the population of which had already been reduced to 15,000 by similar processes, into a sheep-walk. Between 1814 and 1820 these 15,000 inhabitants, about 3,000 families, were systematically hunted and rooted out. All their villages were destroyed and burnt, all their fields turned into pasturage. British soldiers enforced this mass of evictions and came to blows with the inhabitants. One old woman was burnt to death in the flames of the hut she refused to leave. It was in this manner that this fine lady appropriated 794,000 acres of land which had belonged to the clan from time immemorial ... The remnant of the original inhabitants, who had been flung onto the sea-shore, tried to live by catching fish. They became

amphibious, and live, as an English writer says, half on land and half on water. (Marx 1979: 890–892)

The Sutherlanders were then expelled from the seashore, which was rented out to London fishmongers by the Duchess. In formal subsumption the newly-created workers are disciplined by placing them within particular locations of control such as factories, schools, prisons and mental hospitals. Such discipline is direct, the factory is a form of prison and so is the school (Read 2003). No doubt the Glaswegians, a working class swept from the Highlands into the city, recomposed as professional workers on Red Clydeside only to be decomposed by factory closures ... and so on.

Real subsumption occurs when such relatively crude methods cease to be necessary and workers take on their role willingly because they see no alternative to waged work. Social norms – 'values' – keep them at work; they need to earn money for their families to consume and fear of unemployment is used to maintain discipline with a lighter touch. The social factory produces not just commodities but a capitalist society and capitalist subjectivities:

> When capital reaches a high level of development, it no longer limits itself to guaranteeing collaboration of the workers ... something it so badly needs. At significant points it now makes a transition, to the point of expressing its objective needs through the subjective demands of the workers. (Fuller 2001: 66)

The Mayday Monopoly group observed: 'Capitalist society requires a specific social structure and a precise form of "individual". A whole machine is geared to create such a set up' (London Mayday Collective 2001: 38). Our assumptions, beliefs, practices and personality are forged by the capitalist economy. The creation of capitalist subjectivities is never totally complete. Partly this is because different institutions and practices within capitalism may have contradictory demands and produce contradictory effects:

> A somewhat simplistic example of this would be the conflict of the demands of consumption and production – the demand to consume as much as possible – necessary for the realization of surplus value and the demand to live frugally in order to be productive, which is necessary for the production of surplus value ... The dissonance produces possibilities and conditions for subversion. (Read 2003: 143)

Even though education, the media, advertising and other aspects of the social factory work to create a capitalist personality, workers still resist. This belief in resistance, despite a system that seeks to engineer our souls is an important bridge between autonomism and a larger longer anarchist anti-capitalism. Formal subsumption and discipline are never entirely replaced, as Naomi Klein has shown in her accounts of the prison-like conditions of the Export Processing Zones (2001a: 215). The commons is constantly re-enclosed to maintain capitalism (de Angelis 2001).

The autonomist analysis takes us a long way from the approach of Soros and Stiglitz. Yet the autonomists would argue that as representatives of capital Soros and Stiglitz believe that the Washington Consensus provides an unworkable means of controlling the multitude. What we have is not a debate on economics but a discussion between those who would punch us with the iron fist or greet us with a welcoming hand when opening the prison door. Theorists like Negri substitute economics with politics and arguably turn Marx into a bearded anarchist, happier smashing up the street than theorising in his study.

MARXIST ANARCHISM

While Hardt and Negri reject the anarchist label, other autonomists like Cleaver note the importance of anarchist thinkers such as Emma Goldman and Peter Kropotkin within a broadly communist tradition (Cleaver 2000: 14). Anarchists generally see politics as taking precedence over economics, and stress the power of the state rather than the activities of corporations alone. Like the autonomists they see the state as instrument of oppression. Anarchists argue that human beings are cooperative and resourceful. Bursting with potential, they don't need the state to instruct them to do work which is necessary or to channel their creativity. A minority, particularly in the US, are supporters of the market – seeing it, especially in its Smithian original form of small local firms, as a force for liberation. But the majority reject the need for a price mechanism, and view the market as an oppressive tool that restricts human creativity.

The numerous anarchist magazines, networks and quasi-political parties have fed into the anti-globalisation movement, often drawing inspiration (both positively and negatively) from Marxist sources. There is no distinct anarchist analysis of trends in global capitalism: while anarchists have developed descriptions of a utopian anarchist economy that will exist after the 'revolution', their understanding of how the present economy works is often taken from Marx.

The most extreme green anarchists, who reject civilisation and see a society rooted in the primitive, draw heavily upon the work of John Zerzan. Zerzan, originally an autonomist, has argued that even such institutions as written language and agriculture function as instruments of social control (Zerzan 1999). The great refusal demands that we re-create a primitive society. Although such theorising appears insanely extreme, primitivists point to studies such as Marshal Sahlins' *The Original Affluent Society* (1972) that argue for stone age prosperity, as well as archaeological evidence that prehistory may not have been as nasty and brutish as is usually supposed. Zerzan's call for humanity to be wild and free is promoted in journals such as *Green Anarchy*, *Green Anarchist* and *Fifth Estate*, which are often sold on anti-capitalist protests.

Other green anarchists draw upon the ideas of Murray Bookchin. Bookchin argues that ecological destruction is produced by the state and capitalism. He believes that Athenian democracy and the township meetings that brought together American citizens to make decisions during the late eighteenth century provide models for direct democracy. Direct democracy which enables the community to take collective decisions is seen as an anarchist alternative to the state by Bookchin. He is hostile to primitivism, deep ecology and other currents that he dismisses as irrational. Bookchin, one of the most well-known anarchist thinkers of the twentieth century, has challenged Marxism in many ways, but based his understanding of economics largely on *Capital* (Bookchin 1974: 178).

The 'classic' anarchists, writing and agitating, at the beginning of the twentieth century, often promoted green anti-capitalism. Typically, in 1906 writing in her journal *Mother Earth*, Goldman attacked a productivist, ecologically destructive capitalism:

Whoever severs himself from Mother Earth and her flowing sources of life goes into exile. A vast part of civilization has ceased to feel the deep relation with our mother ... Economic necessity causes such hateful pressure. Economic necessity? Why not economic stupidity? This seems a more appropriate name for it. (Goldman 1906: 2)

Peter Kropotkin (1842–1921) produced a guide for cooperative economies based on communal ownership. Kropotkin argued that many goods and services within the economy were already free such as books provided by libraries. Where goods remained in short supply rationing could be introduced. In the end, money could be abolished. He further argued that only five hours' work a day would be necessary if more goods were used communally. And he believed that the desire to be creative and part of the community would tend to encourage work despite the absence of monetary reward (Kropotkin 1972: 122–3). It must nevertheless be admitted that Kropotkin was more interested in gardening than providing a detailed analysis of trends within the global economy of the early twentieth century.

Autonomism is not the only movement which straddles the divide between Marxism and anarchism. Situationism, which originated in France during the 1950s, argued for an autonomous society and challenged the society of the spectacle in which the media shaped and controlled desire. Influential during the student uprising of Paris 1968, the situationists came up with a number of provocative and utopian slogans, along the lines of 'Be realistic, demand the impossible'. Many of its ideas were derived from Marx, particularly Marx's *Paris Manuscripts* that challenged the alienation created by capitalist work (Marx 1977). Such themes were combined with a rejection of parties and unions. Situationism was influenced by the libertarian group Socialisme ou Barbarie (Plant 1992). Situationist use of art can be found in Reclaim the Streets' anti-capitalist actions and the Situationist International is seen as an influence on Italian autonomism by some authors. The council communists who rejected Lenin's creation of a disciplined centralised party and supported workers' control equally combined Marxist theory with anarchist principles (Smart 1978). Anti-capitalist ideas are often a melange of council socialism, situationism, green anarchism and cultural theory.

Michael Albert, editor of *Z* magazine, has developed the concept of 'Parecon', shorthand for participatory economics, based loosely on council communist and anarchistic economics. Property is owned socially instead of by private individuals, and economic decisions are made by a process of dialogue, known as 'iteration', between worker and consumer councils. Albert describes his scheme in the following terms: 'Participatory economics as proposed in this book combines social ownership, participatory planning allocation, council structure, balanced job complexes, remuneration for effort and sacrifice, and participatory self-management with no class differentiation' (Albert 2004: 24). He has argued in some detail that a participatory economy would increase human welfare compared to the present state- and market-based economies (Albert 2004).

The lived anarchy of, say, autonomist squatters in South London or the Zapatistas or unemployed Argentinians organising after the virtual collapse of the formal economy also provides a model of what is possible. For example, the *piqueteros* in Argentina, a network of the unemployed who picket roads, demand subsidies from the government and self-organise their own economies:

> Carlos, an unemployed telephone technician in his fifties, is part of one of the most radical branches of the *piqueteros*, the MTD (Movement of Unemployed Workers). His group is transforming a huge, abandoned electronics factory into a self-managed organic farm, clinic, and media centre. He said that his most profound political moment since the December 2001 uprising was seeing three young *piqueteros* faint from hunger. 'Our main aim now is to have enough bread for each other ... After that, we can concentrate on other things.' (Notes from Nowhere 2003: 394)

Believing in a 'solidarity economy', they get together twice a week, a group of 70-odd people in a circle, and make decisions about what to produce and how to go about it.

> We have a group building sewage systems, and another that helps people who only have tin roofs put proper roofs on their houses. There is a press group that produces our newsletter and makes links with the outside media. We have the *Copa de Leche*, which provides a glass of milk to children and a free meal every day. We have a store that distributes second-hand clothes, two new bakeries, vegetable plots, and a library. (Notes from Nowhere 2003: 394–5)

I have been at meetings of squatters in the UK with 20–30 individuals planning how to open up new flats, create a social centre, or collect fruit and veg thrown out of Covent Garden market. They may not go smoothly but they at least provide an experiment in an economy that seeks to move beyond market and state control. People can get together and make decisions.

During the Spanish Civil War in the 1930s, the country's huge anarchist movement fought against Franco's forces, which were eventually to impose a totalitarian dictatorship. At the same time they collectivised property and built local economies based on anarchist principles. Within industrialised towns and cities, the anarchist union the CNT found it relatively easy to reorganise factory production based on a system of workers' control. In Alcoy, the second largest city in Alicante, 20,000 workers were organised into councils that ran everything from weapons production to hairdressers. 'In spite of all the monumental difficulties, one big fact stands out: in Alcoy 20,000 workers organized in their syndicates administered production, coordinated economic activities, and proved that industry can be operated better in every respect than capitalism, while still assuring freedom and justice for all' (Leval 1990b: 106). In Catalonia the anarchist workers were able to produce millions of rounds of bullets, bombs and hand grenades to fight Franco's armies (Souchy 1990b: 96). In the countryside peasants were more than happy to produce collectively in Spain, and even Marx admitted that peasant communism based on the traditional *mir* (prerevolutionary Russian peasant commune) might have allowed Russia to move from feudalism to socialism in one leap (Desai 2004: 98). At one point half of Spain's oranges were grown by anarchist farmers (Leval 1990c: 124). Many anarchist rural communities abolished money, produced what they felt was needed and redistributed goods from warehouses.

Commenting on anarchist economics in 1930s Spain, Perirats also noted:

> The realization of these libertarian projects was abandoned with the destruction of the collectives by the combined military might of the fascist powers and (to their everlasting disgrace) the attacks of the Communist armies and their civilian allies in August, 1937, six months after the conclusion of the Congress.
>
> It is axiomatic that revolutionary programs, however important, do not make revolutions. The impact of Revolution must be studied at its source: among the people, in the cities and the villages, the factories and the farms, where the creative efforts of the workers shaped the character of the Revolution. (Perirats 1990: 128)

Anarchism almost vanished during the twentieth century. Franco and the Stalinists destroyed the Spanish anarchist movement; it disappeared even earlier in Italy, and Lenin put the Russian anarchists out of action. In Britain the anarchists were largely absorbed by the creation of the Labour and Communist parties. During the last 20 years, particularly since the collapse of the Soviet Union and most other communist states, anarchism has revived. Increasingly, young people alienated from formal politics describe themselves as anarchists. The anarchist approach suggests that protest need not be aimed at achieving minor changes in government policies but may be seen as a way of trying to create a new society. Thus Reclaim the Streets, a key network that helped to kick off the new anti-capitalist movement, proclaimed:

> Direct action enables people to develop a new sense of self-confidence and an awareness of their individual and collective power. Direct action is founded on the idea that people can develop the ability for self-rule only through practice, and proposes that all persons directly decide the important issues facing them. Direct action is not just a tactic, it is individuals asserting their ability to control their own lives and to participate in social life without the need for mediation or control by bureaucrats or professional politicians. Direct action encompasses a whole range of activities, from organising coops to engaging in resistance to authority. Direct action places moral commitment above positive law. Direct action is not a last resort when other methods have failed, but the preferred way of doing things. (RTS leaflet distributed July 1996)

Such an understanding of the anarchic power of grassroots action is apparent in Hardt and Negri's *Empire*, with its emphasis on the actions of the multitude rather than that of limited policy change.

FOUCAULT ON RIOTING

Michael Ryan, an editor of Negri's *Marx Beyond Marx*, suggests that post-modernism is 'the philosophic equivalent of autonomy' and is most strongly associated with 'Deleuze, Derrida, Foucault and Lyotard' (Ryan 1991: 214). Indeed, Hardt and Negri draw heavily upon a number of post-modernist thinkers; especially Michel Foucault and Gilles Deleuze. Deleuze and Foucault, in turn, are largely inspired by a tradition of philosophy opposed to the grand theorising of Hegel. Given the autonomists' Marxist credentials, this is something of a paradox because Hegel is usually seen as Marx's most important philosophical source. Hegel is criticised for his determinism, which is seen as putting people in the service of a grand historical process, which finds spirit achieving its fulfilment in human society. According to post-modernists, Hegel limits human history to a series of laws.

Lyotard argues in *The Postmodern Condition* that post-modernism implies scepticism towards grand narratives or big stories that explain history, such as those of Hegel and Marx (Lyotard 1984). Post-modernism has also tended to argue that language or knowledge is power rather than economic forces. Post-modernism is equally opposed to rationalism, arguing that attempts to scientifically understand human society are flawed and oppressive.

The post-theories tend for a number of reasons to be seen as anti-Marxist. Marxism is normally seen as strongly influenced by Hegel with its emphasis on the historical process of human development. Post-modernism's opposition to grand narratives means that it cannot discuss capitalism as a system that exploits humanity and despoils nature; it tends to consist of anti-political arguing that attempts to liberate humanity lead to oppression. Thus political action to oppose capitalism seems futile from a post-modern perspective.

Such a rejection of grand narratives is linked to a general scepticism. Post-modernists reject the idea that human societies can be investigated so as to produce truth claims. It is impossible to prove or disprove a particular idea. Scepticism is linked to moral and political relativism, no one stance is seen as being intrinsically 'right' or 'wrong'. The post-modernist Baudrilliard, who most of all is hated by Marxists and others who take in interest in philosophy while struggling for a better world, even went so far as to argue that the First Gulf War was not real but had the status of a video game. Lyotard captures the general post-philosophical distaste for Marxism when he notes: 'The mere recall of the well-known guidelines of Marxist criticism has something obsolete, even tedious, about it ... the ghost has now vanished, dragging the last grand historical narrative with it off the historical stage' (quoted in Dyer-Witheford 1999: 167).

An alternative attempt to use post-modernist insights to create radical politics has been undertaken by the post-Marxists Laclau and Mouffe (1985). Their rather abstract approach to politics suggests that the working class has declined and that instead of seeking communism the goal should be radical democracy. They argue that economic grievances have become secondary to struggles for identity and believe that movements can only succeed through processes of articulation to create new political subjects. Such high theory has been closely linked to the disintegration of the Communist Party of Great Britain and even to the rise of Blairism. While there are similarities between post-Marxism and autonomism, particularly when it comes to their understanding of modern capitalism, they seem diametrically opposed in most respects. The autonomists continue to seek resistance; the post-Marxists largely reject the politics of class conflict.

Hardt and Negri utilise thinkers normally seen as post-modern for an understanding of how power is produced. Foucault, Deleuze and Guattari argue that power develops on a small scale (the 'micro') as much as on a large scale (the 'molar'), through the use of surveillance and language. Foucault suggests that power, more properly termed 'biopower', rather than being primarily exercised at a macro level by the state, works in socially sophisticated societies at a micro level, producing subjects. Foucault argues that society has become governed by the logic of the panoptikon, which means 'all-(*pan*) seeing eye (*optikon*)'. He derived this metaphor from a prison design, where the guards could view prisoners from a tower situated in the centre of the structure. Discourse, a term equally key to Foucault's perspective, is normally understood as a form of socially situated speech such as the disempowering jargon of economists or the phraseology of priests (Foucault 1979, 1980, 1991). In a disciplinary society, Foucault suggests, repression is used to maintain domination by an elite, in a more advanced system of 'control' individual personalities are shaped so as to maintain rule (Foucault 1980). Foucault's argument – that a disciplinary society has made way for one based upon control – is mirrored in Negri's work by Marx's distinction between formal and real subsumption of labour. Capitalism produces personalities as well as laptops, pet food and exotic package holidays.

Gilles Deleuze supplies the authors of *Empire* with the concept of the multitude, which he borrowed along with the all-important distinction between power as domination and power as creativity from Spinoza. Indeed, Hardt and Negri claim that the two inspirations for their book are Marx's *Capital* and Deleuze and Guattari's *A Thousand Plateaus* (Hardt 2004: 169).

The idea that we have moved to a post-Fordist economy is also shared with the post-Marxists and derived from post-modern thinkers. Such an economy is based on knowledge, physical factory production is less significant, work is outsourced to distant parts of the globe and the traditional Western working class largely disappears. While for post-Marxists such as Laclau and Mouffe (1985) political opposition is based on the demands of new social movements no longer primarily concerned with economic need, for the autonomists the whole of society becomes a factory and the demands of the social movements can only be met by destroying capitalism. The creation of a new post-modern economy hinted at by authors like Naomi Klein in *No Logo* (2001a) is most fully explored in *Empire*.

The Mayday Monopoly group drew upon Foucault's themes of surveillance and biopower when they wrote:

> Our lives are monitored, analysed and regulated today as never before, as the ethos of the prison seeps out into everyday life. But resistance to this Panopticism is still possible; life can still be made spontaneous and free of instrumental control. We can start by following our desires, but in a world where our desires themselves are packaged and sold back to us. (London Mayday Collective 2001: 38)

The anti-capitalist movement at its most playful seems to draw upon notions that the distinction between culture and economics has been eroded in a post-Fordist economy. Brands are subverted through subvertising, which involves stencilling and graffiti to erode the codes of Nike and McDonald's. Deleuze and his co-author Guattari in books such as their *Capitalism and Schizophrenia* advocate nomadic action based on marginal groups (Deleuze and Guattari 1988).

Deleuze and Guattari are also important for autonomism in their emphasis on 'immanence', which means finding hope in the material and the present rather than seeking salvation in transcending mundane human efforts. They reject all grand plans that see an external hand guiding humanity. Such an emphasis on immanence is a rather pagan virtue that, despite their complex, some would say mad, theorising, roots them to the struggle of human beings to build a less oppressive and alien society. Immanence is broadly speaking a product of their understanding of Spinoza and is set against the transcendence of Hegel (Hardt and Negri 2001a: 326; Ryan 1991: 216). The materialism of Deleuze and Guattari provides an alternative to the transcendent analysis of Hegal which sees the real world as a vehicle for the movement of the world spirit.

EMPIRE AS A PURE MODEL OF CAPITAL

Having outlined the sources of autonomist ideas it is now tentatively possible to discuss some of the main themes presented within *Empire* and the broader autonomist approach to globalisation. First, working-class resistance explains globalisation. Workers have pushed up pay and conditions, so multinational corporations relocate or outsource so as to push wages back down. Firms exploit the low-cost conditions of Export Processing Zones where repression can be used to prevent wages rising. Globalisation is a product of working-class victory rather than defeat. The Vietcong, the Fiat workers, the British miners and other working-class insurgents have propelled it. These forces wrecked the Keynesian system, which maintained economic peace by providing higher pay linked to productivity; a measure of state intervention in the market and welfare state. When Keynesianism no longer worked, the empire evolved as an alternative form of global regulation (Hardt and Negri 2001a: 179). Cleaver notes: 'Capitalist imperialism, fleeing the obstacles created by class struggle at home, spreads its class antagonism across the globe. This is the moment of the world market, but also of the global factory and the international ruling class' (Cleaver 1991: xxv).

Rather than the old imperialism identified by Lenin, Luxemburg and Hobson (see Chapter 6) where various states fought each other for economic and political dominance, the new imperialism is based on one global entity. Empire has no country and exists globally. Nowhere is truly outside of empire, it has run out of frontiers to cross and further colonisation in the geographical sense is impossible. The old imperialism was analogous to Foucault's notion of the disciplinary society, with gunboat diplomacy being used to extend and maintain exploitation. While the US looks as if it dominates the globe, domination has largely escaped from state control and now circulates on a global basis (Hardt and Negri 2001a: xiv). The WTO, the IMF and the UN act as judicial institutions of Empire; thus even the world's one superpower prefers to act in 'collaboration with others under the umbrella of the United Nations' (Hardt and Negri 2001a: 309).

Empire runs on fear of unemployment and poverty through the operation of global markets in finance and investment. A country that resists the market is consigned to the discipline created by falling share values, currency and investment. A truly national economic policy is impossible. Even the US is threatened by the sovereignty of empire: if debt grows too high, for example, market forces make economic growth unsustainable for the country. *Do or Die!* noted:

Speculation is directed at those countries whose domestic policies are in some way incompatible with global competitivity requirements, i.e. those who have not made sufficient attempts to subjugate or co-opt workers or who display any weakness by bowing to pressure over controlling public finance and social expenditure. Those countries which have begun a 'healthy restructuring' program are rewarded with currency stability and the loyalty of the speculators. (Anon. 1999b: 49)

Instead of using external territories to offload excess production that cannot be sold to domestic populations who lack purchasing power, as in Rosa Luxemburg's analysis, exploitation has moved inwards. Thus as the price and profits generated from manufactured goods fall, capitalism commodifies new areas of life to maintain profit: 'Capital no longer looks outside but rather inside its domain and its expansion is thus intensive rather than extensive' (Hardt and Negri 2001a: 272). Instead of selling to new markets, within empire, we are increasingly sold the services of personal trainers and encouraged to buy brands produced symbolically as well as physically.

The global sovereignty of empire has been made possible both by deregulation (privatisation plus the removal of governmental controls on business) and the creation of new communication technologies such as the Internet. It has created a new global economy where the social factory rather than old-style mass production is key. Work is increasingly based not on production but knowledge and care:

> [T]he role of industrial factory labor has been reduced and priority given instead to communicative, cooperative, and affective labor. In the postmodernization of the global economy, the creation of wealth tends ever more toward what we will call biopolitical production, the production of social life itself, in which the economic, the political, and the cultural increasingly overlap and invest one another. (Hardt and Negri 2001a: xiii)

An economy based on intellectual and emotional work leads to the multitude. The multitude can produce because of their ability to manipulate knowledge and care. Empire generates resistance to itself in the form of highly skilled, highly mobile workers who have both grievances against the social factory and the ability to produce autonomously. The multitude are the new face of the international working class: peasants in Mexico who can use the internet; squatters in Peckham who can exploit their law degrees to live a little longer without paying rent; old ladies who sit in the road to protest for pension rises; anarchists who can climb buildings and break locks on government doors; call-centre operatives who know how to sabotage the phones without being caught; students who can operate pirate radio stations; cyclists who can use webcams to broadcast their actions against car culture on the internet. The new anti-capitalism has no need of parties, NGOs, pressure groups or leaders. It is energetic and endlessly mobile. The multitude 'is in fact the foundation of all social creativity' (Hardt 2004: 173). Cyber-capitalism creates a cyber-proletariat busy digging the grave of empire.

STRATEGY

Autonomists do not believe in constructing a blueprint for a post-capitalist society, nor do Hardt and Negri develop a detailed strategy for getting there. Alternatives, they believe, will emerge from the struggles of the multitude; it is foolish for writers to think that they can produce great plans that their readers will then translate smoothly into reality. Nonetheless, a number of assumptions about how neo-liberal globalisation can be challenged emerge from *Empire*. For Hardt and Negri, the resort to localism is impossible; globalisation must be accelerated with workers migrating in waves and technologies speeding away. Instead of looking to past certainties because capitalism cannot be reined in, we must seek the security of an utterly mobile and constantly mutating world. Nation states, far from being better than global sovereignty, were equally repressive. The process of globalisation creates the multitude. The multitude has the power to create another world. Hardt and Negri insist time after time that nowhere is outside empire, rejecting measures to create local economies insulated from the world market.

There is a tacit assumption that mobile (both socially and geographically) individuals are able to develop new social codes appropriate to a post-capitalist society. This notion of nomadism is drawn from Deleuze and reflects the title of Melucci's study of social movements *Nomads of the Present* (Melucci 1989). The nomads living on the margins create new ways of life; the squats and protest camps are high-pressure factories where experimenters can forge alternative ways of life. Negri notes in *Marx Beyond Marx*, 'to be a Communist today now means to live as a Communist' (Negri 1991: xvi)

The vision in *Empire* often looks like a re-coding of Marx's *Capital* read rather superficially. Capitalism/empire is a product of class struggle and in turn creates the conditions via a global market, technological development and the construction of new subjectivities for its own destruction and the introduction of communist utopia. Sometimes *Empire* looks like a parody rather than a recoding, a giant joke from the post-modern Marxist anarchist intellectuals at the expense of the rest of us. For example, towards the end of *Empire*, having long rejected notions of liberal democracy such as universal rights, parliamentary representation and the mediation of political organisations, Hardt and Negri suddenly produce three political demands to petition from representative governments. The sudden insertion of reforms to be gained from the state or empire seems to cut across all the militancy and sophistication of their prose, suggesting that they don't take their profoundest ideas seriously and are merely testing us with contradiction to see if we can read a big book to the end.

Perhaps the joke is really upon the moderate defenders of capitalism, the likes of Soros and Stiglitz whom we met in Chapter 2. The three demands are: the right to universal migration; a basic income scheme; and finally the right to economic reappropriation, control over and self-management of one's economic existence (Hardt and Negri 2001a: 396–407). Each demand is 'reasonable' and follows from the economic case made in *Empire*. How can capital, that demands the dismantling of borders for goods and finance, fix peoples in one place? The basic income scheme, long promoted by social creditors, greens and other radicals, is almost mainstream. In a mild form it was supported by Milton Friedman, and in the form of tax credits by Gordon Brown, British finance minister in the first two Blair governments. Given the nature of the social factory where society as a whole helps produce all goods and services, why should those outside the formal economy not be paid as they help sustain economic activity, particularly where they care for others such as elderly relatives and children? Finally individuals should control the process by which they produce goods and services. Three very moderate demands that cannot reasonably be denied, but lead to a society where individuals are free to move where they like, where income is separated from work and work is controlled by the multitude.

Hardt and Negri seem to have produced a set of anti-capitalist rights that can be put to the mainstream. Autonomism has long advocated the virtues of refusal, seeing resistance as productive. Resistance rather than negotiating for rights is a feature of the more radical elements of the anti-capitalist movement. The black bloc more directly participate in the great refusal, damaging property and fighting with the police. They argue that far from being mindless vandals, they are motivated by an autonomist philosophy that rejects both the market and the state as innately oppressive. A black bloc communiqué after the Seattle protest, where the bloc were widely criticised as being destructive and distracting from the aims of more moderate activists, is instructive:

Property destruction isn't a violent activity, unless it destroys lives or causes pain. Private (especially corporate) property is thus infinitely more violent than any action taken against it.

Personal property is distinguished from private property. The former is based upon use – each having what s/he needs. The premise of private property is that we have something someone else needs. Those who accrue more of what others need (or want) can wield greater control over others (and what others perceive as needs/desires), thereby increasing profits to themselves.

Advocates of 'free trade' want to push this process to its logical conclusion: a few industry monopolists with ultimate control over everyone else. Advocates of 'fair trade' want to mitigate this process via government regulations, which superficially impose 'humanitarian standards'. We despise both positions. Private property – and capitalism, by extension – is intrinsically violent and repressive ... When we smash a window, we aim to destroy the thin veneer of legitimacy that surrounds private property rights. At the same time, we exorcise the set of violent and destructive social relationships which has been imbued in almost everything around us. (ACME 1999: 125)

Such strategies of property destruction rest not only on high spirits or hooliganism, but on a particular reading of political economy. While the politics of refusal remain necessary Hardt and Negri argue that 'the creative forces of the multitude that sustain empire are also capable of autonomously constructing ... a new constituent power that will one day take us through and beyond Empire' (Hardt and Negri 2001a: xv). With added ecological gloss, and a note of transcendence, *Do or Die!* writes:

It's time to celebrate our resistance: digger diving, window smashing, pleasant picnicking, office occupying, hoody wearing, GM trashing, squat cracking, sun lit lovin', machine burning, treeliving – total fucking anarchy ... It's time to strategise how to make a real impact on this apocalypse. Look seriously at our strengths and weaknesses and pull together to resist. The empire is powerful but the spring is growing. It's a challenge like no other, but with love, luck and hard resolve we can transcend. (Anon. 2003: 1)

Ryan is also optimistic, 'Productive force, once liberated from the constraints of bourgeois productive relations, shows itself to be immediately constitutive, and it shows the possibility that the world can be transformed according to desire' (Ryan 1991: 219).

CRITICISM IS PRAISE

Criticism is praise. Well, perhaps not, but the autonomist tradition was almost entirely ignored by other Marxists and the academic world. In contrast *Empire* has given rise to a mass of often bitter denigration, including two entire book-length collections of critical reviews, indicating that at the very least it is seen as important enough to challenge (Balakrishnan 2003; Passavant and Dean 2004). Post-Marxists have noticed that they have a rival form of analysis that uses the insights of post-modernism, while other Marxists have been stung by the ability of anarchists to mobilise on the streets and autonomists to attempt to explain the trajectory of class conflict. Academic and political rivalry help to explain the venom heaped upon Hardt and Negri but do not disguise the fact that their ambitious approach contains a number of flaws.

First, Hardt and Negri have been seen as parroting the hyperglobalist thesis that is put most strongly by the fervent defenders of capitalism. Indeed, Ellen Meiksins Wood asks whether they have produced 'A Manifesto for Global Capitalism' (Wood 2003a). If markets are all-powerful it is impossible to defend welfare states and workers' rights or to prevent environmental standards from sliding. Hardt and Negri provide an exaggerated and pessimistic account borrowed from the political enemies of the left. Clearly the European Union has managed (despite economic decline in Germany during the early years of the third millennium) to maintain a social chapter, which defends working conditions without capital simply fleeing to Cambodia or El Salvador. Their analysis, which swings dialectically from pessimism to unbridled optimism, could be interpreted as a call to support capitalism, so as to allow capitalism to continue growing until it collapses. They can be seen as reinventing a sort of simplistic Marxism that challenges any attempt to fight for change now as ineffective.

The dismissal of imperialism seems inappropriate given the Second Gulf war and US attempts to control states across the globe, often for nakedly material and rather traditional economic motives. Even in the Clinton era when *Empire* was being written, rather than the Bush presidency when it was published and read, the US appeared rather dominant and domineering. The global institutions of the IMF, the UN and the World Bank are powerless in comparison. The empirical evidence for sovereignty of Empire seems thin, when even currency movements can be resisted by powerful states, at least temporarily.

Critics argue that since nation states have a great deal of power, global politics is best understood by looking at the conflict between rival empires or the domination of the US empire (Bull 2003). Capitalism is not one smooth global wired project, especially not in Iraq or Cuba. Unfortunately, their analysis 'aligns Hardt and Negri against other leftists who call for resistance against global forces' (Tilly 2003: 27).

Equally, the economic analysis of *Empire* seems to be based on the rather superficial assumptions of a post-Fordist knowledge-based economy. While drawing diametrically opposed political conclusions (that capitalism is triumphant and basically benevolent) post-Marxists advocating a new society of post-modern knowledge-based work, equally seemed to ignore the fact that even in a supposedly virtual economy farmers have to grow yams and old-style mass workers have to make the computers used in the social factory. Brands may be virtual but trainers and burgers remain physical. In short, the political economy of *Empire* is incomplete.

Academic critics have had no serious comment to make on the productivism of *Empire*. Read literally, it takes us back to the worst excess of socialism that celebrates the maturing of productive forces. The excess of capitalism in ruining rivers, chopping down forests, building autobahns and poisoning our DNA remains necessary to pull us towards utopia. A grand narrative indeed.

The subjective reading of Marxism, while stressing that human beings make history rather than being victims of structural change, unfortunately produces a very reductionist approach to political economy. For social creditors, everything is about money; for autonomists, everything can be reduced to rising labour costs. However, capitalism is not just a boxing match. Working-class struggle is mediated and the crises of capitalism are plural, not singular.

The strategic assumptions of autonomism can also be challenged. Negri, in particular from the 1970s to date, has overestimated the militancy of the working class. In an era where the traditional left has appeared to suffer defeat time after time, autonomism reminds us that capitalism is shaped by the resistance it faces. Unfortunately revolutionary optimism is no substitute for cool analysis. Hardt and Negri rightly bemoan the conservative uses Gramsci has been put to by the post-modernists, observing:

> Communist and militant before all else, tortured and killed by fascism and ultimately by the bosses who financed fascism – poor Gramsci was given the gift of being considered the founder of a strange notion of hegemony

that leaves no place for a Marxian politics. (see, for example, Ernesto Laclau and Chantel Mouffe, *Hegemony and Socialist Strategy: Towards a Radical Democratic Politics*). (Hardt and Negri 2001a: 451)

Yet is it not also a secular Marxist sin to reverse Gramsci's dictum that proclaims the need for 'optimism of the will, pessimism of the intellect'? Whatever happens, the working class is strong and the autonomists keep smiling as the police smash down their doors, burn their books, bulldoze their squats, kill their pets and imprison their children. Hardt and Negri reimport the Hegelian grand narrative of capitalism as a process that creates its own collapse. Indeed, Sergio Bologna, who coined the term 'tribe of moles', attacked Negri along these lines, noting:

> There have been many small (or big) battles, but in their course the political composition of the class has changed substantially in the factories, and certainly not in the direction indicated by Negri ... In sum there has been a reassertion of reformist hegemony over the factories, one that is brutal and relentless in its efforts to dismember the class left and expel it from the factory. (quoted in Callinicos 2001: 44)

All forms of organised opposition, such as Communist or Green parties, and even anarchist federations, are seen as serving the capitalist powers. Strategy involves removing all such organisational forms of mediation, so the priests and communists and squatters can unite as the multitude. This approach leaves an ocean of questions unanswered. One of the lessons of organising anarchist economics in Spain is that prior organisation is vital. Anarchist trade unions active for decades found it relatively easy to socialise the means of production (Dolgoff 1990).

Equally if postmodern theory from Deleuze teaches that we are desiring machines that lack an unchanging ego or solid identity, how can we be oppressed, let alone seek liberation? While the evidence is against the existence of the ego and human psychology may be the study of our internal multitude, such issues demand further examination. Nomadism is necessary to generate new social codes, but can constantly mobile populations create the community cohesion necessary to make a non-capitalist economy work? Maybe not. Less extravagant praise for the marginal and mad might lead to a more plausible account of how a new economy can be created. Vast generalisations are the order of the day together with poetic homilies that seem to owe something to a kind of utopian Catholicism. *Empire* finishes both beautifully and (for those with a distaste for theology) rather alarmingly, with a comparison between St Francis of Assisi and the communist militant:

> Consider his work. To denounce the poverty of the multitude he adopted that common condition and discovered there the ontological power of a new society. The communist militant does the same, identifying in the common condition of the multitude its enormous wealth. Francis in opposition to nascent capitalism refused every instrumental discipline, and in opposition to the mortification of the flesh (in poverty and in the constituted order) he posed a joyous life, including all of being and nature, the animals, sister moon, brother sun, the birds of the field, the poor and exploited humans, together against the will of power and corruption. Once again in postmodernity we find ourselves in St Francis's situation, posing against the misery of power the joy of being. This is a revolution that no power will control – because biopower and communism, cooperation and revolution remain together, in love, simplicity, and also innocence. This is the irrepressible lightness and joy of being communist. (Hardt and Negri 2001a: 413)

For all the flaws, rhetoric and avoided issues, *Empire* and the broader autonomist tradition should be praised as intellectually productive and engaged. The autonomists are orientated to activism and will work to promote the analysis appropriate to accelerate change. They are not afraid to think because thinking must proceed fighting. Their integration of post-modern thought and Marxism at times seems unconvincing, but it is necessary and brave, providing ways of examining both the molar and micro of change. In exploring autonomism one is provoked to reflect deeply, which can be no bad thing.

Autonomism is hostile in one important sense to the very notion of economics. Economics, rather than being a neutral method of regulating activity to produce goods and services as efficiently as possible, is simply a method of control. The insight/suggestion is that economics is in fact always a form of politics, a way of constraining the power of the working class/multitude to allow capitalism to survive. Marx, while he bitterly fought with anarchists like Bakunin, argued that the state would wither away in a communist order. Despite the authoritarianism developed in his name by the likes of Stalin, Marx was, in the everyday sense, an anarchist. Hardt, Negri, Marx, Deleuze and the black bloc have their differences, but all agree that both the state and the market distort the realisation of human potential.

Despite the inadequacies of *Empire* and autonomism, at least two other important insights are provided. First, capital rules, to the extent it rules at all, virtually through markets, and such a mechanism, while far from complete, increasingly dominates global politics and society. The US invades, global trading blocs clash as in the old imperialism, nation states have some power, but the market creates global sovereignty above and beyond such localisms. This is *potestas* or constituent power: if one likes, it can be described as force, oppression or 'power over'. Also the notion of *potentia*, creative power, 'power to', rings true to participants of the kinds of protest outlined at the start of this chapter. Unmediated by formal organisation, the revolution is made by loose but intelligent militant networks. *Potentia* fuels empire and can transform it. The market faces the multitude. Academic critics of *Empire* have little appreciation of either *potestas* based on control by the constitution of subjectivity or of the opposition of *potentia* fuelled by a global economy. Any sophisticated account of capitalism can learn from autonomism. Equally, autonomism, in the broadest sense of a reflective, grassroots but occasionally violent anarchism, is a key part of the multitude's movement against neo-liberal capitalism.

8
Marx on the Seashore:
Ecosocialist Alternatives

Beth Collar

At first sight, environmentalists or conservationists are nice, slightly crazy guys whose main purpose in life is to prevent the disappearance of blue whales or pandas. The common people have more important things to think about, for instance how to get their daily bread ... However, there are in Peru a very large number of people who are environmentalists ... they might reply, 'ecologist your mother', or words to that effect ... Are not the town of Ilo and the surrounding villages which are being polluted by the Southern Peru Copper Corporation truly environmentalist? Is not the village of Tambo Grande in Pirura environmentalist when it rises like a closed fist and is ready to die in order to prevent strip-mining in its valley? Also, the people of the Mantaro Valley who saw their little sheep die, because of the smoke and waste from La Oroya smelter. (Hugo Blanco quoted in Guha and Martinez-Alier 1997: 24)

For my own part right glad I am to have got rid of all company, even that of my books. I have taken a private lodging which fronts the sea ... but the air is wonderfully pure and reinvigorating, and you have here at the same time sea air and mountain air. I have become myself a sort of walking stick, running up and down the whole day, and keeping my mind in that state of nothingness which Buddhaism considers the climax of human bliss. (Marx 1987: 241–2)

Anti-globalisation has an ecosocialist shade. Some socialist anti-capitalists are also green and some green anti-capitalists are also red. There are strong socialist currents in most Green parties around the world and there are a number of red-green organisations like the Green Left Party in the Netherlands. Ecosocialists combine aspects of green and socialist thought to argue that capitalism is the cause of ecological crisis. Ecosocialists believe that the green approach has not gone deep enough, while they criticise most of the left for failing to take environmental destruction seriously. Nonetheless, there is a distinct, albeit a minority, ecosocialist tradition that can be traced back through history. The road to a society that is green and red will be a long and hard one with no short cuts based on nationalising the banks or electing a few more green or socialist politicians to office.

The journal *Capitalism Nature Socialism* is one source of such an approach. Its founding editor, James O'Connor, has developed the concept of the second contradiction of capitalism, showing how environmental degradation caused by capitalism feeds back into economic crisis for the system (O'Connor 1991). Joel Kovel's book *The Enemy of Nature* provides a detailed ecosocialist account of globalisation (2002). Kovel, who stood unsuccessfully for the US Green Party presidential nomination in 2000 against Ralph Nader, argues that globalisation is fuelled by capitalism and gives rises to accelerated economic growth that is wrecking the planet. Such growth is not a by-product of corporations or the money power but is built into the very DNA of our economic system. He argues that the basic contradiction between use values and exchange values identified by Marx is at the core of the crisis. John Bellamy Foster (2000, 2002) and Paul Burkett (1999) have suggested that Marx's ideas, especially his theme of a 'metabolism' or interaction between humanity and the rest of nature, is a rich source of ecological ideas.

Ecosocialism has deep roots. William Morris, the poet, designer and novelist, shaped a distinctly English school of ecosocialism in the 1880s and 1890s. Aran Gare has chronicled in some detail the activities of a generation of green scientists and thinkers who tried to shape the Russian Revolution in an ecological direction before being purged (Gare 1996). During the early 1970s Professor Barry Commoner developed a leftist response to the limits to growth thesis suggesting that capitalist technologies rather than overpopulation threatened global ecosystems (1972). Rudolf Bahro, an East Germany intellectual, fused red and green in books like *The Alternative in Eastern Europe* (1978) and *Socialism and Survival* (1982). In Australia the Marxist theorist and activist Alan Roberts showed how unfulfilled human needs fuelled rampant consumerism (Roberts 1979). Another Australian, Ted Trainer in *Abandon Affluence!* (1985), has argued that socialists must embrace a society based on meeting need rather than the wants created by capitalism. Much theoretical work has been done by writers such as Ariel Salleh (1997) and Mary Mellor (1992) to develop a feminist-socialist approach to ecological concern. In many countries in the south of the globe, activists have developed an environmentalism of the poor, which links ecosocialist sentiments to day-to-day struggles against globalisation (Guha and Martinez-Alier 1997).

This chapter provides a survey of the ecosocialist tradition and the environmentalism of the poor, moves onto the red-green approach to globalisation and makes a nod towards the ecological Marx, before evaluating red-green alternatives.

THE ANTI-CAPITALISM OF THE POOR

Ecosocialists argue that the ecological crisis is already with us, particularly in the south of the globe where the capitalist production of basic commodities is degrading the environment. Such degradation inevitably leads to poverty for much of the world's population. Crops are produced for exports that take water from subsistence agriculturalists, thereby increasing the incidence of hunger. Forests are enclosed, felled and replaced with fast-growing cash crop species like eucalyptus. Such development, as we have seen in previous chapters, makes the poor poorer by separating them from their local means of production.

The enclosure of the commons identified by both Marx and the subsistence ecofeminists is an extremely important theme for ecosocialists. They argue that economic growth and the expansion of capitalism far from being necessary to remove poverty leads to poverty. For ecosocialists, it is utterly inappropriate to think of a contradiction between zero growth as a means of reducing environmental damage and the need for increased production to remove the problems of the poorest. The 'poor' have access to the means of production they need to survive and even prosper but such non-monetised communal means of production are unmeasured by GNP figures. Neo-liberal globalisation is just part of the long struggle of the state and commercial interests to steal from those who subsist. Neo-globalisation is destructive of the environment and as such removes access to the resources that sustain ordinary people across the globe.

Authors such as Rumachandra Guha and Juan Martinez-Alier argue in their 'varieties of environmentalism' thesis that there are two environmentalisms: the supposed environmentalism of the wealthy post-materialist north, and the environmentalism of the poor of the south of the globe. The 'environmentalism' of the north is partly a construct of academics and the media. It is based on the assumption that environmentalism is a non-essential and aesthetic demand of the relatively prosperous. As individuals become wealthier, they have the choice of being concerned with non-material issues. In the south, the environment is a source of communal wealth. Peasants and gatherers defend it because they know that if it is enclosed or destroyed they will find it difficult to survive. Globalisation stops people from producing for themselves, accelerates the creation of waste and then pushes the waste onto the very poorest.

The 'varieties of environmentalism' thesis needs to be adapted a little. First, it is not just in the south that global capitalism targets the poorest. In the north too, ecosocialists have identified an environmentalism of the poor, noting how poorer communities with less political influence tend to be dumped on. An environmental justice movement has grown up in the US, made up of working class and ethnic minority activists who are aware that toxic waste dumps, major highways and incinerators tend to be built in locations which are perceived to be socially marginal (Schlosberg 1999). Second, cultural appreciation of nature has long been combined with material demands. Some of the most radical deep ecology movements that reject the idea that non-human nature should primarily act as a resource for the human species come from poor and minority communities. However, the fact that such deep ecology of the poor comes from marginalised voices means that they are almost universally ignored by academics. The mainly African-American radical group/green religion MOVE comes to mind here. MOVE, founded in the 1970s by John Africa, argued for animal rights and ecological revolution from inner-city Philadelphia. Many of their supporters were killed or imprisoned by the US authorities. MOVE is almost universally ignored in histories of the green movement, along with other radical black environmental philosophies (Wall 1993).

THE END OF THE WORLD

Ecosocialists draw strongly upon the Marxist analysis identified in earlier chapters, yet while many Marxists celebrate economic growth as a means of raising the productive forces, the ecosocialists are strongly critical of capitalist growth. James O'Connor argues that capitalist growth tends to degrade the environment it depends upon to sustain growth. Capitalism by polluting drinking water, reducing soil fertility and breeding toxins, weakens the ability of both workers and nature to sustain growth. This second contradiction, like the primarily economic contradictions discussed by Marx, has a tendency to drive the system out of existence. O'Connor notes that to overcome environmental contradictions capitalism introduces new technologies that solve old environmental problems at the expense of creating new ones. Thus nuclear power is posited as an alternative to greenhouse-gas-producing fossil fuels; he also quotes Gary Snyder's contention that capitalism 'spreads its economic support system out far enough that it can afford to wreck one eco-system, and keep moving on' (O'Connor 1998: 181).

Some ecosocialists fear that the globalised economy is running out of fresh ecosystems to kill. Kovel presents a series of terrifying statistics to suggest that planetary ecology is bending if not breaking under the strain of environmental damage fuelled by neo-liberal globalisation. He notes how, between the first Earth Day in 1970 and 2000:

- oil consumption had increased from 46 million barrels a day to 73 million;
- natural gas extraction had increased from 34 trillion cubic feet per year to 95 trillion;

- coal extraction had gone from 2.2 billion metric tonnes to 3.8 billion;
- the global motor vehicle population had almost tripled, from 246 million to 730 million;
- air traffic had increased by a factor of six;
- the rate at which trees are consumed to make paper had doubled, to 200 million metric tonnes per year;
- human carbon emissions had increased from 3.9 million metric tonnes annually to an estimated 6.4 million – this despite the additional impetus to cut back caused by an awarness of global warming, which was not perceived to be a factor in 1970;
- average temperatures increased by 1 degree Fahrenheit – a disarmingly small number that, being unevenly distributed, translates into chaotic weather events (seven of the ten most destructive storms in recorded history having occurred in the last decade), and an unpredictable and uncontrollable cascade of ecological trauma – including now the melting of the North Pole during the summer of 2000, for the first time in 50 million years, and signs of the disappearance of the 'snows of Kilimanjaro' the year following;
- species were vanishing at a rate that has not occurred in 65 million years;
- fish were being taken at twice the rate as in 1970;
- 40 per cent of agricultural soils had been degraded;
- half of the forests had disappeared;
- half of the wetlands had been filled or drained;
- one-half of US coastal waters were unfit for fishing or swimming;
- despite concerted effort to bring to bay the emissions of ozone-depleting substances, the Antarctic ozone hole was the largest ever in 2000, some three times the size of the continental United States; meanwhile, 2000 metric tonnes of the substances that cause it continue to be emitted every day; and
- 7.3 billion metric tons of pollutants were released in the United States during 1999. (Kovel 2002: 3–4)

Kovel is convinced that such appalling statistics can be correlated with and explained by rising economic growth. Echoing the criticism of economic growth by greens noted in Chapter 4, he observes how between 1970 and 2000 global economic product rose by 250 per cent, from $16 trillion to $39 trillion. As we have seen, higher growth has increased global inequality. He argues that environmental damage will gradually rise like a tide. Incrementally, day-by-day, climatic conditions will become worse with the greenhouse effect, toxins will increase in our bodies and new diseases will evolve and spread as ecosystems are disrupted:

> If the world were a living organism, then any sensible observer would conclude that this 'growth' is a cancer that, if not somehow treated, means the destruction of human society, and even raises the question of the extinction of our species. The details are important and interesting, but less so that the chief conclusion – that irresistible growth, and the evident fact that this growth destabilizes and breaks down the natural ground necessary for human existence, means, in the plainest terms, that we are doomed under the present social order, and that we had better change it as soon as possible. (Kovel 2002: 5)

It is a sad irony that Kovel had to write the obituary of his eco-socialist co-worker Walt Sheasby who died of the effects of the West Nile virus, a disease spread by mosquitos that have travelled north through the state with rising temperatures. Sheasby wrote extensively on ecosocialism, was a founder of the Green Party in California and chronicled Marx's love of the environment and affinities with Zen. I come to the end of a sentence, scratch my head and think Walt will know, only to remember he won't be answering my emails any more.

While ecosocialists agree that capitalism is characterised in the third millennium by the activities of transnationals and the finance capital needs of the bank, even without such forces the market would tend to be destructive. Ecosocialists have a tradition of using the term 'imperialism', but imperialism based on the activities of monopolistic corporations is not enough to explain ecological destruction. For Kovel, the conflict between Islamic Jihadists and the Bush administration since the destruction of the Twin Towers in 2001 is a product of oil imperialism. However, things go deeper:

> As organized by the capitalist-industrial economy, progress and modernity require the limitless exploitation of energy resources: in a word, oil; and in another word, imperialist control over the oil-soaked parts of the earth, the chief parts of which happen to be inhabited by Islamic peoples. Thus the fundamentalists do not hate us because of our free life-style. They hate

us because of the ruin brought upon their societies in order to fuel that life style.

Nor does the ruin end with the direct effects of imperialism on the peoples of one region. The whole of terrestrial nature is afflicted with the by-products of capitalist expansion. The same process that brings corrupt dictatorships and violence from the skies also gives us global warming, indeed, the entire ecological crisis, that destabilization of the natural ground of society which puts the very idea of a future at risk.

The planes that slammed into the World Trade Center brought down more than great buildings and thousands of lives. They brought us up against the unfaced contradictions of our civilization. (<www.joelkovel.org> Beyond The Deadly Dance)

Kovel argues that the distinction between exchange values and use values outlined by Marx in chapter one of *Capital* is the essential insight for understanding both globalisation and the ecological and social ills that it unleashes. In an economy based upon the market, we do not directly produce goods because they are useful to us. We produce goods that we exchange for money that we can then use to exchange for other goods. This seems a sensible and convenient arrangement. However, we constantly have to sell if we are to buy. This means that we have to persuade others to buy our goods if we are to survive. A contradiction tends to develop between the usefulness of goods and their value from exchange. We thus have to sell goods that previously had no use to maintain our ability to buy goods and services. This tendency has a tendency to get out of hand.

In the third millennium, the contradiction between use and exchange values has accelerated to an astonishing gap. Abstract economic activity with no apparent use value commands billions, while concrete useful activity, particularly in the 'domestic' sphere of caring for kids, relatives, preparing basic foodstuffs (the subject of subsistence discussed in Chapter 4), is largely unrewarded. Producing for use is no priority at all. If goods were quite useless one might be reluctant to exchange them and this would lead to economic problems, For the moment, however, society is focused on exchange. If you buy this book instead of borrowing it from the library this increases exchange value, but it would be better ecologically and socially to provide books, CDs, DVDs, children's toys, tools, and so on, via libraries because this would circulate use values more widely. Anything that increases exchange values is encouraged in our society because it allows the market economy to function; however, this means that use values are largely ignored or achieved through duplication and waste.

For ecosocialists it is clearly not enough to reform the worst aspects of capitalism or to define capitalism in such a way that mild change is possible. Many of the anti-capitalists examined in these pages see capitalism as the poisoned out-growth of what is a basically sane system. The abolition of fractional reserve banking, localisation of economies, an element of state or community planning, for example, can be used to heal the system. Ecosocialists see the need for economic growth as built into the market. This takes us a long way from all of the elite theories of capitalism. Such elite theories are political rather than economic. They suggest that a particular class or even group of conspirators get together to design a globalising system that brings them immense personal wealth and power at the expense of poor and planet. Ecosocialist approaches suggest that the reality is even more worrying. Rather than there being a particular group who could be replaced, the system tends to self-perpetuate and is driven by apparently extra-human forces.

Kovel illustrates this contention with a discussion of the Bhopal disaster in India, when an incident at the Union Carbide plant led to the worst industrial accident of human history. This might be thought to be just another example of the many cases of transnationals wrecking people and planet for reasons of personal greed. Tens of thousands were killed and many more blinded, and nearly 20 years later the death toll is still mounting. Union Carbide blamed an unknown saboteur. Kovel has suggested that the reality is that a downturn in sales led to falling profits for Union Carbide. Like the virtual movements of power catalogued by Hardt and Negri, the malign magic of the stock market meant that falling profits were likely to translate into falling share values. Lower share values would encourage shareholders to sell, weakening the company. Therefore cuts were made in the operating costs of the Bhopal plant and, Kovel suggests, these cuts led to disaster: the abstract pressure of the market rather than the concrete activities of plotters led to this catastrophe. This is not to say that the catastrophe was inevitable, but it provides an example of how hunger for exchange values can lead to disaster (Kovel 2002: 28). John Bellamy Foster quotes Noam Chomsky to make this point:

> The Chairman of the board will always tell you that he spends his every waking hour laboring so that people will get the best possible products at the

cheapest possible price and work in the best possible conditions. But it is an institutional fact, independent of who the chairman of the board is, that he'd better be trying to maximize profit and market share, and if he doesn't do that, he's not going to be chairman of the board any more. If he were ever to succumb to the delusions that he expresses, he'd be out. (Foster 2002: 48)

Kovel argues that capitalism is like a virus spreading through the world, that moves extensively through geographical space and intensively into our very souls. Globalisation is driven by the crises of capitalism. To maintain profit firms must sell more and exploit labour with greater vigor. A falling profit rate can be overcome by a combination of exploiting labour more intensively (getting them to work harder) or extensively (getting them to worker for longer) and selling to new markets. To survive, capitalism therefore has to grow for ever. New economic niches must be exploited by constructing new needs. Capitalism, Luxemburg (1971) argued, needs an outside to colonise. Nature must be commodified by enclosing and exploiting new habitats. People must constantly consume more and work harder:

In 1992 alone U.S. business spent perhaps $1 trillion on marketing, simply convincing people to consume more and more goods. This exceeded by about $600 billion the amount spent on education – public and private – at all levels. Under these circumstances we can expect people to grow up with their heads full of information about saleable commodities, and empty of knowledge about human history, morality, culture, science, and the environment. What is most valued in such a society is the latest style, the most expensive clothing, the finest car. Hence, it is not surprising that more than 93 percent of teenage girls questioned in a survey conducted in the late 1980s indicated that their favorite leisure activity was to go shopping. (Foster 2002: 46–7)

Clearly, as the many activists and writers discussed in these pages show, capitalism keeps moving on to new areas. The process of privatisation encouraged by the WTO, IMF and World Bank means that new areas of corporate economic activity are developed to attempt to maintain profits.

Capitalism also has a psychological dimension. The system tends to select those who are most aggressive and inspired at increasing profit. Individuals in firms who decide that there is a kinder, gentler way of doing things or who have priorities other than profit trying to produce what is most ecological or useful, for example, either fail to rise to the top or are replaced:

> People who are genuinely forthcoming and disinterestedly helpful do not become managers of large capitalist firms. The tender-hearted are pushed off far down the ladder on which one ascends to such positions of power. For capital shapes as well as selects the kinds of people who create these events. (Kovel 2002: 38)

Every member of a capitalist firm could be replaced by another and the system would still maintain its trajectory. Capitalism colonises us internally and makes us dream of shopping.

Capitalism is a system that has evolved out of human action but seems to have developed its own inhuman power. Capitalists recognising that the end of the world may ultimately be bad for business will try to find ways of creating sustainable growth. Companies will seek corporate solutions to the ecological crisis. However, as far as market players are concerned, declining profits are a threat today and pollution a threat tomorrow, so share values are likely to take precedence over indices of species destruction.

John Bellamy Foster summaries the ecosocialist account of globalisation by comparing it to a giant treadmill:

> First, built into this global system, and constituting its central rationale, is the increasing accumulation of wealth by a relatively small section of the population at the top of the social pyramid. Second, there is a long-term movement of workers away from self-employment and into wage jobs that are contingent on the continual expansion of production. Third, the competitive struggle between businesses necessitates on pain of extinction of the allocation of accumulated wealth to new, revolutionary technologies that serve to expand production. Fourth, wants are manufactured in a manner that creates an insatiable hunger for more. Fifth, government becomes increasingly responsible for promoting national economic development, while ensuring some degree of "social security" for a least a portion of its citizens. Sixth, the dominant means of communication and education are part of the treadmill, serving to reinforce its priorities and values.
>
> [...] Everyone, or nearly everyone, is part of this treadmill and is unable or unwilling to get off. Investors and managers are driven by the need to accumulate wealth and to expand the scale of their operations in order to prosper within a globally competitive milieu. For the vast majority the commitment to the treadmill is more limited and indirect: they simply need

to obtain jobs at liveable wages. But to retain those jobs and to maintain a given standard of living in these circumstances it is necessary, like the Red Queen in *Through the Looking Glass*, to run faster and faster in order to stay in the same place. (Foster 2002: 44–5)

The market keeps us marching to the clock, ecosocialists are at one with the autonomists and subsistence ecofeminists on this point. Boredom, the commute to work, Export Processing Zones and injury because of poor health and safety are just some of the worst symptoms of a disease called 'paid employment'. The market must be broken not only because it kills the planet, but also because it kills those of us who work a little every day.

SOCIALISM AND ECOLOGY

Simply moving to a planned socialist economy will not suffice for thinkers like Kovel and Bellamy Foster. Environmental concern seems to be on a tick list of modern socialist virtues but rarely goes very deep. Kovel notes how David McNally in his book *Against the Market* (McNally 1993) argues that production should be expanded without any thought of the environmental ill effects (Kovel 2002: 209). For example, the need for a car, let alone a four-wheel-drive should be questioned critically given the ecological, social and psychological damage done by capitalism.

Ecosocialists are somewhat divided on the question of Marx's green credentials. He can (see Chapter 6), be interpreted as a productivist concerned only with expanding the economy; indeed, Marx argued that capitalism created the expansion of the means of production necessary to create surplus. Without surplus, communism would simply be the sharing of poverty. Globalisation, again, is a double-edged sword. It creates poverty and need, subsuming the whole globe to the dictates of profit. Equally, it breaks up settled hierarchical communities, sweeps away petty tyrants, expands human need positively, removes superstitions, creates a communication system and finally puts together the multitude/working class who will introduce a new society. Communism is impossible perhaps without capitalism.

However, Marx noted, in Russia it might be possible for the peasant *mir*, a form of communal village, to provide the basis for communism without a capitalist production phase (Desai 2004: 98). While this may have been a throwaway thought in a draft of a discarded letter, there is more solid evidence for a greener Marx. In one of his earliest essays he noted:

> The view of nature which has grown up under the regime of private property and of money is an actual contempt for and practical degradation of nature … In this sense Thomas Munzer declares it intolerable that 'all creatures have been made into property, the fish in the water, the birds in the air, the plants on the earth – all living things must become free.' (Marx 1977: 239)

For Marx, capitalism and globalisation, produced from the expansion of the market, are both good and bad. The green Marx would only be a half-Marx, and so too the productivist Marx. Even if Marx was no green, his analysis of how capitalism works, his philosophy based on subtle dialectics and his vision of a society no longer dominated by economics makes him indispensable to any form of green anti-capitalism. However, John Bellamy Foster and Paul Burkett argue that Marx was an early green. Foster notes:

> I discovered that Marx's systematic investigation into the work of the great German agricultural chemist Justus von Liebig, which grew out of his critique of Malthusianism, was what led him to his central concept of the 'metabolic rift' in the human relation to nature – his mature analysis of the alienation of nature. To understand this fully, however, it became necessary to reconstruct the historical debate over the degradation of the soil that had emerged in the mid-nineteenth century in the context of the 'second agricultural revolution,' and that extends down to our time. Herein lay Marx's most direct contribution to the ecological discussion. (Foster 2000: ix)

Ecosocialists argue that his notion of a metabolism between humanity and the rest of nature is key to recreating a more ecologically conscious connection. Marx's materialism based on sensuous interaction with the rest of nature is vital to green awareness. Marx and Engels also made numerous statements on ecological issues; indeed, Engels was politicised partly as a result of concern over river pollution, while soil erosion and sewage were significant issues for both writers (Parsons 1977).

Engels noted:

> Let us not, however, flatter ourselves overmuch on account of our human victories over nature. For each such victory nature takes its revenge on us. Each victory, it is true, in the first place brings about the results we expected,

but in the second and third places it has quite different, unforeseen effects which only too often cancel the first. The people who, in Mesopotamia, Greece, Asia Minor and elsewhere, destroyed the forests to obtain cultivable land, never dreamed that by removing along with the forests the collecting centres and reservoirs of moisture they were laying the basis for the present forelorn state of those countries. When the Italians of the Alps used up the pine forests on the southern slopes, so carefully cherished on the northern slopes, they had no inkling that they were thereby depriving their mountain springs of water for the greater part of the year, and making possible for them to pour still more furious torrents on the plains during the rainy season [...] Thus at every step we are reminded that we by no means rule over nature like a conqueror over a foreign people, like someone standing outside nature – but that we, with flesh, blood and brain, belong to nature, and exist in its midst, and that all our mastery of it consists in the fact that we have the advantage of all other creatures of being able to learn its laws and apply them correctly. (quoted in Foster 2000: 235–6)

While there is a minority ecosocialist tradition and more recently mainstream Marxists from Castro onwards have been showing a green side, Kovel suggests that socialists need to catch up. He believes that socialism without ecological concern is no basis for a sane world, socialists need to take their founding concepts and apply them far more deeply.

MALTHUSIANISM AS MURDER

Ecosocialists certainly see a range of opinions with the green movement as regressive and damaging. As we have seen, green politics at its most radical can engage a very fundamental critique of economics. However, particularly as regards an ideology that is put into practice by politicians struggling to change the society we live in on a daily basis, according to ecosocialists other greens step back or are even ignorant of their radicalism. Localism, support for small businesses and demands for a range of ecotaxes are the kind of policies that can be used to gather votes without alienating support. Demands for zero growth, opposition to the tyranny of the clock and fears that quantitive measurements are leading to an instrumental and arid way of living are not the stuff of local election leaflets.

Green concerns with population growth inspired by the economics of Malthus are also strongly criticised by ecosocialists (Kovel 2002: 23; Foster 2002). Thomas Malthus, a nineteenth-century Somerset vicar, argued that poverty could not be removed by social reform; the poor would always tend to use up their resources and remain in misery because of their fertility. Paradoxically, ecosocialists like many political greens can be easily labelled as neo-Malthusian because they criticise growth. Malthus was stringently criticised by Marx for blaming poverty not on class injustice but upon the breeding habits of the poor. Neo-Malthusianism tends to suggest that natural resources are running out and ecosystems are being devastated because people (especially poor people) have too many babies. Human greed rather than a system that nurtures overconsumption is also blamed.

Ecosocialists point out that Malthus had nothing to say about ecology himself and that his ideas were used to force peasants from the land into workhouses. The notion of the tragedy of the commons, developed by Garrett Hardin, is a key neo-Malthusian notion used to justify enclosure. Hardin argued that overgrazing would occur if common land was not owned privately. Herders would graze as many animals as possible, even though they knew this would result in soil erosion and disaster, and a free-rider problem would prevent conservation. For example, if any one herdsman or herdswomen were to graze their cattle less, others would exploit their good will by putting more of their cattle on the common. The solution is to abolish all commons and turn them into private property, which will not be abused. Hardin's ecological solution is a clarion cry for the privatisation of the last bits of non-commodified land.

Guha and Martinez-Alier, in arguing for the often mistakenly termed Malthusian demand to limit capitalist growth, believe that commons rather than private property are likely to lead to conservation. This is because market-based decision-makers tend to value short-term gain rather than thinking of longer-term needs. In reality, commons regimes have been managed locally by stints or systems of communally agreed use to prevent disaster. There are thousands of well-catalogued examples of well-maintained commons throughout history and right across the world (see Chapter 9). The real tragedy of the commons has been the fact that communal resources have been taken from local people to help create markets and accelerate neo-liberal globalisation (Roberts 1979; *Ecologist* 1992).

Ecosocialist feminists argue that the material circumstances of women's existence from giving birth to largely sustaining economic activity via care and subsistence activities mean that women bare the brunt of ecological crisis and enclosure (Mellor 1992, 1997). Feminist ecosocialists are wary of the essentialist claims of subsistence ecofeminists, suspicious of statements that women are essentially greener than men and critical of the peasant path to utopia. However, neither differences over the epistemological status of gender nor geographical separation should prevent global ecofeminists' solidarity and ecosocialist networks from actively resisting neo-liberalism. Calling for a revolutionary ecology movement, Carolyn Merchant notes:

> A socialist ecofeminists movement in the developed world can work in solidarity with women's movements to save the environment ... It can support scientifically-based ecological actions that also promote social justice. Like cultural ecofeminism, socialist ecofeminism protests chemical assaults on women's reproductive health, puts them in the border context of the relations between reproduction and production. It can thus support point of production actions such as the Chipko and Greenbelt movements in the Third World, protests by Native American women over cancer-causing radioactive uranium mining on reservations, and protest by working class women over toxic dumps in urban neighbourhoods. (Merchant 1992: 200)

ECOTOPIA

Kovel is fascinated by a variety of ecological ensembles. Each such ensemble bring together human activities in interaction with the rest of nature. For Kovel they can be green or destructive, ranging from a community based around nuclear power to permaculturalists. Ecology ensembles that create environmental sustainability put use value before exchange value. As we have noted, this is because exchange values demand continual economic growth, which wrecks ecosystems. Ecosocialists argue that with 'usufruct', the principle of using but not privately owning goods, we could all have access to far more useful things without expanding production. To achieve ensembles that are ecologically sustainable demands not just removing the market but engaging with psychological issues as well as constructing new practices.

Kovel concludes that we need to create or recreate a sensual concern with our surroundings and our products. This radical materialism values what is physically present rather than viewing consumption, production and distribution as goals in themselves or ways of sublimating hidden or semi-hidden psychological needs. Kovel moves on to an implicit theological critique that argues that over centuries we have tended to ignore the real material world of living things.

Ecosocialism draws consciously or unconsciously upon Freud as well as Marx and the greens. Norman O. Brown's book *Life Against Death* (1960) illustrates the theme that unconscious drives are sublimated into the desire for consumer items and economic power. Ecosocialists use Marx to show that capitalism, far from being rational and based on maximising human benefit, is a system of organised madness. Kovel argues that the dynamics of a capitalist economy tend to encourage the growth of a specifically capitalist personality based on competitiveness, violence and greed.

> The domain of use-values will be the sight of contestation. To restore use value means to take things concretely and sensuously, as befits an authentic relation of ownership – but by the same gesture, lightly, since things are enjoyed for themselves and not as buttresses for shaky ego. Under capital, as Marx famously saw, what is produced is fetishized by the shroud of exchange-value – made remote and magical. In the fetishized world, nothing is ever really owned, since everything can be exchanged, taken away and abstracted. This stimulates the thirst for possessions that rages under capitalist rule. The unappeasable craving for things – and money to get things – is the necessary underpinning of accumulation and the subjective dynamic of the ecological crisis. The circuits of capitalist society are defined by having – and excluding others from having – until we arrive at a society of gated communities inhabited by lonely egos, each split from all and the atomised selves split from nature. They can only be resolved in a society that permits this hunger to wither, and this requires the release of labour from the bondage imposed by exchange values. (Kovel 2002: 239–40)

BACK TO THE FUTURE

Ecosocialist strategies are diverse. Guha and Martinez-Alier celebrate struggles to maintain and restore the commons, an approach largely shared with the subsistence ecofeminism of authors like Mies and Shiva. Other ecosocialists have looked to the traditional working class. After all, toxic industrial processes most directly affect workers and there is a history of working-class resistance to ecologically destructive processes. Australian ecosocialists, for example, have been associated with the green ban movement, where workers in the construction industry refused to build projects that were environmentally damaging (Roberts 1979). Globalisation makes these struggles potentially more difficult, because firms can move to areas of the globe where resistance is weaker, playing communities off against one another. However, as the autonomists have noted, new technologies have the potential to create powerful global solidarity.

Kovel argues for working-class action and the construction of ecosocialist parties, although in practice this mainly involves the difficult task of greening green parties. He suggests that prefigurative projects must also be constructed around forms of production based on use values to provide examples of a post-capitalist world. He cites Indy Media, the internet-based alternative media network and other projects associated with the recent wave of anti-globalisation protest. Religious communities, such as the Hutterite Bruderhof who seem to exist outside of capitalist consciousness, also fascinate him.

Ecosocialism provides a critique of what is wrong with contemporary globalisation by bringing together both red and green insights. With the exceptions of Stiglitz et al. and of far-right conspiracy anti-capitalism, anti-capitalist protest tends to be inspired by some form of socialist or green discourse. Kovel and other ecosocialists take from the most radical elements of both to show that not only is neo-liberal globalisation profoundly destructive, but that a deep critique of economics is needed if we are to heal the world. Nonetheless, while ecosocialism is necessary, it is not sufficient; to transcend capitalist globalisation it is crucial to go further still.

9
Life after Capitalism:
Alternatives, Structures, Strategies

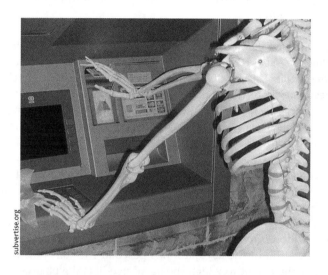

subvertise.org

The Times of November 1857 contains an utterly delightful cry of outrage on the part of a West Indian plantation owner. This advocate argues with great moral indignation – as a plea for the re-introduction of Negro slavery – how the *Quashees* (the free blacks of Jamaica) content themselves with producing only what is strictly necessary for their own consumption, and, alongside this 'use value,' regard loafing (indulgence and idleness) as the real luxury good; how they do not care a damn for the sugar and the fixed capital invested in the plantations, but rather observe the planters' impending bankruptcy with an ironic grin of malicious pleasure … As far as they are concerned, capital does not exist as capital. (Marx 1973: 325–6)

On the wall outside the Doctor's room was written up: OUR NEEDS BEAR NO RELATION TO OUR DESIRES. He let it stay there for several weeks. 'But how can one tell which is which,' Marianne asked herself and thought no more about the slogan. (Carter 1988: 89)

Conventional economics is surprisingly dangerous for a subject normally portrayed as a neutral science. Neo-liberal globalisation takes the economic orthodoxies taught in university departments and applies them to the real world. The result should be prosperity; the consequences are instead growing inequality, severe ecological problems and the colonisation of inner space. Doug Henwood, editor of *Left Business Observer,* believes studying economics makes 'you a nastier person':

> studies have shown that economics graduate students are more likely to 'free ride' – shirk contributions to an experimental 'public goods' account in the pursuit of higher returns – than the general public. Economists also are less generous than other academics in charitable giving ... on other tests, students grow less honest – expressing less of a tendency, for example, to return found money – after studying economics, but not after studying a control subject like astronomy. (Henwood 1998: 144)

However, economics in the sense it is normally conceived is just one way of running society. There are, despite what the apologists for the market suggest, others. Protest has put anti-capitalism on the map. However, solid liveable alternatives to neo-liberal globalisation are also necessary. The construction of such alternatives demands consideration of the key questions posed at the start of the book, namely the extent to which the ills of neo-liberal globalisation are a product of conspiracy or the result of the workings of abstract economic concepts; the dilemma of whether economic growth is appropriate in a post-capitalist society, and the vexed question of strategy. The final question of how effective change is to be organised is the most important and interesting. This chapter revisits these issues and considers alternatives to capitalism, including embedded markets, liberated states, commons regimes, open source and materialist experiments.

WARM CONSPIRACIES

If you search for global justice monetary reform on the internet, you may find a Canadian site with typical anti-globalisation information plus full reproduction of *Billions for the Bankers*, a pamphlet by American pastor Sheldon Emry, which blames bankers from 'Eastern Europe' for a globalising 'new world order':

The 'almost hidden' conspirators in politics, religion, education, entertainment, and the news media are working for the banker-owned United States, in a banker-owned World under a banker-owned World Government! This is what all the talk of a New World Order promoted by Presidents Bush and Clinton is all about.

America will not shake off her Banker-controlled dictatorship as long as the people are ignorant of the hidden controllers. Banking concerns, which control most of the governments of the nations, and most sources of information, seem to have us completely within their grasp. (<www.justiceplus.org/bankers.htm>)

Emry's sentiments, although archaically worded, seem to chime with some anti-capitalists. Amory Starr, author of *Naming the Enemy,* argues that figures on the right and even the religious right are part of the anti-capitalist movement:

Like religious nationalism elsewhere, the Christian/Patriot movement has racist elements, and, like movements elsewhere, panicked accusations of racism are being used to delegitimise core concerns and proposals, which are democracy, populism and the rights of localities.

Both the Freeman and the militias subscribe to conspiracy theories that not only are not anti-Semitic but differ little from left-wing analyses, emphasizing the Trilateral Commission, the New World Order and GATT. (Starr 2000: 142)

In the light of Starr's contentions, Pastor Emry's biography makes interesting reading:

Emry was a major figure in the Christian Identity movement that argues that the White peoples are the Old Testament Israelites and, therefore, God's chosen people, Jews are Satanic in origin, and people of color are intended by God to be the servants of the Whites. Emry allied himself with the armed Identity group, the Citizens Emergency Defense System, and was frequently published in 'Spotlight', the magazine of the anti-Semitic Liberty Lobby ... [He] accused the Jews of starting World Wars One and Two, the Vietnam War, and the assassination of President Lincoln. Emry has also written denying the Holocaust. (Lethbridge 1999)

Reviewing a book by the conspiracy theorist David Icke, the British National Party-linked magazine *Spearhead* noted how anti-globalisation concerns could be fitted to a nationalist agenda:

Free trade, GATT, the European Union, United Nations, Club of Rome, Trilateral Commission and the sinister Bilderberg Group all come under the microscope, fitting together like pieces of a jigsaw in a global vision of a nightmare world of asset strippers, political spivs, thieves and liars of cataclysmic proportions. Readers on the idealist liberal-left will lose their rose tinted spectacles when ingesting the full horror to which world events are rapidly moving. (Noble 1996: 1)

Conspiracy theory is, of course, rarely racist and is popular on the left as well as the right. The anti-corporate vision of Korten articulates with elite conspiracy, and much of what passes for Marxism is conspiracy-orientated. Greens can be valiant foes of what they perceived to be a conspiracy by US imperialism and its corporate controllers. Conspiracies are attractive because they frame the complexities of capitalism in personal terms. Instead of examining abstract concepts, they generate a personal enemy with a human face who can be challenged. Good people can tackle the bad, but social causes remain invisible.

Conspiracies exist. Between their intellectual defeat by Keynesians in the 1940s and their revival in the 1980s, free market liberals built an intellectual movement and moved from academia into politics (Cockett 1995). This revolution of the right, which created 'neo' liberalism, while far from hidden, was planned, plotted and organised. We could call it a conspiracy. Corporate lobbyists spend billions to get their own way. The US neo-conservatives have manipulated public opinion, co-opted America's religious nationalists and quite cynically used the threat of radical Islam to assert the dominance of the right over the US and the authority of the US over the rest of the globe (Frank 2004). Such plots are plain facts and hardly secret. The rich and powerful act to increase their power and riches, as they have always done.

The pro-globalisers deny conspiracy. They argue that theirs is not an ideology but a truth based on economic axioms. However, it is amusing to find that Martin Wolf, author of perhaps the most sophisticated of the pro-neo-liberal books, has attended at least one Bilderberg meeting (*Financial Times*, 21 May 2003). Yet capitalism has a structural element, it is not just a plot by wicked capitalists, let alone the 'East European' bankers and 'spivs' dreamt up by the racist far right. The nicest capitalist still has to exploit labour and promote ecocidal consumerism to survive. The market has it's own gravitational pull but this gravity is a little abstract so the cartoon of a cigar-smoking plutocrat comes into play in cited propaganda.

Roy Bhaskar's critical realist philosophy, while no easy ride, provides useful insights here (1989). Bhaskar has developed a method of understanding reality that rejects 'what you see is what you get' positivism and the relativism of post-modernism. He argues that social reality is based on underlying and often invisible structures – capitalism being an excellent example; language another. These provide the DNA of social systems helping to explain what is going on. However, unlike structures in nature such as DNA, social structures can, though this is often difficult, be changed by human action. They decay over time and are shaped by human meaning but they shape society. Language is a social structural, but we cannot easily talk a different language and hope to be understood. Language illustrates the observation that structures are operated and shaped by people, but gain relative autonomy, perhaps even absolute autonomy, when internalised by human subjects. This concept of structural causation is explicit in the ecosocialist accounts of Joel Kovel and John Bellamy Foster who see capitalism as a kind of force-field or matrix that it is difficult to resist. Bhaskar's critical realism provides a sword to cut through the knotted conspiracy/concept dilemma. The conspirators construct, where they are successful, new structures, but as capitalists they are themselves bearers of deeper structural imperatives to exploit labour, subjectivity and the earth. The marketers plot but are also plotted.

COLD CONCEPT

A very useful supporting metaphor is the notion of icenine from Kurt Vonnegut's novel *Cats Cradle* (1971). Icenine is built from a special kind of water molecule that turns any water it meets into ice. Icenine is a crystal seed that freezes water. In Vonnegut's novel, a fragment of icenine held in a thermos flask is let out, threatening to extinguish life. Icenine is capital, moving through the world, freezing everything in its path. It is invented, in the novel, so the US marines can bridge rivers, useful for the Tigris and Euphrates, the Jordan or Thames.

Polanyi, writing prophetically in 1944, argues that the extension of the market brings such icy destruction that

> To allow the market mechanism to be the sole director of the fate of human beings and their natural environment, indeed, even of the amount and use of purchasing power, would result in the demolition of society. For the alleged

commodity 'labour power' cannot be shoved about, used indiscriminately, or even left unused, without affecting also the bearer of this peculiar commodity. In disposing of a man's labour power the system would, incidentally, dispose of the physical, psychological, and moral entity 'man' attached to that tag. Robbed of the protective covering of cultural institutions, human beings would perish from the effects of social exposure; they would die as the victims of acute social dislocation through vice, perversion, crime and starvation. Nature would be reduced to its elements, neighbourhoods and landscapes defiled, rivers polluted, military safety jeopardized, the power to produce food and raw materials destroyed. (Polanyi 1957: 73)

Anti-capitalism must roll back icenine. The market is hugely destructive, it creates inequality, has an inbuilt tendency to growth, enslaves us and wrecks ecology. Anti-capitalism demands an antidote to icenine. We need to stop economics, a series of abstractions, based upon what Polanyi calls fictitious commodities, from giving us the runaround.

ITALISM

Productivism is problematic since only a few decades of high economic growth are already leading to severe ecological problems. Indeed, as greens and ecosocialists argue, one of the most troubling features of capitalism is that it demands continual growth. However, poverty remains suggesting that further growth is needed, a point taken up by many NGOs and the moderate critics of the Washington Consensus like Soros and Stiglitz.

For Marx in a future society based on global growth, rich human needs are developed, technology advances and equality can be based on surplus rather than shortage. Hardt and Negri sing the same tune, celebrating the dialectic of globalisation and looking to their cybertariat in the form of the multitude to liberate humanity from Fox TV. Shiva and Mies believe that in peasant societies needs can be met from gathering and nurturing local resources. Many of the various anti-capitalisms have an implicit stance on a political economy of time and progress, arguing that there is a stage of human development which is particularly desirable. This anti-capitalist politics of time is concerned with appropriate regulation, technology, prosperity and human development. All perspectives look to a time where decisions can be made cooperatively without the corporations. Korten likewise looks backwards to the time of the small-scale market of the eighteenth century. Marx waited for tomorrow, as do the autonomists Hardt and Negri; subsistence ecofeminists celebrate the yesterday of peasant production.

History does not march to a predictable narrative. Despite the prophecy of many Marxists, the promotion of hyperglobalisation seems unlikely to flip society neatly into a socialist order. While there are contradictions inherent in capitalism, it is a not a system based on clockwork that will strike twelve and chime in revolution. Capitalism has crisis tendencies but capitalism uses barriers as a pole vaulter uses obstacles to practice jumping ever higher. The regressive vision of subsistence perspectives are just as flawed as hyperglobalisation, we cannot move back to an earlier stage in human history. Much human suffering and ecological damage has to be forgotten to sustain the subsistence approach to progress and time. The march of the warlords like Hitler or the Mogul emperors cannot be ignored in praise of goat breeding.

A bold constructive approach is appropriate, we need to reinvent entirely new economic arrangements as well as knitting together alternatives to the market and the state from a range of cultures. The politics of periodised time cannot be forgotten, we live with particular potentialities. However, history should furnish raw materials to construct alternatives rather than to legitimise determinist schemes which are often little more than myth. The cybertariat and the peasant commons have the potential to make a new society. Economics can be made political through choice. The struggle must be to reject productivism and to pursue in different contexts economic arrangements that fulfil need equitably, develop humanity, sustain ecosystems and lead to cooperation.

Here the ecosocialists via Joel Kovel provide a useful insight in their distinction, derived from Marx, between exchange values and use values. The use of what is useful and beautiful must be pursued, while exchange values must be rejected. Economics can be bent towards serving the needs of humanity and nature rather than its own violent abstract growth. The rejection of exchange values is essential to reducing resource consumption and human alienation. Goods can be made to last longer, to be shared, to be easily repaired, so less will mean more. Libraries can be extended. Ecological agricultural systems such as permaculture that reduce work and replace exchange with diversity are important (Mollison 1991). Such measures that diminish poverty and economic growth, enhance the fertility of the soil and respect the land, are impossible within a profit-orientated system.

Localism is part of the process. This is not because everything can be produced locally; economies of scale mean that some goods are likely to generate fewer greenhouse gases if produced in bulk. Neither is localism an analytical tool for understanding how capitalism functions. Nonetheless, local production for local need reduces transport costs and more significantly works with the ecological grain. Diverse local food production, use of local building materials, locally grown herbs to heal the sick, provide work that has a sensual connection with the material. Shit has to be shovelled and there is a danger of romanticising the joys of manual labour, but the local also has the ability to cut the chains of unnecessary added value.

Marx's localism from the *Grundrisse*, cited at the head of this chapter, celebrates the fact that land can be freedom. Access to the means of production provides true liberty. Before Marx read *The Times*, the Maroons, escaped Jamaican slaves, had been taking to the hills to live independently (Genovese 1992). Maroon anti-capitalism, rejecting fixed capital for freedom is implicit in the Rastafarian notion of localism known as ital. In ital what is sacred is what comes from the earth and is grown locally. People can be footloose. Rastafarianism, at its best, shows how religion can inspire both internationalism and localism without building walls between sects. Ital is a neat metaphor because it is derived from what is vital and dismembers cap-ital (see Nander Tanczos' foreword to this volume). Italism is a worldwide rooted cosmopolitanism. Typically in the UK, while only a minority of Caribbean diaspora in Britain are adherents of Rastafarianism, there is interesting hybridisation, with traditional Jamaican gardening practised on allotments in London and Birmingham (see, for example, <www.movinghere.org.uk/galleries/histories/caribbean/culture/culture>). Religious metaphors, where useful, can sometimes be taken and adapted.

Caution remains. Rastafarianism, like Christianity, Islam, Pantheism and the rest, has strains that are oppressive and intolerant. However, as the activism of New Zealand Green Party MP and Rastafarian Nandor Tanczos shows, italism has the potential to energise anti-capitalism and provide an anti-racist localist practice.

AMPHIBIANS

Strategy, whether in Kentucky or Ulan Bator, must be amphibious, half in the dirty water of the present but seeking to move on to a new, unexplored territory. Anti-capitalist alternatives should be assessed in terms of their ability to address present concerns but also to move society in a new direction. This is one of the virtues of ital and the better forms of localism, which should not be thought of as going backwards but as moving forward to an alternative society with a different rhythm. Such projects have cultural resonance today. Amphibious alternatives act as a bridge. 'Anti-capitalism' such as that of Soros and Stiglitz that seeks to preserve the present economic system illustrates the truth that a bridge that stands on only one side of the river is no bridge at all.

Anti-capitalist strategy demands struggle in some very cold climates, yet even in the US, despite Republican corporate domination, there are some hopeful signs. In 2003, a Green candidate came within a couple of percentage points of becoming Mayor of San Francisco, gaining 47 per cent of the vote – astonishing given the influence of European greens who average 8 per cent in states they govern like Germany (*The Economist*, 11 September 2003). It is worth remembering that the anti-capitalist movement was given a kickstart in Seattle which is, after all, in the US. In China, the world's emerging market-based superpower, despite the icy grip of the Communist Party, workers strike, walk out and oppose the brutalities of the Export Processing Zones. Greens are organising too, although with extreme caution as locally based environmentalists (*Guardian*, 11 June 2002). Peasant protest is significant:

> About 40,000 farmers staged protests last week against a dam project in the south-western province of Sichuan. 100,000 villagers' homes would be flooded if the plan went ahead, according to media reports.
>
> Two villagers were killed in the protests, and at least one police officer is reported dead. Sichuan Province's party secretary Zhang Xuezhong was briefly confronted and held up by around 10,000 villagers in Dashu Township demanding a halt in construction of the dam.
>
> The violence broke out in Hanyuan County on 5 November when up to 30,000 people tried to block thousands of armed police deployed to the area to quell days of protests against the construction of the Pubugou dam. The government has deployed as many as 10,000 soldiers to areas near the dam. (*China Labour Bulletin*, November 2004)

November 2004 also saw workers walk out of a newly privatised store in protest at wage cuts and Inner Mongolian civil servants striking to preserve pensions. China is viewed as an opaque and obedient state but inevitably, anti-capitalism is developing because while growth fuels consumer demand, peasants, workers and the environment are trampled. Anti-capitalists in other parts of the globe can aid Chinese and US movements where necessary with asylum, translation and dialogue. Solidarity sometimes works to prevent bloodshed, as the example of the Zapatistas has shown. One of the attractions of Naomi Klein's work has been her investigations of workers' struggles in EPZs in the emerging capitalist economies across the globe.

EMBEDDED MARKETS AND ANTI-CAPITALIST STATES?

One approach to amphibious politics is to adapt markets as a way of beginning to move beyond the market. Markets can be embedded in society and state provision decentralised. A strong example comes from Stan Thekaekara, who worked with Indian adivasis, 'first inhabitants', a marginalised group kicked off their land by higher caste groups. Once they had reclaimed their land, they grew tea and sold it directly to Fair Trade outlets in India and the UK. Face-to-face contact was made with working-class communities in Easterhouse Glasgow who were sold ethical and cheap tea. Social preference rather than profit maximisation socialised economic activity:

> In the present market economy, even in the Fair Trade model, the moment we put our tea into the market chain, at the first point of contact a price would be determined and we would lose ownership over the tea. And then the tea would take a life of it's own. We are divorced from that tea. The ownership moves from us to somebody else. And then to somebody else and somebody else, ownership often changing till finally it ends up in a package with a pretty picture on it. And all along the way, the price also changes. And as the tea moves along the market chain the price is increasingly de-linked from the cost of production and the initial payment made to the producer. What you as a consumer pay for your tea has nothing to do with what I as a producer got for that tea. (Thekaekara 2003: 9)

Instead of being 'divorced from that tea', the tea was produced and exchanged under conditions determined by the farmers. The project erased distinctions between the global and the local by being controlled by the producers who built relationships with the consumers based on equity and respect:

The first consignment of tea was due to go out to a group of people who are considered to be untouchable by upper caste Hindus. Because they are the community that does all of the unclean work, cleaning toilets, burying carcasses and so on: totally untouchable. There is terrible discrimination against them. We found that they were also huge tea drinkers. And we said why don't we send the tea to them? And we had a meeting of our tribal people. And asked them if some profit is generated through this transaction how do you think we should distribute it? How much should they get, how much should we get? Now, there were two hundred people at this meeting, and they turned around and said, are you mad? These people are so much worse off than us, they have trouble in every way, why should we take anything of their profit, and we've got the cost of our tea. We've got a fair price. If there is a surplus generated, let them keep it. Market sense? Not at all. (Thekaekara 2003: 9–10)

Embedded markets, as Polanyi suggests, challenge capitalism and growth:

Even those of us who are concerned about and work with the people who are at the bottom of the economic pile are told and tend to believe that growth is inevitable and our task is to ensure that there is fairness and justice in this growth. And so our slogan has become 'growth with equity'. I would like to challenge this. Because it is my personal experience after having come in contact with communities in different parts of the world, that growth is not always desirable and is definitely not inevitable. I went back to the village where I first began my work in the early 1970s. I went back there after 24 years to find the village unchanged – there had not been a single addition in the number of buildings. None of the buildings or huts had become any larger. The land that they owned had not grown any more than what it was back then ... The economies of indigenous people and many rural communities all over the world, are not based on growth. So this presumption that growth is inevitable, is I think, a presumption of an industrialised economy. It is absolutely essential for an industrialised economy that there is growth. Because if people don't consume more, the economy doesn't work. So you have to have growth. It is absolutely necessary for a capital economy. And it is a brilliant way to legitimise consumerism. It is a brilliant way to legitimise unfettered growth in incomes. (Thekaekara 2003: 2)

Thekaekara's work provides a rare and impressive example, but at their most radical a range of ethical and alternative marketing systems provide some hope. The British cooperative movement, started in

1834 by the Rochdale pioneers to provide affordable food for workers exploited by company shops, still survives (Birchall 1997). A once massive mutual-help organisation owned by the workers, many of its stores have shut but it retains an interesting and award-winning cooperative bank. Ethical and green consumption are on the rise. In Argentina, Naomi Klein and Avi Lewis have chronicled how bankrupt factories have been occupied and reopened by their workers under the slogan 'Occupy, Resist, Produce':

> What they do is start small and build gradually. Forja has started working with a local auto repair shop. They don't need the capital to buy raw materials because the client brings them steel that he has purchased from scrap metal and recycling. The Forja workers melt the scrap metal in their ovens and make axle assemblies. They work on very small contracts. So they don't need big capital outlays. And they're building that way. There are other examples of occupied factories that are working at a much higher level. Zanon Ceramics is the largest ceramic tile factory in all of Latin America. They've been under worker control for over three years and they have increased production. (Znet, 8 August 2004)

Such worker- and peasant-orientated projects are significant yet still work within a capitalist system that threatens them. The need to survive can lead to self-exploitation with pay being cut to remain competitive. The embedded market can instead embed the ecological and the social within the oppressive structures of abstract economics. Nonetheless, such projects provide examples of economic projects that seek, however partially, to make growth, profit and exchange secondary goals. We cannot shop or work our way to utopia, but such projects ease present ills and point roughly to a different future. Powerful consumer boycotts such as that of Nike over poor labour conditions or Marks and Spencer over their complicit support for the Israeli domination of the Palestinian Occupied Territories are examples of how protest can be used to struggle to embed the market.

States can advance an anti-globalisation agenda. In Cuba and Venezuela, Castro and Chavez have harnessed popular demands for a decentralised, socialist economy. Both states heavily promote of organic farming:

> Back in Caracas I was curious to witness the parallel 'ruralisation of urban life'. The pilot urban garden project is a vegetable patch down by the Hilton Hotel, on one side of a busy bridge linking a six-lane city highway ... The

city centre garden produces a range of vegetables and medicinal plants sold at below average prices ... 'This is a tool to help change the attitude of ordinary Venezuelans,' explains Angelina. 'You can't put a monetary value on community,' she said, adding, 'garden plots bring people together.' The scale is impressive, with an area of 3,800 square metres capable of producing seven tonnes of vegetables a month (McCaughan 2004: 79)

Both states deserve international solidarity. US capitalism is very keen to snuff out any threat of a good example and anti-capitalists must resist. Thus while anti-imperialism is insufficient alone, it is clearly necessary. It goes without saying that US imperialism in the Middle East must also be challenged: as critics note, the language of rights, democracy and disarmament legitimates a corporate agenda of invasion and domination.

Positive state solutions from health services to social housing and public transport should be defended against the onslaught of the market the world over. Public services are the result of a long history of popular struggles showing a social recognition of the need to meet essential needs outside of the market, whether individuals can pay or not. However, the top-down nature of much state provision demands localisation and democratisation. Hilary Wainwright, editor of the ecosocialist magazine *Red Pepper*, has argued that innovative participatory mechanisms can be used to embed the state in society, reclaiming decision-making for ordinary people. Strong extra-state institutions can also make successful state resistance to neo-liberalism easier. She cites the citizens' budgets introduced by the Brazilian Workers Party as one example of such a mechanism, noting 'participatory decision-making has turned out to be a more socially efficient way of running things, delivering, by all accounts, a better city in which to live' (Wainwright 2003: 68).

One of the virtues of the open source approach discussed below is the principle that the difference between services providers and users should be eroded. Consumers should be able to choose how state services are provided and run. An open source politics would embed states in society and provide people with a stake in them.

DEFEND, EXTEND, DEEPEN THE COMMONS

While state provision can be humanised and markets tamed by the social, the more fundamental task requires that both the state and the market are rolled back. The commons provides an important alternative to both. The anti-capitalist slogan above all others should be 'Defend, extend, and deepen the commons'.

The commons is important because it provides a way of regulating activity without the state or the market. The market, despite the assumptions of some anti-capitalists like David Korten, is icenine with a tendency constantly to expand. It is built on enclosure. The state, even at its best, tends to separate society from self-government. Throughout history, the commons has been the dominant form of regulation providing an alternative almost universally ignored by economists who are reluctant to admit that substitutes to the market and the state even exist. Within the commons, scarcity, if it exists, is usually managed and resources conserved through stinting systems arranged by users.

The commons works best by consensus and does not, unlike market-based exchange systems, depend upon constant growth. It provides shared access to important resources so that human needs can be met with potential equity. Anti-capitalist globalisation could be labelled positively as the movement for the commons. Where anti-capitalists lose, the neo-liberals will constantly advance. Their demands are unlimited because capitalism to survive needs constant commodification. Capitalism seeks to extend commodification, the movement resists by conserving the commons. In South America and South Africa grassroots protest seeks to prevent water being privatised. In cyberspace downloaders, hackers and open source designers seek to maintain free access. Greens and subsistence ecofeminists preserve communal land from private corporations.

Yesterday's satire will describe tomorrow's struggle:

> Say we wake up one morning and discover we'll be getting a new bill each month for air. The Bush administration has decided to privatize the air; corporations will now own it and charge for its use.
>
> Lawrence Lindsey, the White House economics advisor, hails the move as a 'potent stimulus' and a big boost for the GDP. Alan Greenspan offers assurances than any inflationary effects will be minor. The rest of us, meanwhile, would feel stunned, and violated in a way that would be hard to express. Pay for air? What gives them the right to do that? The air is ours, isn't it? But what exactly would we mean by that?
>
> The question is not fantasy. In recent decades, the market has been penetrating into realms previously thought off-limits. It is claiming every inch of physical and psychological space, from the outer reaches of the solar system to the most intimate interiors of daily experience. Billboards in the

heavens, pharmaceutical manipulation of thoughts and moods – through genetic engineering, corporations even are claiming ownership to the genetic code of life itself. If life, then why not the air that sustains life? (Rowe 2002)

Some commons demand little or no regulation, merely preservation from such corporate assaults. However, there are numerous well documented accounts of commons regimes where regulation occurs through local bargaining and shared use. In Canada the Ojibway Nation of Ontario still harvests wild rice from Wabigoon Lake using commons principles:

> Violations of harvest allocations by machine harvesters are dealt with at community meetings: a recent case resulted in one machine harvester being denied harvest rights for the rest of one season. For each canoe harvest area, the community agrees upon 'a field boss' whose responsibilities are to regulate the harvest cycle according to custom, and to arbitrate in any disputes. Where harvesting rules are breached, the offender may be 'grounded', one person in a recent harvest being told to 'relearn the Indian way by sitting on the shore and watching'. (*Ecologist* 1992: 127)

The *Ecologist* claims that while the commons has an old-fashioned feel for many of us in Europe and North America, it is a reality for the 'vast majority of humanity' (*Ecologist* 1992: 127). Around 90 per cent of inshore fisheries are regulated by commons. Depletion is a product of high-tech hoovering by unregulated Japanese and European fleets keen to increase profit rather than more local abuse (*Ecologist* 1992: 127). In Maine, lobster fisheries have long been preserved by the commons; in Finland, many forests are communally regulated, and in Switzerland, grazing is controlled by commoners to prevent 'tragedy' through overexploitation:

> [in] Torbel in Switzerland, a village of some 600 people ... grazing lands, forests, 'waste' lands, irrigation systems and paths and roads connecting privately and communally owned property are all managed as commons ... Under a regulation which dates back to 1517, which applies to many other Swiss mountain villages, no one can send more cows to the communal grazing areas than they can feed during the winter, a rule that is still enforced with a system of fines. (*Ecologist* 1992: 128)

The importance of the commons is noted, as we have seen by greens, autonomists, anarchists and many Marxists from Marx onwards. There is no space here to examine the encyclopaedic variety and success of commons regimes but work by scholars such as Ostrom (1991) can provide the basis for deepening the commons. The best anarchist experiments from the Spanish Civil War to contemporary squatting are based on the reinvention of the commons. There has been a long war against the commons. The earliest poems of Robin Hood, long before the inclusion of Maid Marion and Friar Tuck, show a yeoman resisting enclosure. Where I live in Windsor Forest, the Royal Family privatised the land for hunting. E.P. Thompson in *Whigs and Hunters* recorded how 'the blacks' who darkened their faces before 'poaching' game and resisting the royals fought gunbattles in Winkfield and Wokingham parishes (Thompson 1977). A few miles away at St George's Hill, the Diggers briefly established a communal farm in 1649 (Brockway 1980). Wherever you live, there will, if you dig deep enough, have been a struggle between commoners and the monopolising state or market for control.

A review written with the late Walt Sheasby puts these struggles in context:

> Communes formed more or less briefly under the maverick Wyclifite John Ball in Kent, England, in 1381–82; the Hussite Jan Zizka in Tabor, Bohemia, in 1420–24; the Anabaptists Thomas Muenzer of Muelhausen, Thuringia, in 1524–25, Jacob Hutter in Moravia in 1526–36, Bernard Rothmann in Muenster in 1533–35; and the Quaker layman Gerard Winstanley of the Diggers in Surrey, England, in 1649. A recurrent theme in various European locales over hundreds of years was the attempt to reclaim the 'commons.'
>
> The Taborite communism that sprang up briefly in Bohemia in the 1420s proclaimed: 'As in the city of Tabor there is no "mine" and no "yours" but all is in common, the like it shall be everywhere and nobody shall have a special property, and those who have such property commits a mortal sin.' The Hutterites likewise proclaimed, 'Private property is the enemy of love.' John Ball supposedly preached that 'Things cannot go well in England, nor ever will, until everything shall be in common' (Sheasby and Wall 2002: 160)

While we should be cautious about the balance between religious and political radicalism such accounts provide important evidence of an everlasting struggle. In the third millennium hackers and open source coders strive to conserve the cyber-commons. From land reform to anti-privatisation campaigns, commons can be preserved or restored. Some of Naomi Klein's best insights come from her identification of how corporations have invaded public space: for example, saturating the environment with billboards and using schools to sell fast food.

OPEN SOURCE

New commons regimes are created with technological and social change. The internet has heralded the arrival of open source, a new form of commons regime in cyberspace. Software is designed and put on the web for free. Open source software designers, perhaps part of Negri and Hardt's multitude, produce for the pleasure of invention:

> Because their actions patently do not 'prevent good software from being written,' they implicitly call into question the very basis of the Microsoft Empire: If good software can be written and given away like this, who needs Microsoft or companies like it? (Moody 2001: 3)

The open source movement produces programmes, recipes, designs and other forms of information which are developed, passed around, adapted and used for free. There is no isolated genius who creates alone, huge tasks can be undertaken and flexibility is key:

> The Wikipedia project <www.wikipedia.org> stemmed from a conversation between Larry Sanger, editor-in-chief of the online encyclopaedia Nupedia, and Ben Kovitz, a computer programmer. The idea was to create a complete encyclopaedia that could be updated with new information provided by readers almost every minute of every day. You may think such a site would be a magnet for spam, drivel and abusive graffiti, but the quality has been very high, with people adding useful, expert knowledge in thousands of different areas. Wikipedia hit half a million articles earlier this year, including information in anything from Afrikaans to Serbo-Croat. (*Spark 3*, 2004)

Days from finishing this book, I read the following leader in the *Guardian*:

> Today marks a milestone in the history of the 'open source' movement, the extraordinary unpaid community of volunteers all over the world who work together to produce software which is placed in the public domain without commercial gain. Today sees the official launch of Firefox (www. getfirefox.com), a free internet browser that is daring to take on Internet

Explorer, owned by Microsoft, which until recently had a market share of over 95%. ... Microsoft has an embedded advantage, not just because of its $50bn-plus cash reserves, but because Windows has a near-monopoly of the operating system inside personal computers. It comes pre-loaded with Explorer – so users need a good reason to overcome inertia and switch to something else.

Firefox believes it has that reason, a nimble, easy-to-install browser that has new features, keeps out irritating 'pop-up' advertisements and claims much more security against most of the bugs and viruses that have riddled Explorer ... Firefox has come from nowhere to 3% of the market before being officially released and Explorer has lost market share for five months to just under 93%. In response to an appeal to buy an advertisement in the *New York Times*, more than 10,000 Firefox users donated more than $250,000, much more than asked for. (*Guardian*, 9 November 2004)

Open source is obviously amphibious, it works in the world we have but is a viral antidote to the prevailing icenine. It means we have access to resources without exchange, it is a fast growing means of decommodifying society. Open source is an excellent example of how something that does not directly increase GNP can fuel real prosperity: for example, it provides citizens and governments in developing countries with free access to vital computer software. Open source is, of course, contested: some wish to institutionalise and commercialise it. It is part of a wider power struggle between corporations and the rest of us for power over the internet. From music companies who prosecute free file users to hackers who assault Microsoft, cyberspace provides one front in an open, global struggle. It is a struggle that we can virtually all participate in. The very key to a different economy is the open source principle. Instruments such as copy left and 'creative commons' allow individuals to copy software, recipes, articles and much else for free, thus being released from the prison of individual ownership. Open source encourages users to add their own touches, focusing attention on the quality of the product. It is a stunning example of how both the market and the state can be bypassed by cooperative creativity. The barrier between user and provider is eroded; a direct agreement between society members is maintained.

Marx links the open source principle to socialism and use. We should take what we want but nurture what we use for the benefit of the next generation:

From the standpoint of a higher economic form of society, private ownership of the globe by single individuals will appear quite absurd as private ownership of one man by another. Even a whole society, a nation, or even all simultaneously existing societies taken together, are not the owners of the globe. They are only its possessors, its usufructuries, and like *boni patres familias*, they must hand it down to succeeding generations in an improved condition. (Marx quoted in Kovel 2002: 238)

Marx would have been a Firefox user.

SEX AND ZEN

Materialism has acquired a bad name, but sincere enjoyment of the world can be a way of resisting a throwaway economy and associated commodification. Valuing the real material word and taking a sensual pleasure in it is one of the most attractive aspects of Kovel's ecosocialist anti-capitalism. The understated celebration of sexuality in the ecosocialist heritage from Freud and Wilhelm Reich through to Norman O. Brown and Marcuse gives rise to such an ethos:

The resurrection of the body is a social project facing mankind as a whole, and it will become a practical political problem when the statesmen of the world are called upon to deliver happiness instead of power, when political economy becomes a science of use-values instead of exchange-values – a science of enjoyment instead of science of accumulation … The human physical senses must be emancipated from the sense of possession, and then the humanity of the senses and the human enjoyment of the senses will be achieved for the first time. Here is the point of contact between Marx and Freud. (Brown 1960: 318)

The aim is to enjoy the world without consuming it or being consumed. The slow food movement established in Italy in 1986 is a splendid example. It is anti-capitalist yet celebrates global food diversity. It is the culinary complement of green localism and an Italian variety of italism. Food should be savoured, not thrown down the gullet. It was inspired by opposition to the construction of a McDonald's outlet. It believes instead in locally produced high-quality food. When a McDonald's was planned for the Piazza di Spagna in Rome in 1986, Carlo Petrini turned up to protest, wielding bowls of pasta with his friends. The movement is worldwide, opposes the invasion of Iraq on culinary grounds and lobbies governments to preserve peasant culture and endangered food (Petrini 2003).

There are dangers here too. William Morris, the English ecosocialist, helped launch an arts and crafts movement which might be termed a slow manufacturing campaign. High-quality individually produced items of furniture were built by highly skilled cooperative workers in neo-medieval guilds. A century later I cycle past the remnants of Morris-inspired guilds in Chelsea, London, whose products can only be afforded by the superrich in the third millennium. Quality can be quantified into exclusivity and high profit margins. Nonetheless, a positive emphasis on materialism provides a useful and enjoyable strategy for opposing the tyranny of exchange values.

Zen practice is based on being in the world rather than escaping from it. It helps those who practice to focus on the moment rather than on discriminating in terms of accumulating costs and benefits. To write about Zen is generally discouraged because it is often a substitute for Zen and can be a source of division, misinterpretation and confusion. However, Marshall Sahlins, criticising conventional economics, makes the suggestion that Zen minimises need and provides an alternative road to affluence:

> There are two possible courses to affluence. Wants may be 'easily satisfied' either by producing much or desiring little. The familiar conception ... based on the concept of market economies- states that man's wants are great, not to say infinite, whereas his means are limited, although they can be improved. Thus, the gap between means and ends can be narrowed by industrial productivity, at least to the point that 'urgent goods' become plentiful. But there is also a Zen road to affluence, which states that human material wants are finite and few, and technical means unchanging but on the whole adequate. Adopting the Zen strategy, a people can enjoy an unparalleled material plenty – with a low standard of living ... Modern capitalist societies, however richly endowed, dedicate themselves to the proposition of scarcity. Inadequacy of economic means is the first principle of the world's wealthiest peoples.
>
> The market-industrial system institutes scarcity, in a manner completely without parallel. Where production and distribution are arranged through the behaviour of prices, and all livelihoods depend on getting and spending, insufficiency of material means becomes the explicit, calculable starting point of all economic activity. (Sahlins 1972: 1–2)

Zen, slow food and allied italist practices provide practical ways of bringing our desires a little closer to our needs. All such practices are pagan in a rather rationalist sense, requiring no elaborate belief structure but instead a direct orientation to what is. Like the commons and open source, such practices do not reside within a particular stage of human society or a unique cultural setting. They can be combined and constructed using an open source approach of adaptation and adoption.

MAKE SOME NOISE

'Chrisha', a squatter and community activist from Deptford, London, has suggested, in the spirit of open source composure, that 'The system adapts and lives in and through each one of us. Maybe the biggest revolution is to realise that it is actually our creation, so it is transformable, although at the moment we are slaves to our own creation' (personal communication). To this end I would argue that to get control over such structures, anti-capitalists need to keep making noise. Street protest from Seattle onwards has made millions question economic orthodoxy, and direct action using humour and disruption is needed to maintain the process. Paul Kingsnorth, an editor of the *Ecologist*, catalogues dozens of examples of vibrant protest against the present economic system in his book *One No, Many Yeses*. My personal favourite is the Revd Billy and his Church of Stop Shopping, which mimics the evangelical love of obsessive consumption apparent in capitalist society. Starbucks, McDonald's and even the Disney store are terrified that he and his flock will descend, sermonising: '"MICKEY MOUSE IS THE ANTI-CHRIST, CHILD! DON'T GO INTO THAT STORE! DON'T GIVE YOUR MONEY TO THE PEOPLE WHO PAY THEIR SWEATSHOP WORKERS A DOLLAR FOR AN EIGHTEEN-HOUR DAY. SAVE YOUR SOUL!"' (Kingsnorth 2004: 131)

Modest reform of the system can be transformed into rejection and the demand for a different world, which puts creativity in control. This will be a long fight and anti-capitalism may fail. Nevertheless, at the very worst, even in failure we might succeed in bearing witness to the pathological absurdities of world where money makes human beings and the rest of nature a means rather than an end:

> 'I am thinking, young man, about the final sentence for The Books of Bokonon. The time for the final sentence has come.'

'Any luck?'
He shrugged and handed me a piece of paper.
This is what I read:

If I were a younger man, I would write a history of human stupidity; and I would climb to the top of Mount McCabe and lie down on my back with my history for a pillow; and I would take from the ground some of the blue-white poison that makes statues of men; and I would make a statue of myself, lying on my back, grinning horribly, and thumbing my nose at You Know Who. (Vonnegut 1971: 179)

Bibliography

Achebe, C. (1971) *Things Fall Apart.* London: Heinemann.

ACME (1999) *Against Capital and the State.* Seattle: ACME Collective.

Albert, M. (2004) *Parecon. Life After Capitalism.* London: Verso.

Albritton, R. (1999) *Dialectics and Deconstruction in Political Economy.* London: Palgrave.

Albritton, R., Itoh, M., Westra, R. and Zuege, A. (2001) *Phases of Capitalist Development: Booms, Crises and Globalizations.* Basingstoke: Palgrave.

Anon. (1998) Behind the Balaclavas: Breaking Bread with the Zapatistas. *Do or Die!,* 5: 110–17.

Anon. (1999a) Friday June 18th 1999 Confronting Capital and Smashing the State. *Do or Die!,* 8:1–12.

Anon. (1999b) Globalisation: Origins-History-Resistance. *Do or Die!,* 8: 35–55.

Anon. (2000) Resisting the WTO. *Do or Die!,* 7: 111–39.

Anon. (ed.) (2001a) *On Fire: The Battle of Genoa and the Anti-Capitalist Movement.* London: One-Off Press.

Anon. (2001b) Genoa: War Against Capitalism. *Fight Racism Fight Imperialism,* 162: 1–3.

Anon. (2001c) Vampires. *Do or Die!,* 9: 133–5.

Anon. (2003) Down with the Empire, Up with the Spring. *Do or Die!,* 10: 1–102.

Avineri, S. (1972) *Hegel's Theory of the Modern State.* Cambridge: Cambridge University Press.

Bahro, R. (1978) *The Alternative in Eastern Europe.* London: New Left Books.

Bahro, R. (1982) *Socialism and Survival.* London: Heretic.

Balakrishan, G. (2003) *Debating Empire.* London: Verso.

Baker, D. (1996) *Ideology of Obssession: A.K. Chesterton and British Fascism.* London: Tauris Academic Studies.

Barber, B. (2001) *Jihad vs. McWorld: Terrorism's Challenge to Democracy.* New York: Ballantine Books.

Barlow, M. and Clarke, T. (2002) *Blue Gold: The Battle Against Corporate Theft of the World's Water.* Toronto: Stoddart.

Barry, J. (1999) *Rethinking Green Politics.* Thousand Oaks, California: Sage.

Baudrillard, J. (1995) *The Gulf War Did Not Take Place.* Sydney: Power Publications.

Bateson, G. (1972) *Notes Toward an Ecology of Mind.* New York: Ballantine Books.

Bell, E. (1993) *Social Classes and Social Credit in Alberta.* Montreal: McGill-Queens University Press.

Bennholdt-Thomsen, V., Faraclas, N. and von Werlhof, C. (2001) *There is an Alternative: Subsistence and Worldwide Resistance to Corporate Globalization.* London: Zed Press.

Bennholdt-Thomsen, V. and Mies, M. (1999) *The Subsistence Perspective: Beyond the Globalised Economy.* London: Zed Press.

Benton, E. (ed.) (1996) *The Greening of Marxism*. London: Guilford Press.

Berlet, C. and Lyons, M. (2000) *Right-Wing Populism in America*. New York: Guilford Press.

Beynon, J. and Dunkerley, D. (2000) *Globalization: The Reader*. New York: Routledge.

Bhagwati, J. (2004) *In Defence of Globalization*. New York: Oxford University Press.

Bhaskar, R. (1989) *Reclaiming Reality*. London: Verso.

Birchall, J. (1997) *The International Co-operative Movement*. Manchester: Manchester University Press.

Black, E. (2001) *IBM and the Holocaust*. London: Little, Brown and Co.

Bobbitt, P. (2002) *The Shield of Achilles*. Harmondsworth: Penguin.

Bookchin, M. (1974) *Post-Scarcity Anarchism*. London: Wildwood.

Boyle, D. (ed.) (2002) *The Money Changers: Currency Reform from Aristole to E-Cash*. London: Earthscan.

Braverman, H. (1974) *Labour and Monopoly Capitalism*. New York: Monthly Review Press.

Brewer, A. (1990) *Marxist Theories of Imperialism: A Critical Survey*. London: Routledge.

Brockway, F. (1980) *Britain's First Socialist: The Levellers, Agitators and Diggers of the English Revolution*. London: Quartet.

Bronner, S. (1987) *Rosa Luxemburg: Revolutionary For Our Times*. New York: Columbia University Press.

Brown, B. (1974) *Protest in Paris: Anatomy of a Revolt*. Morristown, New Jersey: General Learning Press.

Brown, N. (1960) *Life Against Death: The Psychoanalytical Meaning of History*. London: Routledge and Kegan Paul.

Buchan, J. (1997) *Frozen Desire: An Inquiry into the Meaning of Money*. London: Picador.

Bukharin, N. (1973) *Imperialism and the World Economy*. New York: Monthly Review Press.

Bull, M. (2003) You Can't Build a New Society With A Stanley Knife, in Balakrishnan, G. (ed.) *Debating Empire*. London: Verso.

Burbach, R. (2001) *Globalization and Postmodern Politics: From Zapatistas to High-Tech Robber Barons*. London and Sterling, Virginia: Pluto Press, and Kingston, Jamaica: Arawak.

Burkett, P. (1999) *Marx and Nature: A Red and Green Perspective*. New York: St. Martin's Press.

Burns, H. (2001) May Day Protest against Capitalism. *Fight Racism Fight Imperialism*, 161: 6–7.

Cable, V. (1995) The Diminished Nation-State: A Study in the Loss of Economic Power'. *Daedalus*, 124: 22–53.

Callinicos, A. (2001) Toni Negri in Perspective. *International Socialist*, 92: 33–67.

Callinicos, A. (2003) *An Anti-Capitalist Manifesto*. Cambridge: Polity Press.

Callinicos, A. and Rees, J. (2004) *Building the Party in the Age of Mass Movements*. London: Socialist Workers Party.

Canovan, M. (1981) *Populism*. New York: Harcourt Brace Jovanovich.

Carchedi, G. (1991) *Frontiers of Political Economy.* London and New York: Verso.

Carter, A. (1988) *Heroes and Villians.* Harmondsworth: Penguin.

Castells, M. (1997) *The Information Age: Economy, Society and Culture. Volume II: The Power of Identity.* Oxford: Blackwell.

Castro, F. (2003) *On Imperialist Globalization: Two Speeches.* London: Zed Press.

Caulfield, C. (1997) *Masters of Illusion: The World Bank and the Poverty of Nations.* New York: Henry Holt.

Chesters, G. (2000) The New Intemperance: Protest, Imagination and Carnival. *Ecos,* 21, 1: 2–9.

Chesterton, A. (1970) *The New Unhappy Lords. An Exposure of Power Politics.* Boring, Oregon: CPA Book Publisher.

Chossudovsky, M. (1997*) The Globalisation of Poverty: Impacts of IMF and World Bank Reforms.* London: Zed Press.

Christian Aid (2000) Mind the Gap: How Globalisation is Failing the World's Poor. London: Christian Aid.

Chua, A. (2003) *World on Fire: How Exporting Free Market Democracy Breeds Ethnic Hatred and Global Instability.* New York: Doubleday.

Cleaver, H. (1981) Technology as Political Weaponry Anderson, R. (ed.) *Science, Politics and the Agricultural Revolution in Asia.* Boulder, Colorado: Westview Press.

Cleaver, H. (1991) Introduction to Negri, A., *Marx Beyond Marx: Lessons on the Grundrisse.* London: Pluto Press.

Cleaver, H. (2000) *Reading Capital Politically.* Leeds: Antithuses.

Cleaver, H. (2003) Marxian Categories, the Crisis of Capital, and the Constitution of Social Subjectivity Today, in Bonefeld, W. (ed.) *Revolutionary Writing,* New York: Autonomedia.

Cockett, R. (1995) *Thinking the Unthinkable: Think-Tanks and the Economic Counter Revolution, 1931–1983.* London: HarperCollins.

Commoner, B. (1972) *The Closing Circle.* New York: Alfred A. Knopf and Bantam.

Coogan, K. (1999) *Dreamer of the Day: Francis Parker Yockey and the Post-War Fascist International.* Brooklyn: Autonomedia.

Danaher, K. (1994) *50 Years is Enough: The Case against the World Bank and the International Monetary Fund.* Boston, Massachusetts: South End Press.

Danaher, K. and Burbach, R. (2000*) Globalize This!: The Battle against the World Trade Organization and Corporate Rule.* Monroe, Maine: Common Courage Press.

de Angelis, M. (2001) Marx and Primitive Accumulation: The Continuous Character of Capital's 'Enclosures'. *The Commoner,* 2.

de Brie, C. (2000) Crime, the World's Biggest Free Enterprise. *Le Monde Diplomatique,* April.

Deleuze, G. and Guattari, F. (1988) *A Thousand Plateaus: Capitalism and Schizophrenia.* London: Athlone Press.

Derber, C. (2002) *Corporation Nation.* New York: St Martin's Press.

Derber, C. (2003) *People Before Profit.* New York: St Martin's Press.

Desai, M. (2004) *Marx's Revenge: The Resurgence of Capitalism and the Death of State Socialism.* London: Verso.

Devine, P. (1988) *Democracy and Economic Planning*. Cambridge: Polity Press.

Diani, M. (1994) *Green Networks*. Edinburgh: Edinburgh University Press.

Dobson, A. (1991) *The Green Reader*. London: Andre Deutsch.

Dobson, A. (2000) *Green Political Thought*. London: Routledge.

Doherty, B. (2002) *Ideas and Actions in the Green Movement*. London: Routledge.

Doherty, B., Paterson, M., Plows, A. and Wall, D. (2000a) Constructing the Fuel Protests: New Populist Movements in British Politics. Presented to the ISA/BSA Conference on Social Movements, Manchester, 3–5 November.

Doherty, B., Paterson, M. and Seel, B. (eds) (2000b) *Direct Action in British Environmentalism*. London: Routledge.

Dolgoff, S. (ed.) (1990) *The Anarchist Collectives*. New York: Black Rose Books.

Dostoevsky, F. (1993) *Crime and Punishment*. London: Vintage.

Douglas, C. (1979) *The Monopoly of Credit*. Sudbury, Suffolk: Bloomfield Books.

Douthwaite, R. (1993) *The Growth Illusion*. Bideford: Green Books.

Douthwaite, R. (2000) *The Ecology of Money*. Totnes, Devon: Green Books.

Drakeford, M. (1997) *Social Movements and Their Supporters: The Greenshirts in England*. Basingstoke: Macmillan.

Dunkley, G. (1997) *The Free Trade Adventure, the Uruquay Round and Globalism: A Critique*. Melbourne: Melbourne University Press.

Dunleavy, P., Gamble, A., Holliday, F. and Peele, G. (2000) *Developments in British Politics 6*, London: Macmillan.

Dyer-Witheford, N. (1999) *Cyber-Marx: Cycles and Circuits of Struggle in High-Technology Capitalism*. Urbana and Chicago: University of Illinois Press.

Ecologist (1992) Whose Common Future? *Ecologist*, 22, 4.

Elliot, D. (2003) *A Solar World: Climate Change and the Green Energy Revolution*. Totnes: Green Books.

Elliott, L. (1998) *The Global Politics of the Environment*. New York: New York University Press.

Elliott, L. and Atkinson, D. (1998) *The Age of Insecurity*. London: Verso.

Falk, R. (1999) *Predatory Globalization: A Critique*. Cambridge: Polity Press.

Fast, H. (1970) *Spartacus*. London: Panther.

Fast, H. (1990) *Being Red*. Boston, Massachusetts: Houghton Mifflin.

Featherstone, L. (2002) *Students Against Sweatshops*. London: Verso.

Fine, B. and Saad-Filho, A. (2004) *Marx's Capital*. London: Pluto Press.

Firor, J. and Jacobsen, J. (2002) *The Crowded Greenhouse. Population, Climate Change, and Creating a Sustainable World*. Yale: Yale University Press.

Foster, J. (2000) *Marx's Ecology*. New York: Monthly Review Press.

Foster, J. (2002) *Ecology Against Capitalism*. New York: Monthly Review Press.

Foucault, M. (1979) *Discipline and Punish: The Birth of the Prison*. Harmondsworth: Penguin.

Foucault, M. (1980) *Power/Knowledge: Selected Interviews and Other Writings*. New York: Pantheon.

Foucault, M. (1991) Governmentality, in Burchell, G., Gordon, P. and Miller, P. (eds) *The Foucault Effect*. London: Harvester.

Frank, T. (2004) *What's the Matter with America? The Resistible Rise of the American Right*. New York: Secker.

French, H. (2000) *Vanishing Borders*. London: Earthscan.

Fromm, E. (1979) *To Have or To Be?* London: Abacus.

Fuller, J. (2001) The New Workerism: The Politics of the Italian Autonomists. *International Socialist*, 92: 63–76.

Galbraith, J. (1975) *Money: Whence it Came, Where it Went*. London: Penguin.

Galeano, E. (1973) *The Open Veins of Latin America*. New York: Monthly Review Press.

Gamble, A. (1988) *The Free Economy and the Strong State*. Basingstoke: Macmillan.

Gare, A. (1996) Soviet Environmentalism: The Path Not Taken, in Benton, E. (ed.) *The Greening of Marxism*. London: Guilford Press.

Genovese, E. (1992) *From Rebellion to Revolution: Afro-American Slave Revolts in the Making of the Modern World*. New Orleans: Louisiana State University Press.

George, S. (1990) *A Fate Worse Than Debt*. London: Penguin.

George, S. (1999) *The Lugano Report: On Preserving Capitalism in the Twenty-First Century*. London: Pluto Press.

George, S. and Sabelli, F. (1994) *Faith and Credit: The World Bank's Secular Empire*. New York: Penguin.

Gerhards, J. and Rucht, D. (1992) Mesomobilization: Organizing and Framing in Two Protest Campaigns in West Germany. *American Journal of Sociology*, 98: 555–95.

German Green Party (1983) *The Programme of the German Green Party*. London: Heretic.

Gilman, P. and Marx, G. (2000) Complexity and Irony in Policing and Protesting: The World Trade Organisation in Seattle. *Social Justice*, 27, 2: 212–36.

Goldman, E. (1906) Observations and Comments. *Mother Earth*, 1: 2.

Goldsmith, E. (ed.) (1972) *A Blueprint for Survival*. London: Tom Stacy.

Goldsmith, E. (1988) *The Great U-Turn: De-Industrializing Society*. Bideford: Green Books.

Goldsmith, J. (1994) *The Trap*. London: Macmillan.

Gould, P. (1988) *Early Green Politics*. Brighton: Harvester.

Gray, J. (2002) *False Dawn*. London: Granta.

Greco, T. (2001) *Money: Understanding and Creating Alternatives to Legal Tender*. New York: Chelsea Green Publishing.

Greenpeace (2001) *Getting to Zero Waste: A Citizens' Resource Recovery Strategy for Anyshire County Council*. London: Greenpeace.

Greider, W. (1997) *One World, Ready or Not: The Maniac Logic of Global Capitalism*. New York: Simon and Schuster.

Guérin, D. (1973) *Fascism and Big Business*. New York: Pathfinder Press.

Guha, R. and Martinez-Alier, J. (1997) *Varieties of Environmentalism: Essays North and South*. London: Earthscan.

Hall, S. and Jacques, M. (1989) *New Times*. London: Lawrence and Wishart.

Hardt, M. (2004) 'Intermezzo' in Passavant, P. and Dean, J. (eds) *Empire's New Clothes*. London: Routledge.

Hardt, M. and Negri, A. (2001a) *Empire*. New York: Harvard University Press.

Hardt, M. and Negri, A. (2001b) From Movement to Society, in Anon. (ed.) *On Fire: The Battle of Genoa and the Anti-Capitalist Movement*. London: One-Off Press.

Harman, C. (2000a) Globalisation: A Critique of a New Orthodoxy. *International Socialist*, 73

Harman, C. (2000b) *The IMF, Globalisation and Resistance*. London: Socialist Worker.

Harris, N. (2003) *The Return of Cosmopolitan Capital: Globalisation, the State and War*. London: I.B. Tauris.

Harvey, D. (1990) *The Condition of Postmodernity*. Oxford: Blackwell.

Harvey, D. (1996) *Justice, Nature and the Geography of Difference*. Oxford: Blackwell.

Harvey, D. (1999) *The Limits to Capital*. London: Verso.

Hawken, P., Lovins, A.B. and Hunter Lovins, L. (1999) *Natural Capitalism – The Next Industrial Revolution*. London: Earthscan.

Hayden, A. (2000) *Sharing the Work, Sparing the Planet*. London: Zed Press.

Hayek, F. (1976) *The Road to Serfdom*. London: Routledge and Kegan Paul.

Henwood, D. (1998) *Wall Street*. London: Verso.

Herman, E. and McChesney, R. (1997) *The Global Media: The New Missionaries of Global Capitalism*. London: Cassell.

Herman, P. and Kuper, R. (2003) *Food for Thought: Towards a Future for Farming*. London: Pluto Press.

Hertz, N. (2001) *The Silent Takeover*. London: Heinemann.

Hilferding, R. (1981) *Finance Capital: A Study in the Latest Phase of Capitalist Development*. London: Routledge.

Hines, C. (2000) *Localization: A Global Manifesto*. London: Earthscan.

Hirsch, F. (1977) *Social Limits to Growth*. London: Routledge and Kegan Paul.

Hirst, P. and Thompson, G. (1999) *Globalization in Question: The International Economy and the Possibilities of Governance*. Oxford: Polity Press.

Hiskett, W. and Franklin, J. (1939) *Searchlight on Social Credit*. London: P.S. King and Son Ltd.

Hoffman, Y. (1998) *Japanese Death Poems: Written by Zen Masters and Haiku Poets on the Verge of Death*. Tokyo: Charles Tuttle.

Holloway, J. (2002) *Change the World: Without Taking Power*. London: Pluto Press.

Holloway, J. and Pelaez, E. (eds) (1998) *Zapatista! Reinventing Revolution in Mexico*. London: Pluto Press.

Horkheimer, M. and Adorno, T. (1973) *The Dialectic of Enlightenment*. London: Allen Lane.

Houellebecq, M. (2000) *Atomised*. London: Vintage.

Houellebecq, M. (2003) *Platform*. London: Vintage.

Howard, M. and King, J. (1989) *A History of Marxian Economics. Vol. 1*. London: Macmillan.

Howard, M. and King, J. (1991) *A History of Marxian Economics. Vol.2*. London: Macmillan.

Huber, J. and Robertson, J. (2000) *Creating New Money: A Monetary Reform for the Information Age*. London: New Economics Foundation.

Huffington, A. (2003) *Pigs at the Trough: How Corporate Greed and Political Corruption are Undermining America*. New York: Crown.

Hughes, J. (1994) *Pan's Travail: Environmental Problems of the Ancient Greeks and Romans*. London: Johns Hopkins University Press.

Hulme, D. and Mosley, P. (1996) *Finance Against Poverty*. London: Routledge.

Hutchinson, F. and Burkitt, B. (1997) *The Political Economy of Social Credit and Guild Socialism*. London: Routledge.

Hutchinson, F., Mellor, M. and Olsen, W. (2002) *The Politics of Money: Towards Sustainability and Economic Democracy*. London: Pluto Press.

Hutton, W. (2001) *The World We're In*. London: Little, Brown.

Icke, D. (1994) *The Robots' Rebellion*. Bath: Gateway.

Illich, I. (1973) *Deschooling Society*. Harmondsworth: Penguin.

Illich, I. (1975) *Medical Nemesis*. London: Calder and Boyars.

Illich, I. (1978) *The Right to Useful Unemployment and its Professional Enemies*. London: Marion Boyars.

Inglehart, R. (1977) *The Silent Revolution: Changing Values and Political Styles Among Western Publics*. Princeton: Princeton University Press.

Jay, M. (1973) *The Dialectical Imagination. A History of the Frankfurt School and the Institute of Social Research, 1923–1950*. London: Heinemann Educational Books.

Katsiaficas, G. (1997) *The Subversion of Politics: European Autonomous Movements and the Decolonization of Everyday Life*. New Jersey: Humanities Press.

Kean, H. (1998) *Animal Rights: Political and Social Change in Britain since 1800*. London: Reaktion Books.

Keynes, J. (1960) *The General Theory of Employment, Interest and Money*. London: Macmillan.

Keynes, J. (1972) *Essays in Persuasion. Volume IX, The Collected Works of John Maynard Keynes*. Cambridge: Cambridge University Press.

King, J. (1988) *Economic Exiles*. London: Macmillan.

Kingsnorth, P. (2004) *One No, Many Yeses*. London: Free Press.

Klein, N. (2001a) *No Logo*. London: Flamingo.

Klein, N. (2001b) Reclaiming the Commons. *New Left Review*, 2, 9 (May–June): 86.

Kolakowski, L. (1988) *Main Currents of Marxism: The Founders*. Oxford: Oxford University Press.

Korten, D. (1998) *The Post-Corporate World- Life after Capitalism*. West Hartford, Connecticut: Kumarian Press.

Korten, D. (2001) *When Corporations Rule the World*. San Francisco: Kumarian Press.

Kovel, J. (2002) *The Enemy of Nature*. New York: Zed Press.

Kropotkin, P. (1972) *The Conquest of Bread*. New York: New York University Press.

Laclau, E. and Mouffe, C. (1985) *Hegemony and Socialist Strategy: Towards a Radical Democratic Politics*. London: Verso.

Lamy, P. (1996) *Millennium Rage: Survivalists, White Supremacists, and the Doomsday Prophecy*. New York: Plenum.

Lang, T. and Hines, C. (1993) *The New Protectionism*. London: Earthscan.

Larsson, T. (2001) *The Race to the Top: The Real Story of Globalization*. Washington, DC: CATO Institute.

Latham, R. (1997) Globalization and Democratic Provisionism; Re-reading Polanyi. *New Political Economy*, 2: 53–63.

Lechner, F. and Boli, J. (2000) *The Globalization Reader*. Malden, Massachusetts: Blackwell.

Lees, C. (2002) *The Red-Green Coalition in Germany*. Manchester: Manchester University Press.

Legrain, P. (2003) *Open World: Truth About Globalisation*. New York: Little, Brown.

Lenin, V. (1982) *Imperialism: The Highest Stage of Capitalism*. Moscow: Progress.

Lethbridge, D. (1999) Jew-Haters and Red-Baiters: The Canadian League of Rights. *AntiFa Info-Bulletin* (2 February).

Leval, G. (1990a) Collectivization in Magdalena de Pulpis, in Dolgoff, S. (ed.) *The Anarchist Collectives*. New York: Black Rose Books.

Leval, G. (1990b) Industrial Collectivization in Alcoy, Dolgoff, S. (ed.) *The Anarchist Collectives*. New York: Black Rose Books.

Leval, G. (1990c) The Peasant Federation of Levant, in Dolgoff, S (ed.) *The Anarchist Collectives*. New York: Black Rose Books.

Lietaer, B. (2001) *The Future of Money: A New Way to Create Wealth, Work and a Wiser World*. London: Century.

Light, A. (ed.) (1998) *Social Ecology after Bookchin*. London: Guilford Press.

Loader, B. (1997) *The Governance Of Cyberspace: Politics, Technology and Global Restructuring*. London: Routledge.

Lomborg, B. (2001) *The Skeptical Environmentalist*. Cambridge: Cambridge University Press.

London Mayday Collective (2001) Mayday Monopoly Game: Anti-Capitalist Actions Across London on Tuesday 1 May 2001. London BM Mayday.

Lowry, M. (1967) *Under the Volcano*. London: Jonathan Cape.

Lowry, M. (1972) *Dark as the Grave Wherein My Friend is Laid*. Harmondsworth: Penguin.

Lutz, M. (1998) *Economics for the Common Good*. London: Routledge.

Luxemburg, R. (1971) *The Accumulation of Capital*. London: Routledge.

Lyotard, J. (1984) *The Postmodern Condition*. Manchester: Manchester University Press.

Maag, B. (1997) Forests and Trees in the World of Two Tamang Villages in Central Nepal: Observations with Special Reference to the Role of Tamang Women in Forest Management, in Seeland, K. (ed.) *Nature is Culture: Indigenous Knowledge and Socio-cultural Aspects of Trees and Forests in Non-European Cultures*. London: Intermediate Technology Publications.

Macpherson, C. (1953) *Democracy in Alberta*. Toronto: Toronto University Press.

Malos, E. (1980) *The Politics of Housework*. London: Alison and Busby.

Mander, J. and Goldsmith, E. (eds) (1996) *The Case Against the Global Economy: And for a Turn Towards the Local*. San Francisco: Sierra Club.

Marcuse, H. (1964) *One Dimensional Man*. London: Routledge and Kegan Paul.

Marquez, G. (1989) *Love in the Time of Cholera*. Harmondsworth: Penguin.

Marx, K. (1973) *Grundrisse*. Harmondsworth: Penguin.

Marx, K. (1977) *Early Writings*. Harmondsworth: Pelican.

Marx, K. (1979) *Capital. Vol. 1*. Harmondsworth: Penguin.

Marx, K. (1987) *Marx and Engels Collected Works*. Volume 42. New York: International Publishers.

Marx, K. and Engels, F. (1985) *The Communist Manifesto*. Harmondsworth: Penguin.

McCaughan, M. (2004) *The Battle for Venezuela*. London: Latin America Bureau.

McLellan, D. (1980a) *Marx before Marxism*. London: PaperMac.

McLellan, D. (1980b) *Marxism after Marx*. London: PaperMac.

McMurtry, J. (1999) *The Cancer Stage of Capitalism*. London: Pluto Press.

McMurtry, J. (2002) *Value Wars: The Global Market Versus the Life Economy*. London: Pluto Press.

McNally, D. (1993) *Against the Market: Political Economy, Market Socialism and the Marxist Critique*. London: Verso.

McNally, D. (2002) *Another World is Possible: Globalization and Anti-Capitalism*, Winnipeg: Arbeiter Ring Publishing.

Meadows, D. (1974) *Limits to Growth: A Report for the Club of Rome's Project on the Predicament of Mankind*. New York: Universe.

Mellor, M. (1992) *Breaking the Boundaries: Towards a Feminist, Green Socialism*. London: Virago.

Mellor, M. (1997) *Feminism and Ecology*. Cambridge: Polity Press.

Melucci, A. (1989) *Nomads of the Present*. London: Radius.

Melucci, A. (1996) *Challenging Codes*. Cambridge: Cambridge University Press.

Merchant, C. (1992) *Radical Ecology*. London: Routledge.

Moggridge, D. (1976) *Keynes*. London: Fontana.

Mol, A. and Spaarrgaren, G. (2000) Ecological Modernisation Theory in Debate: A Review. *Environmental Politics*, 9, 1: 17–49.

Mollison, B. (1991) *Introduction to Permaculture*. Tyalgum, New South Wales: Tagai.

Monbiot, G. (2003a) *Captive State: The Corporate Takeover of Britain*. London: Macmillan.

Monbiot, G. (2003b) *The Age of Consent: A Manifesto for a New World Order*. London: Flamingo.

Moody, G. (2001) *Rebel Code: Linux and the Open Source Revolution*. Harmondsworth: Penguin.

Moody, K. (1997) *Workers in a Lean World*. London: Verso.

Moody, R. (1992) *The Gulliver File: Mines, People and Land*. London: Pluto Press.

Moore, M. (1996) *Downsize This! Random Threats from an Unarmed American*. New York: Crown Publishers.

Moses, M. (1995) *The Novel and the Globalization of Culture*. New York: Oxford University Press.

Morris, D. (1996) Free Trade: The Great Destroyer, in Mander, J. and Goldsmith, E. (eds) *The Case Against the Global Economy: And for a Turn Towards the Local*. San Francisco: Sierra Club.

Nader, R. (1965) *Unsafe at Any Speed: The Designed-in Dangers of the American Automobile*. New York: Grossman.

Nader, R. (2002) *Crashing the Party: Taking on the Corporate Government in an Age of Surrender*. New York: St. Martin's Griffin /Thomas Dunne.

Negri, A. (1991) *Marx Beyond Marx: Lessons on the Grundrisse*. London: Pluto Press.

Negri, A. (1989) *The Politics of Subversion*. Oxford: Polity Press.

Noble, S. (1996) And the Truth Shall Set You Free. *Spearhead*, 331: 11.

Notes from Nowhere (ed.) (2003) *We Are Everywhere*. London: Verso.

O'Connor, J. (1973) *The Fiscal Crisis of the State*. New York: St Martin's.

O'Connor, J. (1984) *Accumulation Crisis*. Oxford: Blackwell.

O'Connor, J. (1991) On the Two Contradictions of Capitalism. *Capitalism Nature Socialism*, 2, 3: 107–9.

O'Connor, J. (ed.) (1995) *Is Capitalism Sustainable? Political Economy and the Politics of Ecology*. New York: Guilford Press.

O'Connor, J. (1998) *Natural Causes: Essays in Ecological Marxism*. New York: Guilford Press.

Ostrom, E. (1991) *Governing the Commons: The Evolution of Institutions for Collective Action*. Cambridge: Cambridge University Press.

Palast, G. (2003) *The Best Democracy Money Can Buy*. London: Robinson.

Papadakis, E. (1998) *Historical Dictionary of the Green Movement*. Lanham, Maryland: Scarecrow Press.

Parsons, H. (ed.) (1977) *Marx and Engels on Ecology*. Westport, Connecticut: Greenwood Press.

Passavant, P. and Dean, J. (2004) *Empire's New Clothes*. London: Routledge.

Patomaki, H. (2001) *Democratising Globalization: The Leverage of the Tobin Tax*. London: Zed Press.

Pearce, F. (1976) *Crimes of the Powerful. Marxism, Crime and Deviance*. London: Pluto Press.

Perirats, J. (1990) The Aragon Federation of Collectives: The Final Congress, in Dolgoff, S. (ed.) *The Anarchist Collectives*. New York: Black Rose Books.

Perlman, F. (1992) *Anything Can Happen*. London: Phoenix Press.

Peterson, J. and Lewis, M. (1999) *The Elgar Companion to Feminist Economics*. Cheltenham: Edward Elgar.

Petras, J. and Morley, M. (1975) *The United States and Chile: Imperialism and the Overthrow of the Allende Government*. New York: Monthly Review Press.

Petras, J. and Veltmeyer, H. (2001) *Globalisation Unmasked*. London: Zed Press.

Petras, J. and Veltmeyer, H. (2003) *System in Crisis*. London: Zed Press.

Petrini, C. (2003) *Slow Food*. London: Grubb Street.

Pigou, A. (2002) *The Economics of Welfare*. New Brunswick: Transaction Publishers.

Pilot, A. (2001) Blossom from the Wasteland. *Social Credit International*, 23: 3.

Plant, S. (1992) *The Most Radical Gesture*. London: Routledge.

Plows, A. (2004) Activist Networks in the UK: Mapping the Build-Up to the Anti-Globalization Movement, in Carter, J. and Morland, D. (eds) *Anti-Capitalist Britain*. London: New Clarion Press.

Poguntke, T. (1993) *Alternative Politics: The German Green Party*. Edinburgh: Edinburgh University Press.

Polanyi, K. (1957) *The Great Transformation*. Boston: Beacon Press.

Porritt, J. (1984) *Seeing Green: The Politics of Ecology Explained*. Oxford: Blackwell.

Prawer, S. (1976) *Karl Marx and World Literature*. Oxford: Clarendon Press.

Price, W. (1981) *Social Credit and the Leisure State: Key to the Green Revolution*. Hebden Bridge: Social Credit Union.

Purkis, J. (2000) Modern Millenarians? in Doherty, B., Paterson, M. and Seel, B. (eds) *Direct Action in British Environmentalism*. London: Routledge.

Rainbow, S. (1993) *Green Politics*. Oxford: Oxford University Press.

Read, J. (2003) *The Micro-Politics of Capital*. State University of New York Press.

Rees, J. (2001) Anti-Capitalism, Reformism and Socialism, *International Socialism* 90: 3–40.

Rich, B. (1994) *Mortgaging the Earth*. London: Earthscan.

Rifkin, J. (1995) *The End of Work: The Decline of the Global Labor Force and the Dawn of the Post-market Era*. New York: G.P. Putnam's Sons.

Ritter, G. (1997) *Goldbugs and Greenbacks: The Antimonopoly Tradition and the Politics of Finance in America*. Cambridge: Cambridge University Press.

Ritzer, G. (1995) *The McDonaldisation of Society*. London: Pine Forge Press.

Roberts, A. (1979) *The Self-Managing Environment*. London: Allison and Busby.

Ronson, J. (2000) *Them: Adventures with Extremists*. London: Picador.

Rosset, P. and Benjamin, M. (1994) *The Greening of the Revolution: Cuba's Experiment with Organic Farming*. Melbourne: Ocean.

Rowbotham, M. (1998) *The Grip of Death: A Study of Modern Money, Debt Slavery and Destructive Economics*. Charlbury, Oxfordshire: Jon Carpenter Books.

Rowbotham, M. (2000) *Goodbye America: Globalisation, Debt and the Dollar Empire*. Charlbury, Oxfordshire: Jon Carpenter Books.

Rowe, J. (2002) The Majesty of the Commons: A Review of David Bollier's *Silent Theft. Washington Monthly* (April).

Roy, A. (1999) *The Cost of Living*. London: Flamingo.

Roy, A. (2001) *Power Politics*. Boston, Massachusetts: South End Press.

Roy, A. (2002) *The Algebra of Infinite Justice*. London: Flamingo.

Rupert, M. (2000) *Ideologies of Globalization: Contending Visions of a New World Order*. London: Routledge.

Russell, P. (1995) *The Chiapas Rebellion*. Austin, Texas: Mexico Resource Center.

Rustin, M. (2003) Empire: A Postmodern Theory of Revolution, Balakrishnan, G. (ed.) *Debating Empire*. London: Verso.

Ryan, M. (1991) Afterword, Negri, A. (1991) *Marx Beyond Marx: Lessons on the Grundrisse*. London: Pluto Press.

Sahlins, M. (1972) *The Original Affluent Society*. Chicago: Aldine Atherton.

Salleh, A. (1997) *Ecofeminism as Politics: Nature, Marx and the Postmodern*. London: Zed Press.

Schifferes, S. (2003) US Inequality Gap Widens. BBC Business News Online, (25 September).

Schlosberg, D. (1999) *Environmental Justice and the New Pluralism: The Challenge of Difference for Environmentalism*. New York: Oxford University Press.

Schlosser, E. (2001) *Fast Food Nation: The Dark Side Of The All-American Meal*. Boston, Massachusetts: Houghton Mifflin.

Schumacher, E. (1978) *Small is Beautiful. A Study of Economics as if People Mattered*. London: Abacus.

Search, R. (1977) *Lincoln Money Martyred!* Hawthorne, California: Omni Publications.

Seeland, K. (ed.) (1997) *Nature is Culture: Indigenous Knowledge and Socio-cultural Aspects of Trees and Forests in Non-European Cultures*. London: Intermediate Technology Publications.

Sen, A. (1999) *Development as Freedom*. Oxford: Oxford University Press.

Sheasby, W. (2003) George Soros and the Rise of the Neocentrics. *Change Links* (December).

Sheasby, W. (2004) Karl Marx and the Victorians' Nature: The Evolution of a Deeper View: Part One: Oceanus. *Capitalism Nature Socialism*, 15, 2: 47–64.

Sheasby, W. and Wall, D. (2002) The Enemy of Nature and the Nature of the Enemy. *Capitalism Nature Socialism*, 11, 4: 155–66.

Shiva, V. (1988) *Staying Alive: Women, Ecology and Development*. London: Zed Press.

Shiva, V. (2000) *Stolen Harvest: The Hijacking Of The Global Food Supply*. Cambridge, Massachusetts: South End Press.

Sklair, L. (2001) *The Transnational Capitalist Class*. Oxford: Blackwell.

Sklar, H. (1980) *Trilateralism*. Boston, Massachusetts: South End Press.

Sklar, H. (1995) *Chaos or Community: Seeking Solutions, Not Scapegoats for Bad Economics*. Boston, Massachusetts: South End Press.

Smart, D. (1978) *Pannekoek and Gorter's Marxism*. London: Pluto Press.

Smil, V. (1984) *The Bad Earth: Environmental Degradation in China*. London: Zed Press.

Snyder, G. (1974) *Turtle Island*. New York: New Directions Books.

Snyder, G. (1999) *The Gary Snyder Reader: Poetary, Prose, and Translations*. Washington, DC: Counterpoint.

Soros, G. (1998) *The Crisis of Global Capitalism*. London: Little, Brown and Co.

Soros, G. (2004) *The Bubble of American Supremacy*. London: Weidenfeld and Nicolson.

Souchy, A. (1990a) The Collectivization of the Metal and Munitions Industry, in Dolgoff, S. (ed.) *The Anarchist Collectives*. New York: Black Rose Books.

Souchy, A (1990b) Collectivization in Catalonia, Dolgoff, S. (ed.) *The Anarchist Collectives*. Black Rose Books: New York.

Spretnak, C. and Capra, F. (1986) *Green Politics: The Global Promise*. London: Paladin.

Starr, A. (2000) *Naming the Enemy: Anti-Corporate Movements Confront Globalization*. London: Pluto Press.

Stauber, J. and Rampton, S. (1995) *Toxic Sludge is Good for You*. Monroe, Maine: Common Courage Press.

St Clair, J. (1999) Seattle Diary: It's a Gas, Gas, Gas. *New Left Review*, 238: 81–96.

Stiglitz, J. (2002) *Globalization and its Discontents*. London: Allen Lane.

Stiglitz, J. (2003) *The Roaring Nineties: Seeds of Destruction*. London: Allen Lane.

Stingel, J. (2000) *Social Discredit: Anti-Semitism, Social Credit, and the Jewish Response*. Montreal: McGill-Queen's University Press.

Strayer, J. (1991) *The German Peasants' War and Anabaptist Community of Goods*. Montreal: McGill-Queen's University Press.

Taylor, K. (1982) *The Political Ideas of the Utopian Socialist*. London: Cass.

Thekaekara, S. (2003) *Beating the System: Local Solutions to the Globalisation Crisis*. London: New Economics Foundation.

Thompson, E. (1976) *William Morris: From Romantic to Revolutionary*. New York: Pantheon Books.

Thompson, E. (1977) *Whigs and Hunters: The Origin of the Black Act*. Harmondsworth: Penguin.

Tilly, C. (1978) *From Mobilization to Revolution*. Englewood Cliffs, NJ: Prentice-Hall .

Tilly, C. (2003) A Nebulous Empire, in Balakrishnan, G. (ed.) *Debating Empire*. London: Verso.

Tokar, B. (1992) *The Green Alternative*. San Pedro: R. and E. Miles.

Toke, D. (2000) *Green Politics and Neoliberalism*. Basingstoke: Macmillan.

Trainer, E. (1985) *Abandon Affluence!* London: Zed Press.

Trainer, E. (1989) *Developed To Death!* London: Green Print.

Tronti, M. (1976) Workers and Capital, in *The Labour Process and Class Strategies*. London: Conference of Socialist Economics.

UNCTAD (2002) Are Transnationals Bigger than Countries? <www.UNCTAD. org>.

Utsunomiya, F. (1980) *Politics of Development and Environment*. Tokyo: Tokyo University Press.

Veblen, T. (1994) *The Theory of the Leisured Class*. New York: Dover.

Victoria, B. (1998) *Zen at War*. New York: Weatherhill.

Vidal, J. (1997) *McLibel: Burger Culture on Trial*. London: Macmillan.

Vonnegut, K. (1971) *Cat's Cradle*. Harmondsworth: Penguin, 2000.

Wainwright, H. (2003) *Reclaim the State: Experiments in Popular Democracy*. London: Verso.

Waldman, E. (1958) *The Spartacist Uprising of 1919 and the Crisis of the German Socialist Movement: A Study of the Relation of Political Theory and Party Practice*. Milwaukee: Marquette University Press.

Walker, M. (1977) *The National Front*. London: Fontana.

Wall, D. (1990) *Getting There: Steps to a Green Society*. London: Greenprint.

Wall, D. (1993) *Green History*. London: Routledge.

Wall, D. (1994) *Weaving a Bower Against the Endless Night*. London: Green Party.

Wall, D. (1999) *Earth First! and the Anti-roads Movement*. London: Routledge.

Wall, D. (2003) The Ecosocialism of Fools. *Capitalism Nature Socialism*, 14, 2: 99–122.

Wall, D. (2004) Bakhtin and the Carnival Against Capitalism, in Carter, J. and Morland, D. (eds) *Anti-Capitalist Britain*. London: New Clarion Press.

Warren, B. (1980) *Imperialism: Pioneer of Capitalism*. London: New Left Books.

Weizsacker, E., Lovins, A. and Lovis, H. (1997) *Factor Four: Doubling Wealth, Halving Resource Use*. London: Earthscan.

Went, R. (2000) *Globalization: Neo-liberal Challenge, Radical Responses*. London and Sterling, Virginia: Pluto Press.

Wheen, F. (2000) *Karl Marx*. London: Fourth Estate.

Williams, R. (1982) *Socialism and Ecology*. London: Socialist Environmental and Resources Association.

Wilson, E.O. (2002) The Bottleneck. *Scientific America* (February).

Wistrich, R. (1985) *Hitler's Apocalypse: Jews and the Nazi Legacy*. London: Weidenfeld and Nicolson.

Wolf, M. (2004) *Why Globalization Works: The Case for a Global Market Economy*. New Haven: Yale University Press.

Wolfe, T. (1988) *The Bonfire of the Vanities*. London: Pan.

Womack, J. (1969) *Zapata and the Mexican Revolution*. London: Thames & Hudson.

Wood, E. (2003a) A Manifesto for Global Capitalism? in Balakrishnan, G. (ed.) *Debating Empire*. London: Verso.

Wood, E. (2003b) *Empire of Capital*. London: Verso.

Woodcock, G. (1963) *Anarchism. A History of Libertarian Ideas and Movements*. Harmondsworth: Penguin.

Woodin, M. and Lucas, C. (2004) *Green Alternatives to Globalisation: A Manifesto*. London: Pluto Press.

Wright, S. (2002) *Storming Heaven: Class Composition and Struggle in Italian Autonomist Marxism*. London: Pluto Press.

Zerzan, J. (1999) *Elements of Refusal*. Columbia, Missouri: Columbia Alternative.

Zobel, G. (1999) Hidden Agenda. *The Big Issue*, 15th November.

Index

Compiled by Xanthe Bevis

1930s recession 26–8, 116
9/11 *see* Twin Towers

Abandon Affluence (Trainer) 72, 155
Achebe, Chinua 83
Adorno *see* Frankfurt School
Africa 14, 88
Africa, John, founder of MOVE 157
Against the market (McNally) 164
agriculture
    agribusiness 51–2
    allotments 178
    'Green Revolution' 129
    organic 120, 182
    see also farmers *and* subsistence
        and permaculture
AIDS *see* HIV/AIDS
alcoholism 14, 36
alienation 16
Allende, Salvador 50
Alternative in Eastern Europe, The
    (Baldro) 155
Althusser, Louis 104
Anabaptists 4, 186
anarchism 5, 19–20
    American MidWest 3
    anarchist economics 20
    'black bloc' 19, 126, 147
    Cooperation 134–5
    green anarchism 135
    and the market 134
    Marxist anarchism 128–34
    Spanish Civil War 186
    see also autonomism *and*
        Kropotkin, Peter *and*
        primitivists
animal rights 77
anti-capitalism 2–3, 12–22, 102, 176
    anti-capitalist alternatives 177–92
    conspiracies 20–2, 84, 114, 119,
        173–5
    green 64–83

militant 5–8, 19, 172
money-centred 84–100 *see also*
    monetary reform *and* eco-
    socialism
by Maroons 178
Marxist 102–22
as politics of time 176–7
protest 7, 124 *see also* anti-
    globalisation protest
right-wing 170, 173–4
social democratic critique 24
strategy 178–92
see also anarchism *and* anti-
    globalisation *and* economics of
    anti-capitalism
'anti-capitalist capitalists' 18, 23–43
    see also Stigliz, Joseph *and*
    Soros, George
Anti-Capitalist Manifesto (Callinicos)
    116
anti-corporate protest 5, 45
anti-corporatists 5, 44–63
anti-globalisation
    anti-corporate 18, 44–63 *see also*
        Klein, Naomi and Korten,
        David
    autonomist 142–52
    by states 183 *see also* Cuba *and*
        Venezuala
    Marxist 102–22
    protest 1–2, 23, 191
        Cancun 2, 17, 65
        Davos 1, 3, 6, 7
        May Day 2002 45
        Prague 8, 102
        Qatar 8
        Quebec 8
        Seattle 2, 3, 8, 19, 65, 85, 102,
        124, 146, 179, 191
    racist 21
    see also globalise resistance *and*
        ecosocialism

anti-imperialism 4, 183
anti-semitism 21, 44, 94–5, 172–3, 174
Apple 53
Argentina 32, 137, 182
Arthur Andersen 48
Asda 52
Asian crisis *see* crises in capitalism
asymmetric information 25, 32, 43
ATTAC (Association for the Taxation of Transactions and for Aid to Citizens) 19, 84, 85, 89, 90–1, 102 *see also* Tobin Tax
Aufheben (anti-capitalist magazine) 124
autonomism 20, 25, 37, 123–52
  action 125, 127, 131, 144, 147
  approach to globalisation 142–52
  Autonomen 126
  Autonomis Operaia 125–6
  campaigns 5
  communist 127
  feminist autonomists 132
  Italian 125–6
  Marxist 122
  'metropolitan Indians' 126
  on power 141
  piqueteros 137
  Reclaim the Streets 136
  regulation theory 130
  shoplifting 127
  situationism 136
  strategy 145, 150
  see also Empire *and* squatting *and* 'tribe of moles' *and* Cleaver, Harry and Hardt, Michael and Negri, Toni *see also* anarchism

Bahro, Rudolf 155
Bakunin, Mikhail 124
Ball, John 4
Bananas 17
Bank of America 53–4
bankers 21, 44, 95, 173 *see* banks, banking
banking 19, 20, 100
banks 9, 91, 97, 99, 126
Baudrillard, Jean 60, 140

Best Democracy Money Can Buy, The (Palast) 45
Bhaskar, Roy 175
Bhopal Disaster 161
Bilderburg Group 55, 174
Billions for the Bankers (Emry) 172
Bjork-Shiley heart valve *see* Pfizer
'black bloc' *see* anarchism
Blair, Tony 54, 56
Blairite Third Way 37, 41, 45, 68, 140
Blake, William 66, 104
Bolivia 3
Bologna, Sergio 125, 150
Bonfire of the Vanities, The (Wolfe) 89
Bookchin, Murray 135
Botswana 32
Bové, José anti-MacDonald's protestor 45
boycotts, consumer 183
BP Amoco 53
brands 46, 57–8, 60, 149
Brave New World (Huxley) 61
Braverman, Harry 129
Brazil, World Bank lending to 88
Brazilian Landless Movement 7, 8, 102
Brazilian Workers Party 183
Bretton Woods Conference 27, 85 *see* IMF
Bretton Woods Institutions 3, 23, 27–8, 29, 39 *see* GATT *and* WTO, *and* World Bank *and* IMF
bribery 48
British East India Company xiv, 49
British Sugar 52
Brown, Norman O. 169, 189
Buchan, James 99
Buchanan, Pat 21
Buddha (Guatama Siddhartha) 4
Buddhism 67, 105, 154
Bukharin, Nikolai 112, 113
Burkett, Paul 154
Bush, George (Sr) xiii
Bush, George W. 26, 38–9, 45, 53, 85, 87, 173

Callinicos, Alec 116–17, 119

Cancer Stage of Capitalism, The
    (McMurtry) 91
Capital (Marx) 103, 110, 128, 142
capital 124
    finance capital 112
    liberalisation 29–31, 84
    Marx on 107
capitalism 19, 28, 102, 116, 161–4
    as conspiracy 20–2, 172–5
    contradictions within 133
    'second contradiction of
        capitalism' 154, 157
    as exploitation of working class 20
    as favouring elite 20–1, 29, 40–1
    and globalisation 8–12
    as matrix 175
    as organised madness 169
    as totalitarianism 5
    'state capitalism' 9
    alternatives to 172–92
    ecosocialist approach to 161
    see also anti-capitalism *and* neo-
        liberal globalisation *and* crises
        of capitalism
Capitalism and Schizophrenia
    (Deleuze & Guattari) 142
Capitalism Nature Socialism (journal)
    154
Captive State (Monbiot) 45
carbon emissions xii, 77, 157, 158,
    178 *see* climate change *and*
    greenhouse gases
Card, Andrew 53
Cargill 51–2
cars 2, 13, 70, 158, 164
Carson, Rachel 85
Cartels 53
Castillo Armas, Colonel Carlos 50
Castro, Fidel 19, 104, 105–6,
    118–21, 122, 182, 166
Cat's Cradle (Vonnegut) 175
Charles Schwab (corporation) 53
Chavez, Hugo, President of
    Venezuela 50, 113, 182
Chevron 53
Chile 13, 50, 88–9 *see also* Pinochet
    and Allende
China 13, 14, 15, 22, 40, 49, 52, 89
    EPZ workers in 58, 179–80

Chomsky, Noam 161
Chossudovsky, Michel 85, 87
Christian Aid 13, 14
CIA 50
Civilisation and its Discontents
    (Freud) 25
class struggle *see* working class
    struggle
class war 42, 129 *see also* working
    class struggle
Cleaver, Harry 20, 21, 134, 122,
    127, 129, 134, 143 *see also*
    autonomism
climate change xii, 13, 16, 22, 53,
    70, 158, 159
Clinton, Bill 17, 18, 25, 41, 45, 68,
    173
CNT *see* anarchism, Spanish Civil
    War
Coalition of Republican
    Environmental Advocates 53
Cobbett, William 62
Coca-Cola 16, 45, 56
colonisation 162, 172
commodification 116, 144, 161,
    184 *see also* enclosure
Commoner, Professor Barry *see*
    growth, limits to
commons 80–1, 89, 105, 134, 167,
    169, 172, 177, 183–7, 191
    tragedy of 167 *see also* enclosure
        and privitisation *and* open
        source
communism 102, 127, 145, 164
    Taborite communism 186
    see Marxism *and* socialism
        and ecosocialism *see also*
        autonomism
Communist Manifesto (Marx and
    Engels) 105, 106, 119
communist parties 19, 102, 125
    Communist Party of Great Britain
        140
communitarianism 37
community 36
comparative advantage 73–4, 77
competition 11, 53, 71–2,
competitiveness 74, 169 *see also*
    'race to the bottom'

Confédération Paysanne 3
conspicuous consumption 35, 42,
    182
conspiracies 20, 21, 174–5
    inflation 21
    racism 21 see also anti-semiticism
    see also anti-capitalist
        conspiracies
consumer boycotts see boycotts,
    consumer
consumerism 9, 57, 61, 72, 155, 174
    control of working class with 5
    see Marceuse
consumers 33, 57
consumption xiv, 109, 133, 191
consumption, green ethical 182 see
    also underconsumption
cooperation 176, 181–2 see also
    anarchism
Corporate Watch 5
corporations 12, 18, 20, 44–63, 71,
    187
    corporate welfare 57
    and crime 48–9, 51
    and education 56,
    and environmental degradation 60
    and exploitation of labour 58–60,
    and free trade 55–6
    influence on political history
        49–50
    and migration 56,
    and nation states 46–7,49–50, 54
    outsourcing 58–60, 61, 77–8
    poverty 58
    privatisation 56
    see also multinationals
colonialism 13, 49, 83, 110–11 see
    also imperialism
    in Ireland 111
    in India 111
councils 136
Coventry League of the
    Unemployed see social credit
crises of capitalism 19, 99–100,
    108–9, 177
    Asian crisis 31, 40, 89
    underconsumption 112, 130
Crisis of Global Capitalism, The
    (Soros) 26

Cuba 19, 50, 120–1, 182 see Castro,
    Fidel

Dalla Costa, Maria 132
Daly, Herman 91
Davos see anti-globalisation protest
DDT 88
debt 9–10, 14, 19, 20, 29, 84, 86, 95,
    100, 109 see also global credits
    see also monetary reform
    Jubilee movement 19, 84
    debt-free money 19, 85, 97
deep ecology 135, 156–7
deflation 21
deflationary policies 24 see also
    Washington Consensus
Del Monte 17
Deleuze, Gilles 127, 139, 141, 142,
    150 see immanence
demand 10
democracy 5, 11, 15, 121
    Athenian 135
    control of working class with 5
    direct 135
    global 19, 78–9
    parliamentary 5
    participatory decision-making
        183
    radical 140
    representative 5
    subordination of 30
demurrage 95–6
deregulation 144 see also
    privatisation
derivatives 10
Derrida, Jacques 139
Desai, Meghnad 19, 105, 109, 114
determinism 139–40, 177
developing countries 31
development 22, 39
    as enclosure 79
    see also productivism
Diggers 186
direct action 121, 139, 191
    see also Lyminge Forest and Earth
        First! and Reclaim the Streets
discourse 141 see also Foucault
Disney 58, 59, 191
Do or Die! (journal of Earth First!) 7

dot.coms 34
Douglas Social Credit 85
Douglas, Major Clifford 19, 42, 85,
    91–5, 97 *see* social credit
Douthwaite, Richard 91
Dulles, John Foster 50
dumping (by supermarkets) 48
Dutch East India Company xiv, 49
Dylan, Bob 43

Eagleton, Terry 22
Earth First! 7, 65
Ecclestone, Bernie 54
ecofeminism 67, 79–83, 155, 164,
    169, 177, 184 *see also* feminism
    and subsistence
ecological destruction xii, 22, 71,
    93, 125, 163, 155–61, 172, 176,
    177
  neo-liberal denial of 16, 53
  see also environmental
    degradation *and* deep ecology
ecological modernism (Germany)
    69
ecology 67 *see also* deep ecology
economics 170, 172, 176, 177
  of anti-capitalism 20, 171–92
  green economics 66, 68
  as method of control 151
  participatory economics *see*
    'parecon'
  see also free market economists
economies of scale 9, 74, 75, 107,
    178
ecosocialism 20, 22, 189, 153–70,
    109, 122 *see also* Kovel, Joel
  feminist 132, 167–8 *see also*
    subsistence
'ejidos' *see* enclosure
embedded markets 172, 180–3
Empire (Hardt & Negri) 20, 142–52
  on imperialism 148
  globalisation 148
  localism 145
  nomadism 145
  multititude 145
  reforms/demands 146
Emry, Sheldon 172–3

enclosure xiv, xv, 4, 13, 79, 89, 105,
    112, 121, 155–6, 184, 186
  'ejidos' 6
  Sutherlanders 132–3, 167
encuentro see Zapatistas *see also*
    Peoples Global Action
Enemy of Nature, The (Kovel) 154
Engels, Friedrich 103, 165–8
Enron 47–8, 82
environmental degradation 13, 16,
    22, 60, 69, 70, 75, 84, 155–61
  neo-liberal denial of 11–12
  see also ecological destruction *and*
    deep ecology
environmental justice movement
    156–7
European Union (EU) 15
  subsidies 17
  support for banana producers 17
  stability pact 76, 78
European Commission 55
exchange value 106–7, 108, 109, 154,
    160, 168, 169, 177, 189, 190
Export Processing Zones 15, 58–60,
    132, 134, 142, 164 *see also*
    China *and* Mexico
Exxon 50
Exxon Mobil 46

fair trade *see* trade
Faith and Credit (George and Sabelli)
    89
False Dawn see Gray
farmers 51–2, 80
  see also peasant *and* agriculture
    and subsistence
Fast, Howard 4
feminism 5, 65
  see also ecofeminism *and*
    ecosocialist feminism *and*
    autonomism *and* subsistence
fertility, decline in 14
fetishism 109–10
feudalism 11, 138
Feuerbach, Ludwig 104, 109–10
  see also fetishism
Fifth International 104
Firefox
  see open source 187

First Gulf War 60, 113
   see also Iraq
First World War 112–13
Fischer, Joschka 57
Fleet Boston Financial 53–4
food 17
   'Great Food Swap' 77
forced labour 13, 49
Ford, Henry 47, 53
   see also Fordism *and* post-Fordism
Fordism 60, 113, 130–1
Forum for the Future 57
Foster, John Bellamy 154, 161, 163, 175
Foucault 127, 139, 141, 142
Fourth International 19, 102, 104, 105, 116
Francis of Assisi 151
Frankfurt School 5, 61
   see also Marceuse
Franklin, Benjamin 95
free market economists 27, 174
free trade *see* trade
Freud, Sigmund 25, 169, 189
Friedman, Professor Milton 50, 129, 146
Friedman, Thomas 15
Furedi, Frank 114

G8 3, 8
Galbraith, John Kenneth 92
Gare, Aran 155
gated communities 169
Gates, Bill 45
GATS (General Agreement on Trade in Services) 56
GATT (General Agreement on Tariffs and Trade) xiv, 1, 6, 7, 17, 24, 28
   see WTO
General Motors 47
genetic engineering xiii, 8, 15, 80, 114, 185
George, Susan 89
Gesell, Silvio 19, 42
global credits
   see Soros, George
global neo-liberalism
   see neo-liberal globalisation

globalisation
   global markets, creation of 10
   as treadmill 163–4
   as weapon against moles 128–9
   support from environmentalists 65–6
   see also neo-liberal globalisation
      and capitalism
Globalistion Unmasked (Petras & Veltmeyer) 115–16
Globalization and its Discontents (Stiglitz) 25
GNP 14, 79
gold standard 116
Goldman, Emma 124, 134, 135
Goldsmith, Edward 65, 67, 70
Goldsmith, Sir James 24
Gore, Al 53
Goudie, Andrew 60
government intervention 24, 28
   non-intervention 27
Gramsci 60–1, 104, 149–50
Gray, John 24, 35
   False Dawn 36
Great Transformation see Polyani
greed 11, 41, 102, 169
Green Alternatives to Globalisation (Lucas & Woodin) 19, 65
green economics *see* economics
'green globalistion' 78
Green Left 154 *see also* ecosocialism
green localism *see* localism
green movement 5, 20, 64–83
Green Party 66, 126
   Austria 67
   California 159
   France 67
   Germany 57, 67, 78, 83
   Iran 71
   New Zealand 178
   in the UK 57, 67, 83
   in the US 47, 179
'Green Revolution' *see* agriculture
greenhouse effect *see* climate change
Gresham's law 98
growth
   effects on environment of 157, 158

export led 86
limitless xiv, 5, 16, 22, 41, 62, 72,
    82, 93, 172, 176, 181
limits to 120, 155, 167
opposition to 68–71
and poverty 79
see also zero growth
Guatama Siddhartha see Buddha
Guatemala 50, 58–9
Guattari 141, 142
    immanence 142
Guevara, Che 102
Guha, Rumachandra 156, 167, 169

Halliburton 50
happiness 189
Hardin, Garrett 167
Hardt, Michael 20, 122–52, 161, 176,
    177, 187, see also autonomism
    and Negri and Empire
Harris, Nigel 19
Harvey, David 99
Hawken, Paul 65–6
hedge funds 10, 25, 89
Hegel 50, 99, 104, 109, 110, 139–40,
    142
Henwood, Douglas 39–40
Hertz, Noreena 39
Hilferding, Rudolf 27, 112
Hines, Colin 18, 65, 78, 82
Hirst, Paul 24
history 22, 176–7 see also
    determinism and Hegel
Hitler 26, 27, 44, 48, 177
HIV/AIDS 14, 32, 74
Hobson, John 112
holism 67
Holocaust 44, 48
    revisionism 173 see also anti-
    semitism
homogenised global culture 16, 47
    see also macdonaldisation
Horkheimer see Frankfurt School
'hot money' 10, 30, 89
Hutton, Will 38–9
Huxley, Aldous 61, 67

IMF 3, 8, 22, 23, 26, 28, 29
    case against 85–7

instrument of US policy 86
structural adjustment
    programmes (SAPs) 32, 40,
    76–8, 85, 86–7
    and Russia 38
    and Tobin Tax 39
IBM 44, 48, 53
icenine 175–6, 184, 188
Icke, David 173
    see also conspiracies
immanence 142
    see also Guattari
imperialism 105, 110–14, 143, 148,
    159
Indian Farmers Union 7
industrialisation 19, 66, 72
IndyMedia 170
inequality 13, 30, 120, 172, 176
    see also poverty
inflation 21, 29, 30, 86, 98
information economy 70
    see also internet
Ingham, Bernard 54
International Bank for
    Reconstruction and
    Redevelopment
    see World Bank
International Forum on
    Globalisation 18
internationalism 76
internet 3, 6, 7, 144, 170, 187
interventionism 38, 39
    see also government intervention
Iraq 50, 189
    see also First Gulf War, Second
    Gulf War
italism xv, 178, 179

J18 see anti-capitalism, protest
Jesus 3

Kant, Immanuel 104, 109
Kerry, John 53
Keynes, John Maynard 24, 26–8,
    34–5, 41
    on Gesell 96
    on Douglas 93
Keynesian 37, 39, 41–2, 130
    green Keynesianism 41

Keynesian economists 32
Kibbo Kift Kin 93
    see also social credit and
    monetary reformers
Kingsnorth, Paul 191
Kitson, Arthur 95
Klein, Naomi 18, 70, 44–63, 141,
    182, 186
Korten, David 9, 18, 44–63, 71, 81,
    91, 108, 174, 184
Kovel, Joel 20, 37, 154, 157–63,
    164, 166, 168–9, 170, 175, 189
Kropotkin, Peter 20, 124, 134,
    135–6
Kyoto Protocol 53

Labour Party
    British 54
        opposition to Tobin Tax 90
        shift to right 68
        see also Blairite Third Way
    in New Zealand 68, 93
Land
    communal ownership of 6
    redistribution of 50
    reform 186
    respect for 177
    theft of 63
    see also enclosure and Brazilian
        Landless Movement and soil
Lang, Tim 18
Law, John 85, 95 see also monetary
    reformers
Lenin 103, 104, 113
Lerner, Jaime, Mayor of Cuntiba,
    Brazil 96–7
LETS (Local Exchange and Trading
    Systems) see monetary reform
Lewis, Avi 182
Lexus and the Olive Tree, The
    (Friedman) 15
Liang, Hector, ex-chair of United
    Biscuits 158
liberal economists see free market
    economists
liberalisation of capital, see capital
    liberalisation
Lietaer, Bernard 96–7, 100
Life Against Death (Brown) 169

life expectancy 14
Lincoln, Abraham 95 see also
    monetary reformers
Linton, Michael 96
lobbyists, corporate 53, 174
localisation 121, 161
    see also localism and green
        localism
localism 7, 18, 19, 115, 166, 178,
    179
    green localism 19, 20, 64–83,
        189
Localization (Hines) 18, 75
locally created currencies 78, 96–7
Lomberg, Bjorn 11, 12
Lowry, Malcolm 6
Lucas, Caroline 19, 65, 70, 74–6, 79,
    83, 97, 120 see also localisation
    and Woodin, Mike
Luxemburg, Rosa 4, 111–12, 113,
    144, 162
Lyminge Forest 123
Lyotard, Jean-François 139–40

McDonald's 8, 15, 16, 142
    see also McLibel Trial
macdonaldisation 16 see
    homogenised globalisation
McLibel trial 45
McNally, David 116, 119, 164
Major, John 54
Malthus, Thomas 166–7
Mandelson, Peter 55
Maoism 6, 104, 121
Marcuse, Herbert 5, 60–1, 189 see
    also Frankfurt School
market forces 10–11
market, the 8–12, 28, 32, 35, 46, 54,
    62, 64, 151, 189, 191
    extension of 33–4, 175–6 see also
        enclosure and colonisation
    alternatives to 37
    failure 41
    as myth 35–6
    see also asymmetric information
        and embedded markets and
        reflexivity
marketing 162
Marks and Spencer 182

Maroons 178
Marshall, Alfred 32–3
Martinez-Alier, Juan 156, 167, 169
Marx, Karl 4, 20, 22, 26, 42, 157, 177, 188
    anarchist view 128–34
    Capital 103
    as ecologist 154–5, 159, 164–6
    economic analysis 106–10
    Grundrisse 171, 178
    on labour 108
    on Maltheus 167
    on money 99
    on profit 107
    as prophet 121
    on crises in capitalism 108–9 *see also* exchange value, use value
    on moles 125
    on colonialism 110–11
    on globalisation 110–11, 114–18
    on imperialism 110–14
    as productivist 109, 114, 165, 176
Marx's Revenge (Desai) 105
Marxism 4, 101–22, 174
    autonomist 109, 127–8
        in comparison to anarchism 4
        in comparison to utopian socialism 4
    opposition to globalisation, ecological dimension *see* Castro, Fidel
    see also post-marxism
Marxisms 103–4
Marxist
    accounts of globalisation 101–22
    anarchism 113–14, 139, 151
    anti-capitalism 6, 100, 102–22
    localism 171, 178
    productivism 121–2
    revolutions 4
Marxists 19
    see also Frankfurt School *and* Gramsci *and* Uno School *and* Althusser
materialism 61, 142, 165, 189–91,
Mayday Monopoly group 129, 133, 142 *see also* direct action *and* anti-capitalist protest
Mebyon Kernow 76

Merchant, Carolyn 168
Mexico 52 *see also* Zapatistas
Microsoft 45, 187, 189
Mies, Maria 81, 169, 176
migrants 37, 56, 59
mir 138
Monbiot, George 19, 45, 56, 78–9, 102
monetary reformers 19, 20, 83, 84–100, 85, 112
    basic income 146
    in Curitiba 96–7, 100
    Gesell's demurrage 95–6
    LETS 96, 98
    Lincoln's greenback 95
    micro-credit 96
    Proudhon's labour credits 95
    timedollars 96
    see also social credit *and* Hutchinson, Frances
money 19, 97–9, 126
    abolition of 136
    see also monetary reform *and* monetary reformers *and* debt *and* banks *and* debt-free money *and* locally created currencies
money-lending 9
monopoly 51–3, 74, 112
monopsony 51
Monsanto 8
Moore, Michael 63
Morris, William 155, 190
Mother Earth (Goldman) 135
MOVE 157
Mudiyanselage, Ranjith 59
multinationals 14–15, 18, 20 *see also* corporations
multitude, the 20, 127–8, 131, 139, 141, 144–5, 146, 151–2, 164, 176, 187 *see also* potentia
Murdoch, Rupert 54

Nader, Ralph 47, 63, 65, 68, 154
NAFTA 5–6, 55
Naming the Enemy (Amory Starr) 173
Narmada Dam 81–2
nationalism 111, 173 *see also* Plaid Cymru *and* Mebyon Kernow

Negri, Toni 20, 122–52, 176, 177, 187
  subsumption of labour 132
  see also autonomism 37, 161 *and* Hardt *and* Empire
neo-conservatives 174
neo-Keynesianism 42 *see also* racism *and* anti-semitism
neo-liberal globalisation 3, 8–22, 172
  capitalist criticism of 23–43
  alternatives to 172
  to meet needs of elite 75–6
neo-liberalism 8, 12–13, 174
Nestlé boycott 5
New Economics Foundation 96
New Protectionaists, The (Hines & Lang) 18
News International *see* Murdoch, Rupert
Nigeria 80, 83
Nike 16, 46, 59, 61, 142, 182
No Logo (Klein) 18, 45, 56–7, 61
nomadism 144, 145, 150
non-intervention 27 *see also* free market economists
non-violent civil disobedience 7, 19
Norberg, Johan 12
Norton, Gale 53
nuclear power 68, 157, 168
nuclear waste 13
nuclear weapons 68

Ogoni 7
oil xii–xiii, 50, 57, 69, 85, 113, 157, 159–60
  lobby 53
Olson, Wendy 95
One dimensional man (Marceuse) 61
One no, many yeses (Kingsnorth) 191
OPEC 50
Open Society Institute *see* Soros, George
open source 172, 183, 184, 186, 187–9, 191
  Wikipedia 187
  Firefox 187
  see also commons
Opium Wars 49, 112

options 10
organised crime 38, 49
Owen, Robert 4, 95
Oxfam 17
ozone layer 158

Pakistan 59
Palast, Greg 45, 47
Panoptikon 141, 142
  see also Foucault
'parecon' 136–7
parliamentary democracy
  control of working class with 5
participatory decision-making 183
Patomaki, Heikki 91
peasant revolts 65, 179
  José Bové 3, 8, 65
  France 3
  Britain 4
  Ireland 4
  Mexico 6 *see also* Zapatistas
  against globalisation 79–80
  peasant communism 138 *see also* mir
  see also farmers
pensions 15
Peoples Global Action 2, 6–8, 102
Perlman, Fredy 99
permaculture 168, 177
Petras, James 115–16
Petrini, Carlo 189 *see* slow food movement
Pfizer 47
Philippines 15
Philosopher Kings 26
Pinochet, General 13, 88–9, 129
Plaid Cymru 76
planning
  as alternative to market forces 10, 13, 37
Plato 26, 66
pollution 48 *see also* ecological destruction *and* environmental degradation
pollution *see* ecological degradation
Polyani, Karl 24, *The Great Transformation* 35–8, 43, 175–6, 181
Popper, Karl 26

population 166–7
populism 63
post-capitalism 19, 172
post-Fordism 141–2, 149 *see also*
    Fordism
post-Marxism 139–42
post-modernism 20, 57–8, 60–1,
    127, 139–42, 148, 178 *see also*
    Baudrillard *and* Deleuze *and*
    Foucault
potentia 131, 147, 152 *see also* the
    multitude
poverty 13–15, 32, 72, 76–9, 155–7,
    164, 167, 176, 177
  caused by imperialism 113
  caused by IMF 85
  see also inequality 35
power 151, 152 *see also potentia*
primitivism 22, 80, 82–3
  'primitive accumulation' 132
  anarchist 135; *see also* Zerzen
Privatisation xiv–xv, 14, 24, 29, 30,
    37, 75, 84, 85, 162, 184
  Private Finance Initiatives (PFI)
    56
  of land
    see enclosure
  of state assets 29, 56
  water 3, 14
  see also Washington Consensus
    and commons
producers 33
producerism 63
production, excess 112 *see also*
    productivism
productivism 22, 121–2, 176
  in *Empire* 149
  in Marx 109, 114, 165, 176
  see also growth, limitless
property xiv, 6, 62, 186
  property destruction 146–7
prostitution 32
protectionism 17, 20–1, 31 *see also*
    Hines, Colin
protest 25
  see anti-globalisation protest
    and anti-capitalist protest *and*
    peasant revolt
Proudhon, Pierre 62, 95

public limited companies xiv, 9 *see*
    also corporations
public spending cuts 38–9 *see also*
    Washington Consensus

Quaderni Rossi (journal) *see*
    Autonomia Operaia
Quantum Fund *see* Soros, George

'race to the bottom' 15, 18, 74
racism 16, 21, 173, 174
rainforests 16, 88, 89
Ramonet, Ignacio 90
  see also ATTAC, Tobin Tax
Rastafarianism xv, 178
  see also italism
Reading Capital Politically (Cleaver)
    127
recession (1930s) 26–8
Reclaim the Streets 6, 7, 136
Red Brigade 126
reflexivity
  see Soros, George
reform 38, 66, 118, 121, 146, 191
regulation theory 132
  see autonomists
Reich, Wilhelm 189
relativism 140
  see post modernism
representative democracy 5
repression 141 *see* Foucault
resistance, culture of 125, 134, 140,
    146, 147
Revolutionary Communist Party
    114
revolution 109, 110, 118, 121, 128,
    149, 151–2
  anarchist 135–8
  anti-capitalist 22, 177
  Marxist 4
  Russian 155
  industrial 72 *see also*
    industrialisation
Ricardo, David 73, 74 *see also*
    comparative advantage
Rice, Condoleeza 53
Roberts, Alan 155
Romantics 66–76 *see also* Blake,
    William

Roy, Arundhati 81–2, 87
Ruskin, John 66–7, 73
Russia 14, 27, 29, 38, 40, 54, 85, 155,
   mir 164
   under Stalin 121
Rwanda 85
Ryan, Michael (editor of Negri) 139, 147

Sahlins, Marshall 190
Salleh, Ariel 155
SAPS see IMF structural adjustment programmes
Saro-Wiwa, Ken 5
scepticism 140 see also post-modernism
Schumacher, E.F. 42, 66, 67, 73, 74–5, 107
Schutz, Alfred 34
second contradiction see capitalism
Second Gulf War 50, 113 see also Iraq
Second International 103
Second World War 27
self-sufficiency 19, 78 see also subsistence
Senegal 76–7
sexually transmitted diseases 14
shareholders 108
shares 9, 33, 39, 89
Shell 5
Shiva, Vandana 19, 65, 79–83, 87, 115, 169, 176
shoplifting see autonomism
Sismondi 66, 73
situationism 136 see also Reclaim the Streets
Sklair, Leslie 45, 54, 55, 57, 59, 60
slavery 13, 49, 178
slow food movement 189–90
Small is Beautiful (Schumacher) 42, 67, 73
Smith, Adam 10–11, 33, 62, 73, 74
Snowdon 27
Snyder, Gary 67
social credit 19, 91, 92–5
   Coventry League of the Unemployed 93

Social Credit Greenshirts 93
   see also monetary reformers and Douglas Social Credit
social factory 124, 131, 133, 144, 146, 149
socialism 26
Socialism or Survival (Bahro) 155
Socialist Workers Party 19, 102, 105, 116, 122
socialists 19, 102–3
Soddy, Frederick 95
Soil
   erosion 66, 158
   fertility of 80, 177
Somalia 85, 86
Sons of Cornwall see Mebyon Kernow
Soros, George 18, 22–43, 45, 79, 85, 86, 119, 179, 134, 176
   Crisis of global capitalism, The 26
   global credits 40
   Globalization and its Discontents 25
   Open Society Institute 25
   Quantum Fund 25
   reflexivity 33–4, 43
   see also Stiglitz, Joseph
Soviet Union 10, 14, 30
   see also Russia
Spanish Civil War 20, 137–8
Spartacus revolution 4
speculative currency flows 33, 89
   see also Tobin Tax
Spinoza, Baruch 104, 109, 127, 141, 142
spirituality 61–2, 67, 71
squatting 132, 137, 144, 191
Stalin 26, 27, 103, 121
Starbucks 191
Starr, Amory 173
starvation 14
state intervention
   see government intervention
Staying Alive (Shiva) 65
Stiglitz, Joseph 18, 22–43, 45, 79, 85, 86, 134, 170, 179
Structural Adjustment Programmes
   see IMF
student uprising 5

subsistence 65, 67, 79–83, 160, 164,
    167–8, 169, 177, 184, *see also*
    ecofeminism
Yabo farmers, Japan 81
subsumption of labour 132–3
subvertising 142
    see also brands *and* direct action
Summers, Larry 88
supermarkets 9, 48, 52, 59, 77
supply 10
surplus value 107
Sutherlanders *see* enclosure

Taborite communism *see*
    communism
Tanczos, Nandor xii–xv, 178
Taoism 67, 104
tariffs 17
Tate and Lyle 52
taxation, burden of 30
technology xiv, 61
    transfer 74
Thatcher, Margaret 21, 54, 129, 130
Thekaekara, Stan 180–1
Theories of Social Value (Marx) 103
Things Fall Apart (Achebe)
Thompson, Edward 24
thrift 41
Tobin Tax 19, 39, 43, 84, 90–1, 102
    see also ATTAC
Tobin, James 19, 24
totalitarianism 26
trade 17–18, 19, 20–1, 33, 51, 73–5,
    78, 84, 122
    deficit 33
    fair trade 17, 20–1, 180–1, 147
    free trade 2, 17, 84, 18, 20, 24,
        31, 64, 147
        and corporations 55 *see also*
        Washington Consensus *and*
        neo-liberalism
    liberalisation of 29 *see also*
        Washington Consensus
    see also 'Great Food Swap'
trade unions 14, 15, 19, 21, 77–9,
    102, 116
Trainer, Ted 72, 155
Transamerican Corp 53
transnational capitalist class 57,
    59–50 *see* Sklair

treadmill *see* globalisation
'tribe of moles' 125, 128
    see also squatting *and* Earth First!
    and direct action
'trickle down' 11
Trilateral Commission 55
TRIPS (Trade Related Aspects of
    IPRS) xiv *see also* GATT
Trotsky 102, 104
tuberculosis 14
Twin Towers destruction 159–60

Under the Volcano (Lowry) 6
underconsumption *see* crises of
    capitalism
unemployment 21
Union Carbide *see* Bhopal Disaster
United Biscuits 58
United Fruit Co. 50
United Nations 143
United States 13–14, 15, 63
    dominance 15, 16, 39, 86,
        116, 143, 148–9, 174 *see*
        imperialism 113, 183
    and free trade 17
    and the IMF 86
    and the invasion of Guatemala
        50
    militarism 15
    subsidies to cotton farmers 17
    style of capitalism 24
    threat to Cuba 119, 120
    see also Washington Consensus
    and Bush, George W.
Uno School 104
use value 154, 160–1, 168, 170, 171,
    177, 189
    in Marx 106–7, 108, 109
    see also exchange value
utopia 22, 26, 41, 145, 168
utopian socialists 4, 95 *see* Owen,
    Robert

Varieties of environmentalism
    156–7 *see* Guha, R *and*
    Martinez-Alier, J.
Veblen, Thornstein 35–6
    see also consumption
Veltmeyer, Henry 115–16

Venezuela 50, 113, 119, 182
  see also Chavez, Hugo
Vietcong 129, 143
Vietnam War 45, 86, 129
violence 8, 14, 19, 22, 25, 169
  see also property destruction
Vonnegut, Kurt 175, 192

wages 11, 14, 15
Wages for Housework see feminist
    autonomists
Wainwright, Hilary 183
Wal-Mart 52
Washington Consensus 24, 28–41,
    84, 86–7, 91, 134, 176
Wealth of Nations (Smith) 10–11
welfare 14
  see also corporate welfare and
    pensions
Went, Robert 105, 116–17
When Corporations Rule the World
    (Korten) 9, 18, 45
whistle-blowing 48
Wikipedia see open source
Winstanley, Gerard 186
Wolf, Martin 174
Wolfe, Tom 89
Woodin, Mike 19, 65, 70, 74, 75,
    76–9, 97, 120
  see also localisation and green
    localism
working class 11, 14, 16, 130–4
  control of 5, 20, 128–9

exploitation of 106–8, 110, 124,
    128–32, 174
working class action 129–30, 170
working class struggle 108, 109,
    116–17, 140, 142, 145, 150
  in China 179–80
  in Argentina 182
  against ecological destruction
    169, 170
  see also class war
World Bank xiv, 3, 13, 25, 28, 29, 82
  case against 87–9
  lending to Brazil 88
World Social Forum 8
WTO xiv, 2, 7, 14, 21, 22, 54–6, 58
  and patents 74
  influences on 76
  see also GATT and Bretton Woods
    Institutions

Yabo farmers, Japan see subsistence
Yugoslavia 85, 86

Z (magazine) 136
Zambia 14
Zapata, Emiliano 6
Zapatistas 5–6, 79, 105, 126, 137,
    180
  encuentro 6
Zen 4, 67, 159, 190–1
zero growth 156
zero-waste 69
Zerzen, John 135